Book 2
Mathematical Reasoning™

Through Verbal Analysis

SERIES TITLES
MATHEMATICAL REASONING™ BEGINNING
MATHEMATICAL REASONING™ LEVEL A
MATHEMATICAL REASONING™ BOOK 1
MATHEMATICAL REASONING™ BOOK 2

Warren Hill & Ronald Edwards

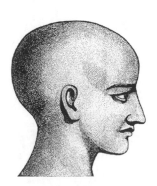

© 2002, 1991
THE CRITICAL THINKING CO.™
(BRIGHT MINDS™ • 800-641-6555)
www.CriticalThinking.com
P.O. Box 1610 • Seaside • CA 93955-1610
Phone 800-458-4849 • FAX 831-393-3277
ISBN 978-0-89455-402-5

ACKNOWLEDGEMENTS

The authors and the publisher are grateful to David Lance Goines
and his publisher, David R. Godine, Publisher, Inc., for permission
to use Mr. Goines' design on the cover of this book.

—— A VERY IMPORTANT COMMENT ——

MATHEMATICAL REASONING THROUGH VERBAL ANALYSIS is a book of math activities designed to be used in a cooperative learning situation. The activities are deceptively simple in appearance, making it essential that the teacher read the Teacher's Manual before beginning the lesson. Only in this way can he/she become fully aware of the multilayered learning that takes place when students explore all the information that can be gleaned from one exercise.

The materials were **not** designed to be used as an independent workbook. After the teacher has thoroughly discussed the example, and introduced and defined any vocabulary that is new to the students, the class may proceed to work the next few exercises independently or in a small group. However, the students will not receive full value from the lesson unless each exercise is discussed in the manner outlined in the Teacher's Manual.

As a result of exploring each exercise to the fullest extent, layer by layer, the students should show significant gains in vocabulary development, increase observation skills substantially, and be able to process mathematical concepts on a much higher level.

TABLE OF CONTENTS

HOW MANY LETTERS?

Find the number of letters in each box. Count the letters only.
Write the answer in the circle.

Example

a	b	e	t
3	2	5	8
c	d	e	f
4	1	6	3

(8)

A–1

A	i	$	?	5
m	t	s	=	4
c	u	E	r	9
M	S	a	p	H

(14)

A–2

D	H	=	?	N	Q
t	u	+		T	
A	F	&	$	O	P
e	f	*		J	

(14)

A–3

=	=	=	=	=	=
=	o	c	t	o	b
=	c	t	o	b	e
=	t	o	b	e	r

(15)

A–4

y	y	y	y	1
w	w	w	2	w
x	x	3	x	x
5	z	z	z	z

A–5

b	+	8	0	L
3	t	1	p	i
E	o	l	d	!
6	B	–	7	$

P.O. BOX 448, PACIFIC GROVE, CA 93950

HOW MANY DIFFERENT LETTERS?

Look at the boxes below. Each box contains a mixture of letters.
Find the number of different letters in each box.
Write the answer in the circle.

Example

```
x   x   y   y   z   z

y   z   z   x   x   y

z   y   x   z   y   x
```

(3)

A–6

```
A   B   C   C   B   A
D   E   F   F   E   D
G   H   I   I   H   G
J   K   L   L   K   J
```

(12)

A–7

```
r r r      s s s      t t t

u u u      v v v      w w w

x x x      y y y      z z z
```

(9)

A–8

```
d   e   f   g   h   i
      j   k   l   m
n   o   p   q   r   s   t
      u   v   w
```

(20)

A–9

```
p   r   f   e   s
c   s   w   p   t
e   p   b   r   p
r   d   f   s   w
```

(11)

A–10

```
THE QUICK
BROWN FOX
JUMPS OVER
THE LAZY DOG
```

(26)

COUNTING THE DOTS

In the triangle write the number of dots pictured in the pattern.
In the circle write the smallest number of dots needed to complete a rectangular pattern of dots.
In the box write the smallest number of dots needed to complete a square pattern of dots.

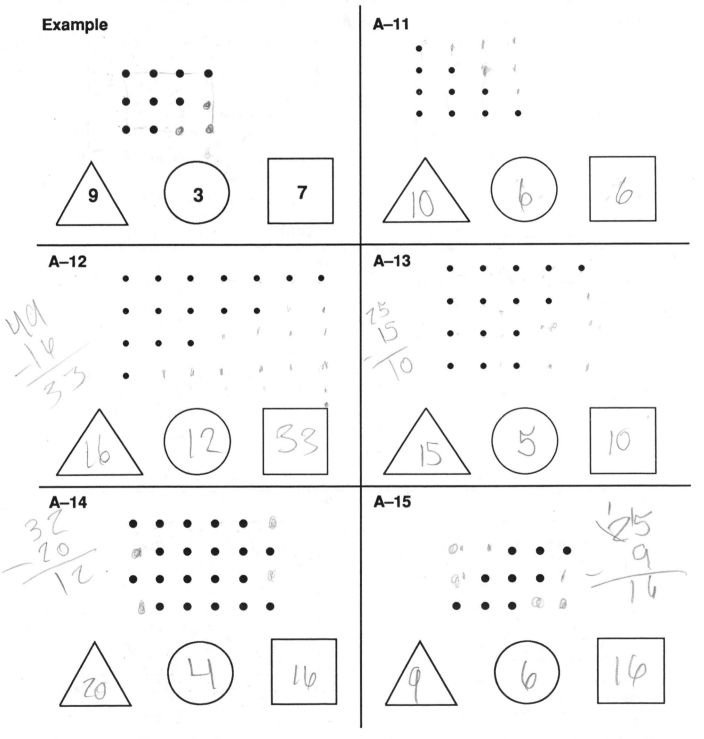

COUNTING THE DOTS

Look at the sets below.
Each circle represents 50 dots, each square represents 25 dots, and each triangle represents 5 dots.
What is the total number of dots in each set?

Example

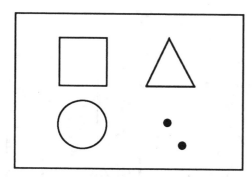

Total = ___**82**___

A–16

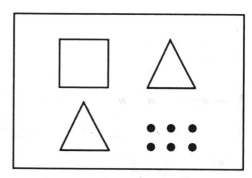

Total = ___41___

A–17

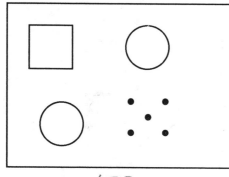

Total = ___130___

A–18

150
50
+ 205

Total = ___205___

A–19

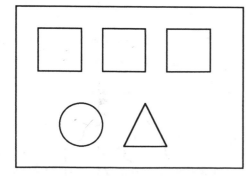

75
50
+ 125

Total = ___130___

A–20

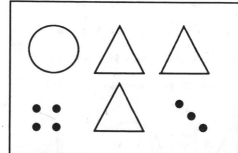

Total = ___72___

P.O. BOX 448, PACIFIC GROVE, CA 93950

WRITE THE NUMBER

A Japanese abacus is pictured below.
The beads above the crossbar have a value of 5; those below have a value of 1.
Beads that have been moved toward the crossbar of the abacus represent a number.
Write the number that is pictured on the abacus.

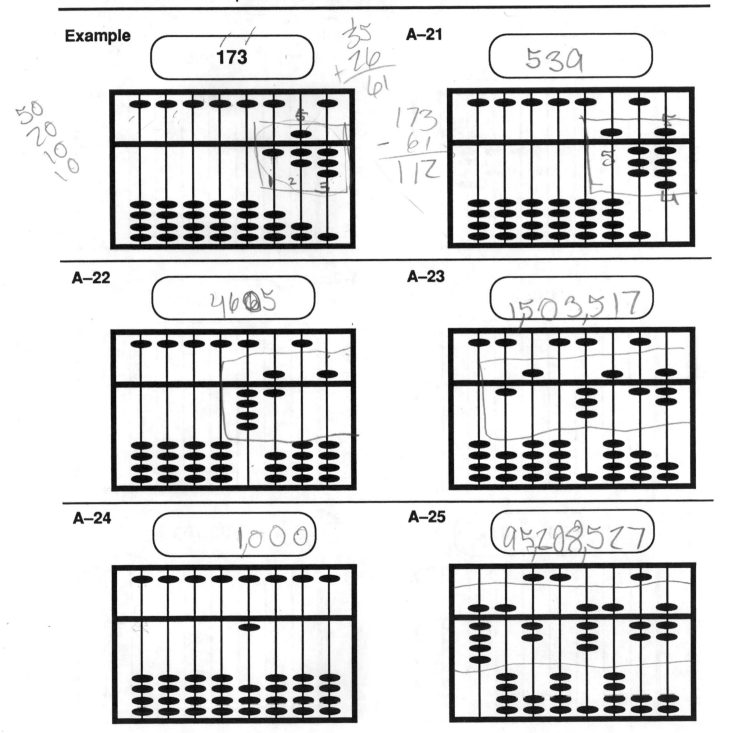

Example

173

A–21

539

A–22

4605

A–23

1503,517

A–24

1,000

A–25

95208,527

CONSTRUCT THE NUMBER

A Japanese abacus is pictured below.
The beads above the crossbar have a value of 5; those below have a value of 1.
Draw the beads at the crossbar of each abacus to represent the number in the box.

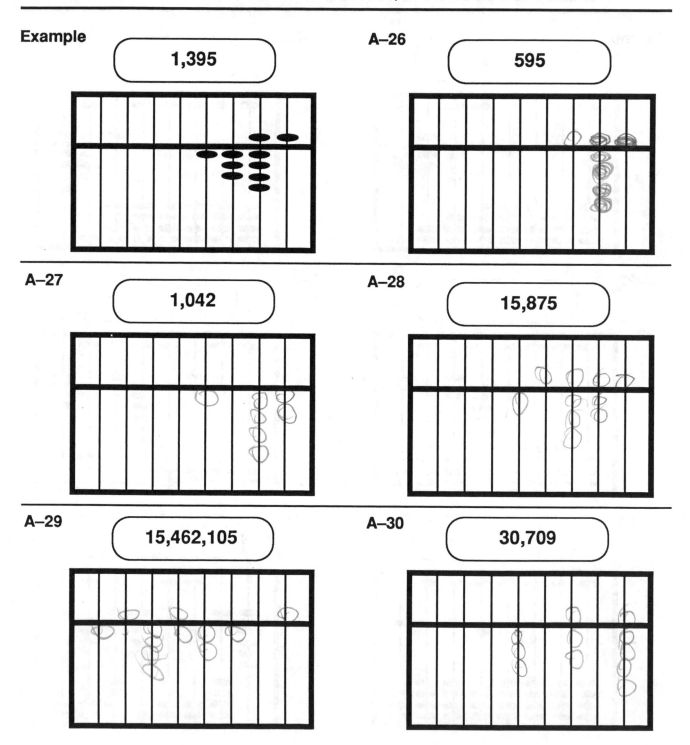

Example   1,395

A–26   595

A–27   1,042

A–28   15,875

A–29   15,462,105

A–30   30,709

CONTINUE THE SEQUENCE

Place numbers in the blank spaces to continue the sequence.

Example	9	11	13	15	**17**	**19**	**21**	**23**
A–31	11	14	17	20	23	26	29	32
A–32	37	44	51	58	65	72	79	86
A–33	50	47	44	41	39	36	33	30
A–34	17	24	31	38	45	52	59	66
A–35	25	28	31	34	37	40	43	46
A–36	97	95	93	91	89	87	85	83
A–37	108	101	94	87	80	73	65	58

CONTINUE THE SEQUENCE

Place numbers in the blank spaces to continue the sequence.

A–38	1	2	4	7	11	_____	_____	_____	_____
A–39	5	6	8	11	15	_____	_____	_____	_____
A–40	1	2	5	10	17	_____	_____	_____	_____
A–41	1	3	6	10	15	_____	_____	_____	_____
A–42	9	11	15	21	29	_____	_____	_____	_____
A–43	5	6	9	14	21	_____	_____	_____	_____
A–44	1	4	9	16	25	_____	_____	_____	_____
A–45	2	4	8	16	32	_____	_____	_____	_____

COMPLETING THE SEQUENCE

Place numbers in the blank spaces to complete the sequence.

Example	2	__4__	6	__8__	10	__12__	14
A–46	3	6	___	___	___	18	21
A–47	36	34	32	___	___	___	24	22
A–48	___	___	20	___	12	8	4
A–49	___	66	___	60	___	54	___	48	45
A–50	___	10	___	20	___	30	___	40
A–51	___	90	___	___	60	___	___	30
A–52	141	___	___	126	___	116	111

COMPLETING THE SEQUENCE

Place numbers in the blank spaces to complete the sequence.

A–53   3   10   17   _____   31   _____   _____   52

A–54   3   _____   9   _____   15   _____   21   _____   27

A–55   4   9   _____   _____   24   _____   _____   39

A–56   95   91   _____   _____   79   _____   _____

A–57   45   _____   31   _____   17   _____   3

A–58   3   _____   _____   18   _____   28   _____   _____   43

A–59   83   _____   _____   74   _____   68   _____

A–60   64   _____   _____   _____   56   _____

SEQUENCES OF NUMBERS

Each exercise below begins a sequence.
The three dots mean that the sequence continues.
Circle the numbers that belong to the sequence.

Example

2, 5, 8, 11, 14, • • •

a. (38)   b. 36

c. 24   d. (23)

A–61

9, 13, 17, 21, • • •

25 29 33
37 41

a. 32   b. (33)

c. 40   d. (41)

A–62

10, 13, 16, 19 • • •

22 25
28 31
34 7

a. 21   b. 36

c. (28)   d. 38

A–63

6, 8, 11, 15, 20, • • •

a. 27   b. 25

c. 33   d. 36

A–64

9, 12, 15, 18, 21, • • •

a. 42   b. 25

c. 44   d. 30

SEQUENCES OF NUMBERS

Each exercise below begins a sequence.
The three dots mean that the sequence continues.
Circle the row that belongs to the sequence.

Example

1, 2, 4, 5, 7, 8, • • •

a.   21, 22, 24, 25

b.   17, 18, 19, 20

c.   22, 23, 25, 26

A–65

1, 2, 3, 5, 6, 7, 9, 10, 11 • • •

a.   28, 29, 30

b.   31, 32, 33

c.   21, 22, 23

A–66

1, 2, 5, 6, 9, 10, 13, 14, • • •

a.   25, 26, 29, 30

b.   19, 20, 23, 24

c.   25, 28, 31, 34

A–67

1, 2, 6, 7, 11, 12, 16, 17, • • •

a.   23, 24, 28, 29

b.   18, 22, 23, 27

c.   31, 32, 36, 37

A–68

1, 2, 4, 7, 8, 11, 13, 14, 16, • • •

a.   18, 19, 22, 25

b.   19, 22, 23, 26

c.   23, 24, 26, 28

NUMBER PROPERTIES

Circle all the numbers that satisfy the rule.

Example: A number that is divisible by 5 and is between 18 and 30.

15   23   **(20)**   30   **(25)**

A–69   A number that is a multiple of 3 and a multiple of 4.

(24)   9   56   42   17

A–70   A number that is even and is between 78 and 85.

77   81   84   86   78

A–71   A number that is greater than the number of days in any month and has a factor of 6.

30   36   54   33   42

A–72   A number that is 2 times a single-digit number and is greater than 14.

14   18   17   15   20

A–73   A number that has a factor of 4 and is between 64 and 74.

60   68   70   88   64

NUMBER PROPERTIES

Circle all the numbers that satisfy the rule.

Example: A number that is odd or is a multiple of 3.

  22   34

A-74   A number that is odd and is a multiple of 3.

72   39   22   34   25

A-75   A number that is divisible by 6 or is between 29 and 31.

27   28   30   36   31

A-76   A number that is divisible by 5 or is divisible by 7

16   35   18   28   20

A-77   A number that is divisible by 5 and is divisible by 7

16   35   18   28   20

A-78   A number that is less than the number of digits in any zip code and is not a prime number.

7   4   3   6   8

NUMBER PROPERTIES

Circle all the numbers that satisfy the rule.

A-79   A number that is a multiple of 2 and has an 8 in tens place.

78   80   8   888   881

A-80   A number that has two digits whose sum is 9 and has a factor of 3.

33   18   182   36   108

A-81   A number that is less than the number of months in the year or is between 37 and 42.

26   41   0   8   12

A-82   A number that is greater than the number of vowels in the alphabet or is between 10 and 15.

4   18   14   5   6

A-83   A number that is less than the number of months in the year and is between 37 and 42.

26   41   0   8   12

A-84   A number that is greater than the number of digits in any local telephone number and is a prime number.

5   7   29   49   53

NUMBER PROPERTIES

All of the numbers in circle A are between 25 and 40.
All of the numbers in circle B are between 30 and 50.
Write each number below in the correct region of the diagram.

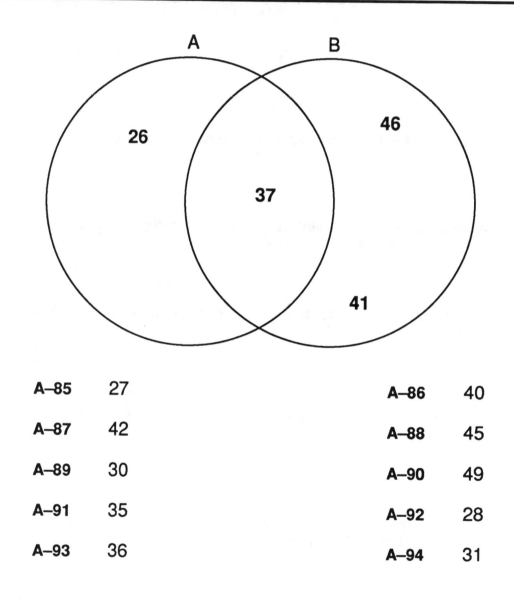

A–85	27	A–86	40
A–87	42	A–88	45
A–89	30	A–90	49
A–91	35	A–92	28
A–93	36	A–94	31

A–95   What numbers are in both circle A and circle B? _____

A–96   What other numbers between 25 and 50 could be placed
        in both circle A and circle B? _____

COMMON FACTORS

All of the numbers in circle A have a factor of 6.
All of the numbers in circle B have a factor of 4.
Write each number below in the correct region of the diagram.

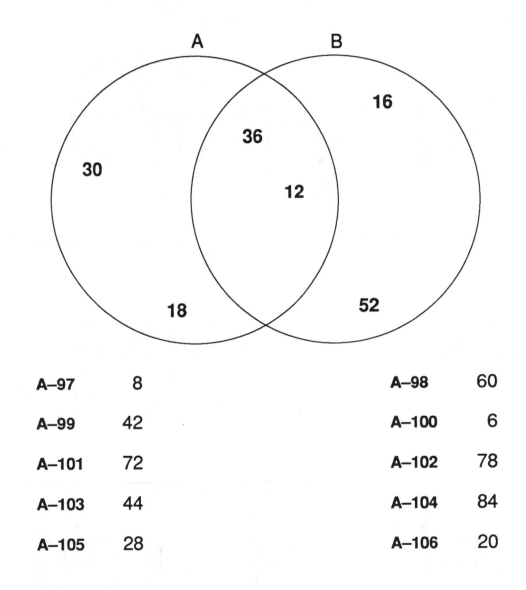

A–97	8	
A–99	42	
A–101	72	
A–103	44	
A–105	28	

A–98	60
A–100	6
A–102	78
A–104	84
A–106	20

A–107   What numbers are in both circle A and circle B? _____

_____

A–108   List two other numbers between 1 and 100 that could be
placed in both circle A and circle B. _____

FRACTIONAL PARTS

In the box write the fraction that tells what part of the figure is shaded.

Example

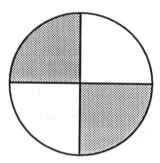

$$\frac{2}{4}$$

A–109

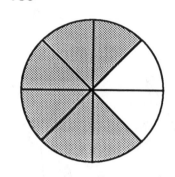

A–110

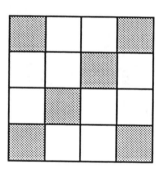

A–111

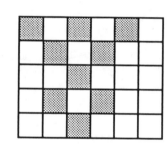

A–112

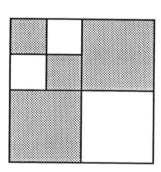

A–113

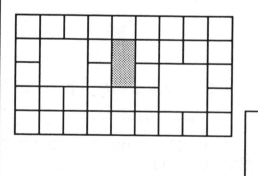

FRACTIONAL PARTS

Shade each figure to match the given fraction.

Example

$\dfrac{3}{4}$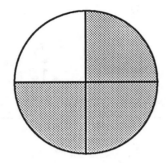

A–114

$\dfrac{5}{8}$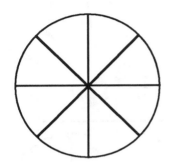

A–115

$\dfrac{7}{12}$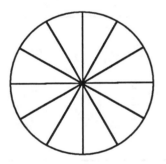

A–116

$\dfrac{2}{3}$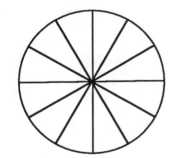

A–117

$\dfrac{3}{8}$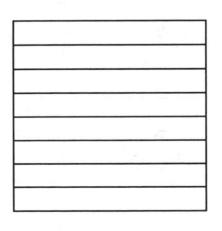

A–118

$\dfrac{3}{5}$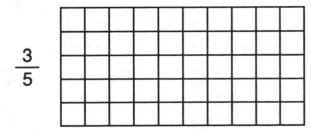

ESTIMATING FRACTIONAL PARTS

Circle the fraction which estimates what part of the figure is shaded.

Example

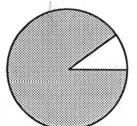

a.

$\dfrac{1}{10}$

b.

$\dfrac{1}{5}$

c.

$\dfrac{5}{10}$

d.

$\dfrac{9}{10}$

A–119

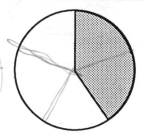

a.

$\dfrac{1}{4}$

b.

$\dfrac{2}{4}$

c.

$\dfrac{3}{5}$

d.

$\dfrac{2}{5}$

A–120

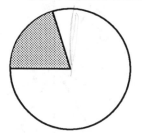

a.

$\dfrac{1}{10}$

b.

$\dfrac{1}{4}$

c.

$\dfrac{4}{5}$

d.

$\dfrac{1}{5}$

A–121

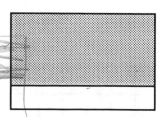

a.

$\dfrac{3}{8}$

b.

$\dfrac{3}{4}$

c.

$\dfrac{1}{4}$

d.

$\dfrac{1}{2}$

A–122

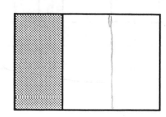

a.

$\dfrac{1}{3}$

b.

$\dfrac{1}{4}$

c.

$\dfrac{2}{3}$

d.

$\dfrac{3}{4}$

20   P.O. BOX 448, PACIFIC GROVE, CA 93950

ESTIMATING FRACTIONAL PARTS

Circle the figure whose shaded part matches the given fraction.

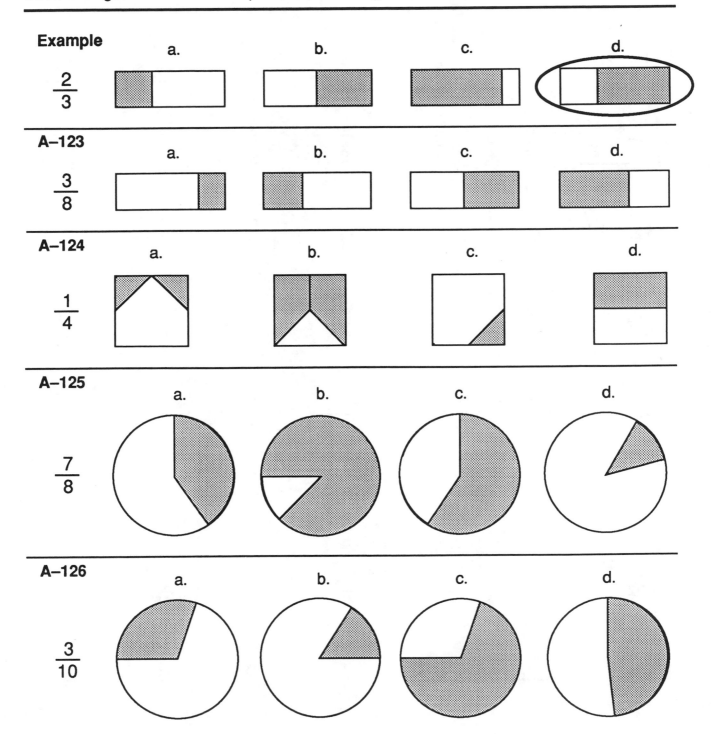

Example

$\dfrac{2}{3}$ a.   b.   c.   d.

A–123

$\dfrac{3}{8}$ a.   b.   c.   d.

A–124

$\dfrac{1}{4}$ a.   b.   c.   d.

A–125

$\dfrac{7}{8}$ a.   b.   c.   d.

A–126

$\dfrac{3}{10}$ a.   b.   c.   d.

SEQUENCES OF FRACTIONS

Place fractions in the blank spaces to complete the sequence.

Example	$\frac{1}{2}$	$\frac{1}{3}$	$\frac{1}{4}$	$\frac{1}{5}$	$\frac{1}{6}$	$\frac{1}{7}$
A–127	$\frac{5}{6}$	$\frac{5}{7}$	$\frac{5}{8}$	$\frac{5}{9}$	——	——
A–128	$\frac{11}{10}$	$\frac{9}{10}$	$\frac{7}{10}$	$\frac{5}{10}$	——	——
A–129	$\frac{2}{4}$	——	$\frac{6}{8}$	——	$\frac{10}{12}$	$\frac{12}{14}$
A–130	$\frac{1}{2}$	$\frac{2}{3}$	——	$\frac{4}{5}$	——	——
A–131	——	——	$\frac{3}{6}$	$\frac{4}{8}$	$\frac{5}{10}$	$\frac{6}{12}$
A–132	$\frac{1}{3}$	——	$\frac{3}{9}$	——	$\frac{5}{15}$	——
A–133	——	——	$\frac{15}{20}$	$\frac{20}{25}$	$\frac{25}{30}$	$\frac{30}{35}$

SEQUENCES AND PATTERNS OF FRACTIONS

Fill in the blanks with the fractions that complete the sequences or patterns of fractions.

Example

$\frac{1}{2}$	$\frac{1}{4}$	$\frac{1}{6}$	$\frac{1}{8}$	$\frac{1}{10}$
$\frac{2}{4}$	$\frac{2}{8}$	$\frac{2}{12}$	$\frac{2}{16}$	$\frac{2}{20}$

A–134

$\frac{1}{3}$		$\frac{1}{5}$	$\frac{1}{6}$	
$\frac{3}{9}$	$\frac{3}{12}$		$\frac{3}{18}$	

A–135

	$\frac{3}{6}$		$\frac{5}{8}$	$\frac{6}{9}$
	$\frac{6}{12}$	$\frac{8}{14}$		$\frac{12}{18}$

A–136

$\frac{1}{2}$		$\frac{3}{4}$
$\frac{2}{4}$	$\frac{4}{6}$	
$\frac{3}{6}$		$\frac{9}{12}$

A–137

	$\frac{1}{6}$	
$\frac{2}{6}$		$\frac{2}{18}$
	$\frac{3}{18}$	

DECIMAL NUMBERS

A Japanese abacus is pictured below.
The beads above the crossbar have a value of 5; those below the bar have a value of 1.
The dotted line represents the **units** column.
Circle the decimal number that is pictured on the abacus.

Example

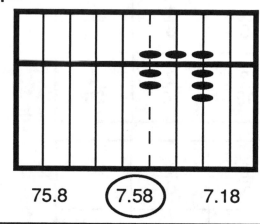

75.8   (7.58)   7.18

A–138

84.42   42.48   42.84

A–139

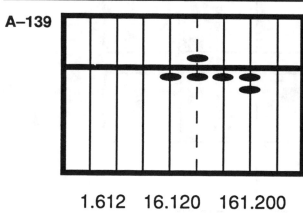

1.612   16.120   161.200

A–140

3.367   33.67   33.067

A–141

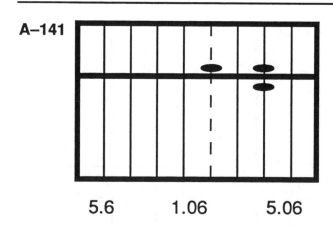

5.6   1.06   5.06

A–142

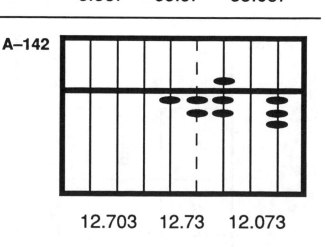

12.703   12.73   12.073

     24   P.O. BOX 448, PACIFIC GROVE, CA 93950

DECIMAL NUMBERS

A Japanese abacus is pictured below.
The beads above the crossbar have a value of 5; those below the bar have a value of 1.
The dotted line represents the **units** column.
Match the decimal number with the value that is pictured on the abacus.

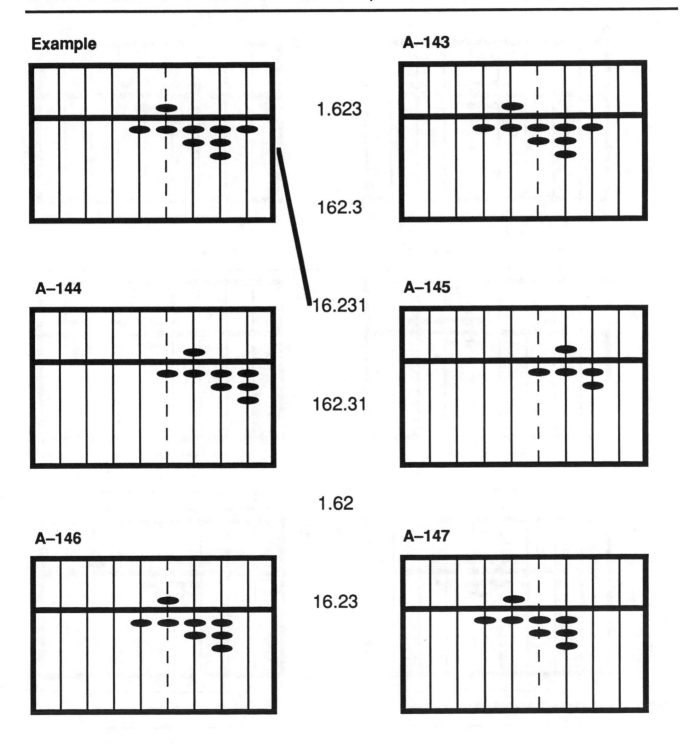

Example

1.623

162.3

16.231

A–143

A–144

162.31

1.62

A–145

A–146

16.23

A–147

DECIMAL NUMBERS

A Japanese abacus is pictured below.
The beads above the crossbar have a value of 5; those below the bar have a value of 1.
The dotted line represents the **units** column.
Write the decimal number that is pictured on the abacus.

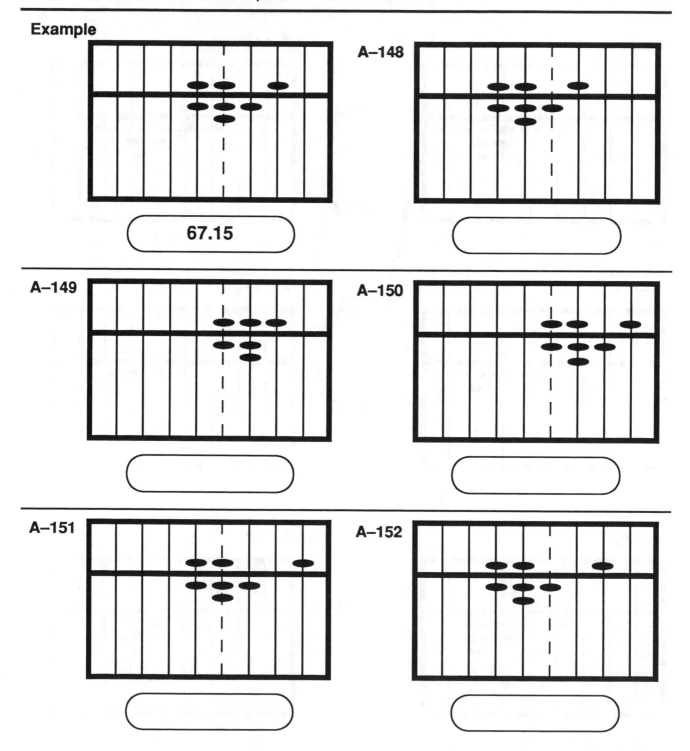

Example

A–148

67.15

A–149

A–150

A–151

A–152

26   P.O. BOX 448, PACIFIC GROVE, CA 93950

DECIMAL NUMBERS

A Japanese abacus is pictured below.
The beads above the crossbar have a value of 5; those below the bar have a value of 1.
The dotted line represents the **units** column.
Draw beads at the crossbar of each abacus to represent the decimal number in the box.

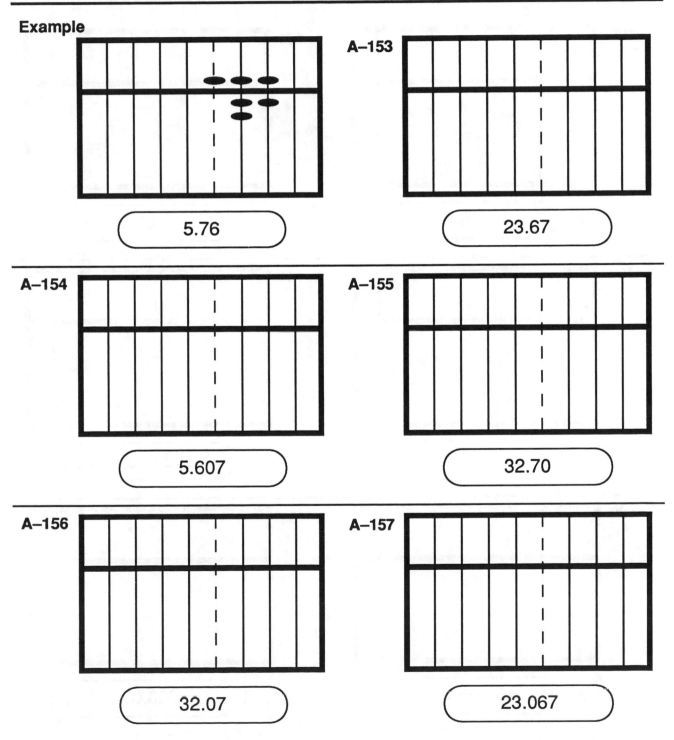

Example

A–153

5.76   23.67

A–154

A–155

5.607   32.70

A–156

A–157

32.07   23.067

DECIMAL NUMBERS

A Japanese abacus is pictured below.
The beads above the crossbar have a value of 5; those below the bar have a value of 1.
The dotted line represents the **units** column.
Draw beads at the crossbar of each abacus to represent the decimal number in the box.

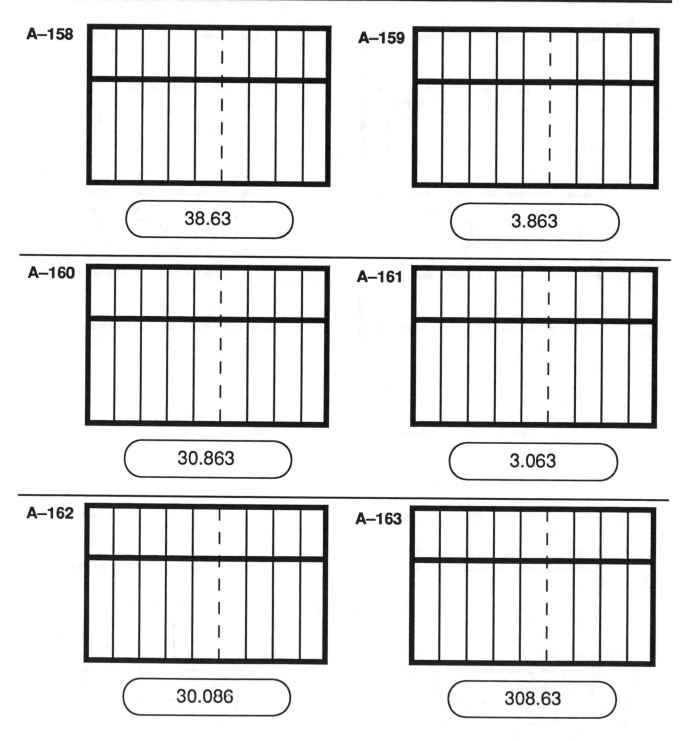

A-158

38.63

A-159

3.863

A-160

30.863

A-161

3.063

A-162

30.086

A-163

308.63

                                       P.O. BOX 448, PACIFIC GROVE, CA 93950

NAMING POINTS ON THE NUMBER LINE

The points on the number line represent consecutive counting numbers.
Fill in the boxes with the correct numbers.

Example

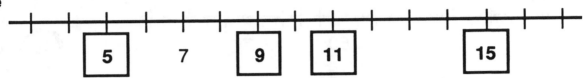

5   7   9   11   15

A–164

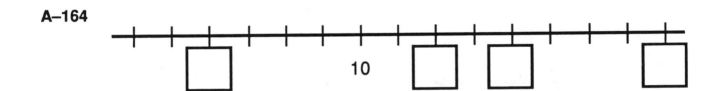

10

A–165

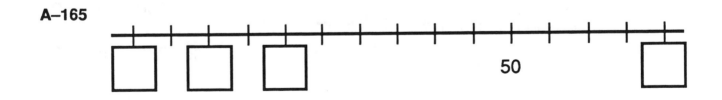

50

A–166

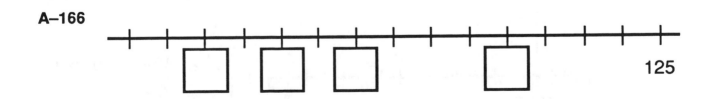

125

29   P.O. BOX 448, PACIFIC GROVE, CA 93950

WHICH NUMBER DOES NOT FIT?

A part of the number line is shown.
Circle all the numbers that do not fit on that part of the number line.

Example

50   60   70

a.   58   b. (78)

c.   (48)   d.   68

A–167

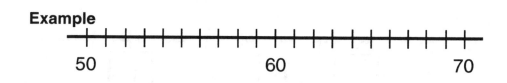

117   127   137

a.   129   b.   201

c.   136   d.   108

A–168

320   340

a.   350   b.   329

c.   318   d.   339

A–169

880   895

a.   950   b.   902

c.   885   d.   897

A–170

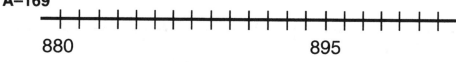

1999   2010

a. 2000   b. 1990

c. 2109   d. 1890

A–171

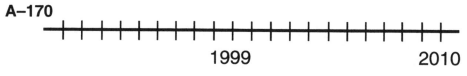

4985   4995

a. 4899   b. 5000

c. 4000   d. 4999

---

30   P.O. BOX 448, PACIFIC GROVE, CA 93950

WHAT IS THE NUMBER?

Look at the numbers on the number line.
The arrow is pointing to a missing number.
Write the missing number as a fraction.

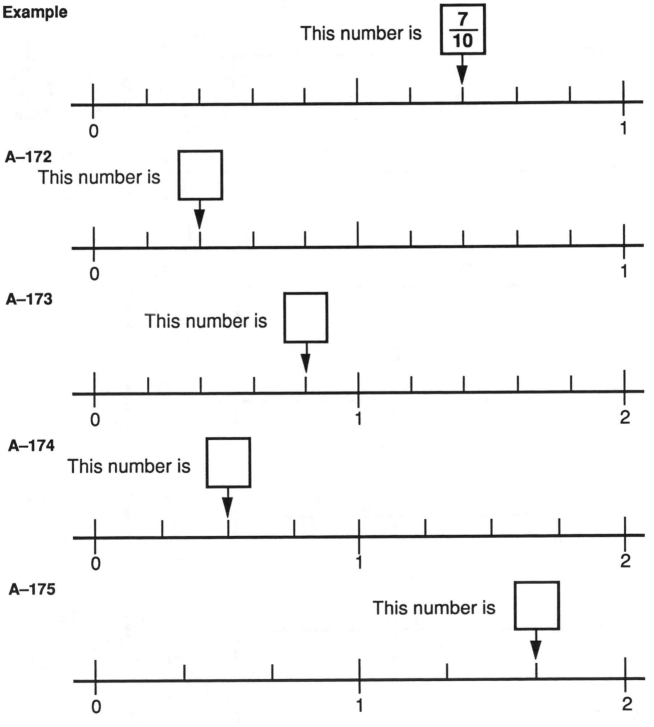

Example

This number is $\dfrac{7}{10}$

0   1

A–172

This number is ☐

0   1

A–173

This number is ☐

0   1   2

A–174

This number is ☐

0   1   2

A–175

This number is ☐

0   1   2

P.O. BOX 448, PACIFIC GROVE, CA 93950

ESTIMATING WITH FRACTIONS

The arrow indicates a point on the number line.
Circle the number that is closest to that point.

Example

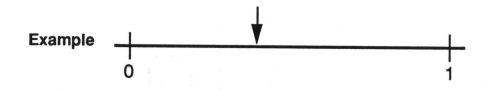

a. $\frac{1}{2}$ b. $\frac{1}{4}$

c. $\frac{2}{3}$ d. $\boxed{\frac{2}{5}}$

A–176

a. $1\frac{1}{4}$ b. $\frac{7}{8}$

c. $\frac{7}{10}$ d. $\frac{1}{3}$

A–177

a. $\frac{1}{4}$ b. $1\frac{1}{2}$

c. $\frac{1}{3}$ d. $\frac{2}{4}$

A–178

a. $\frac{1}{3}$ b. $\frac{1}{2}$

c. $\frac{1}{8}$ d. $\frac{2}{3}$

A–179

a. $\frac{1}{2}$ b. $1\frac{3}{6}$

c. $2\frac{1}{2}$ d. $1\frac{1}{4}$

A–180

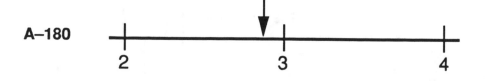

a. $2\frac{2}{3}$ b. $3\frac{1}{8}$

c. $2\frac{7}{8}$ d. $\frac{9}{10}$

                   P.O. BOX 448, PACIFIC GROVE, CA 93950

NAMING POINTS ON THE NUMBER LINE

Two numbers appear on each number line.
Write the missing numbers as decimals.

Example

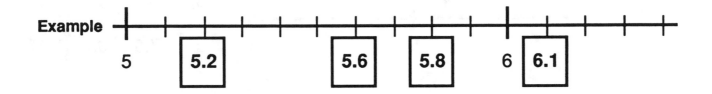

5   **5.2**   **5.6**   **5.8**   6   **6.1**

A–181

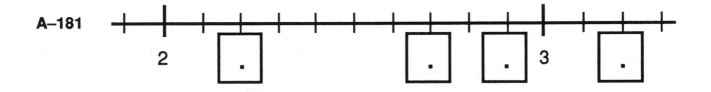

2   .   .   .   3   .

A–182

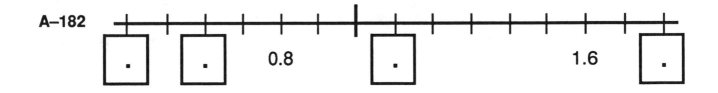

.   .   0.8   .   1.6   .

A–183

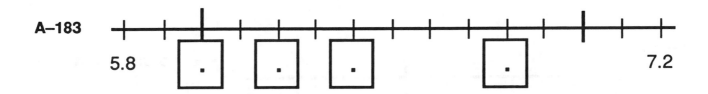

5.8   .   .   .   .   7.2

ESTIMATING WITH DECIMALS

The arrow indicates a point on the number line.
Circle the number that is closest to that point.

Example

a.   8.2   b.   8.8

c.   7.5   d.   (7.8)

A–184

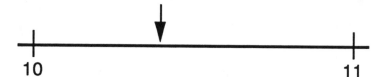

a.   10.1   b.   10.5

c.   10.4   d.   11.6

A–185

a.   23.1   b.   24.5

c.   24.1   d.   23.5

A–186

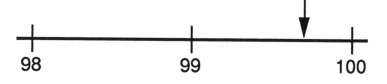

a.   99.7   b.   98.9

c.   100.2   d.   99.5

A–187

a.   1.25   b.   1.75

c.   0.80   d.   0.25

A–188

a. 45.05   b. 45.50

c. 45.30   d. 46.90

WHOLE NUMBER PLACE VALUE

Write the whole number that is described below.

Example	ten greater than 3,587	**3,597**
A–189	one hundred less than 3,642	_____
A–190	one thousand greater than 6,942	_____
A–191	one hundred less than 4,060	_____
A–192	ten thousand greater than 89,742	_____
A–193	ten less than 408	_____
A–194	one hundred less than 3,009	_____
A–195	ten more than 89,990	_____

DECIMAL NUMBER PLACE VALUE

Write the decimal number that is described below.

Example	one-tenth less than 4.24	**4.14**
A–196	one-hundredth more than 0.087	_____
A–197	one-thousandth less than 3.1415	_____
A–198	one-hundredth more than 2.890	_____
A–199	one hundred less than 710.08	_____
A–200	one-tenth more than 3.99	_____
A–201	one-tenth less than 2.075	_____
A–202	one thousand more than 9,888.088	_____

READING NUMERALS

Circle the numeral that is stated in words.

Example: one thousand, forty-two

   1,420   (1,042)   142,000

A–203   two million, eighty thousand, seven hundred five

   2,800,705   280,705   2,080,705

A–204   one hundred eighteen and thirty-four hundredths

   118,340.0   118.034   118.34

A–205   one and five thousandths

   1.050   1.005   0.105

A–206   twenty-six thousand and sixty-two hundredths

   26,000.62   26,000.062   2,600.62

A–207   twenty-six thousand, sixty-two

   2,600,062   260,062   26,062

A–208   five hundred fifty-five and fifty-five thousandths

   555.055   555.550   5,055.055

WRITING NUMERAL NAMES

Write the numerals in words.

Example   29.086   <u>**twenty-nine and eighty-six thousandths**</u>

A–209   2,084.35

A–210   25,025.025

A–211   1.008

A–212   208,750

A–213   9.99

A–214   3.0750

FRACTIONS – GREATER THAN / LESS THAN

Circle all the fractions that are **greater than** the fraction in the square.

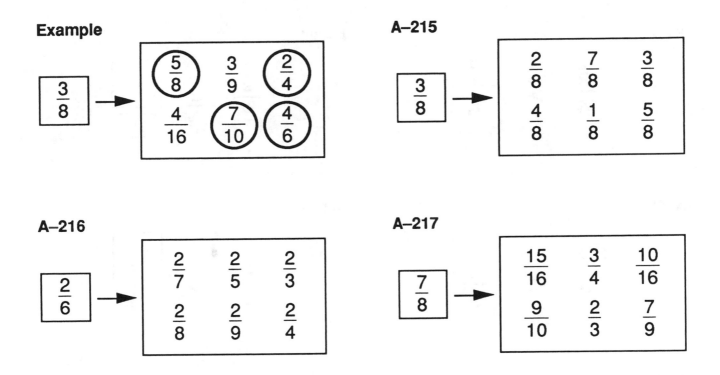

Example

$\frac{3}{8}$ →

$\frac{5}{8}$ $\frac{3}{9}$ $\frac{2}{4}$

$\frac{4}{16}$ $\frac{7}{10}$ $\frac{4}{6}$

A–215

$\frac{3}{8}$ →

$\frac{2}{8}$ $\frac{7}{8}$ $\frac{3}{8}$

$\frac{4}{8}$ $\frac{1}{8}$ $\frac{5}{8}$

A–216

$\frac{2}{6}$ →

$\frac{2}{7}$ $\frac{2}{5}$ $\frac{2}{3}$

$\frac{2}{8}$ $\frac{2}{9}$ $\frac{2}{4}$

A–217

$\frac{7}{8}$ →

$\frac{15}{16}$ $\frac{3}{4}$ $\frac{10}{16}$

$\frac{9}{10}$ $\frac{2}{3}$ $\frac{7}{9}$

Circle all the fractions that are **less than** the fraction in the square.

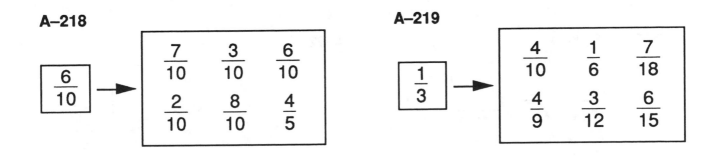

A–218

$\frac{6}{10}$ →

$\frac{7}{10}$ $\frac{3}{10}$ $\frac{6}{10}$

$\frac{2}{10}$ $\frac{8}{10}$ $\frac{4}{5}$

A–219

$\frac{1}{3}$ →

$\frac{4}{10}$ $\frac{1}{6}$ $\frac{7}{18}$

$\frac{4}{9}$ $\frac{3}{12}$ $\frac{6}{15}$

FRACTIONS – GREATER THAN / LESS THAN / EQUAL

Write a whole number in the square to make a true statement.

Example

$$\frac{2}{4} > \frac{2}{\boxed{5}}$$

A–220

$$\frac{2}{3} = \frac{\boxed{}}{12}$$

A–221

$$\frac{5}{9} < \frac{\boxed{}}{9}$$

A–222

$$\frac{5}{6} > \frac{\boxed{}}{6}$$

A–223

$$\frac{1}{2} < \frac{\boxed{}}{8}$$

A–224

$$\frac{4}{\boxed{}} > \frac{4}{6}$$

A–225

$$\frac{12}{15} = \frac{\boxed{}}{5}$$

A–226

$$\frac{5}{\boxed{}} < \frac{\boxed{}}{8}$$

DECIMAL NUMBERS – GREATER THAN / LESS THAN

The dotted line on the abacus represents the **units** column.
A decimal number is pictured on the left abacus.
Draw beads on the right abacus to make a number **less than** the given decimal number.
Write the decimal numbers in the boxes.

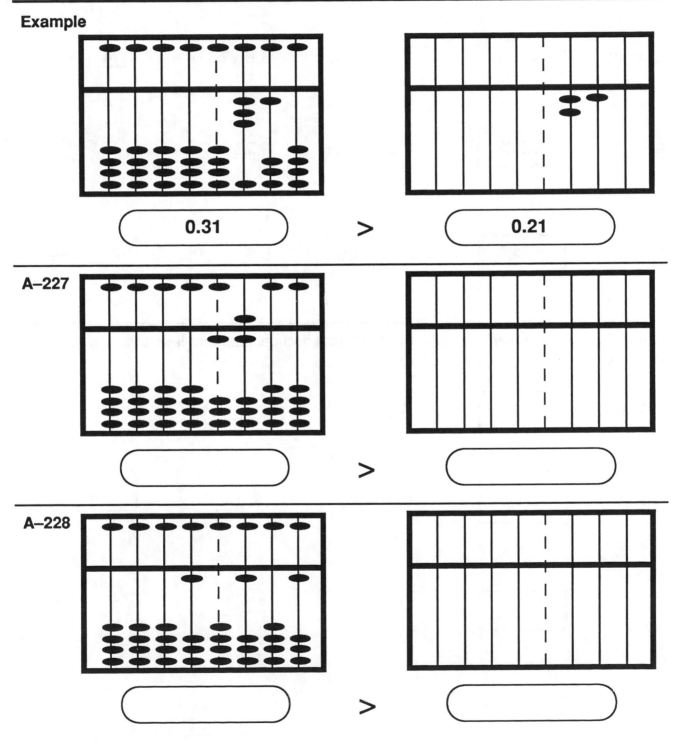

Example

0.31   >   0.21

A–227

>

A–228

>

DECIMAL NUMBERS – GREATER THAN / LESS THAN

Write a digit in each blank to make three different decimal numbers **greater than** the number in the box.

Example	3.819	3._**9**_19	3.8_**2**_0	_**4**_.819
A–229	0.222	0.2____2	0.22____	0.____3____
A–230	5.869	5.____89	5.8____9	5.____89

Write a digit in each blank to make three different decimal numbers **less than** the number in the box.

A–231	1.31	1.____1	____.31	1.3____
A–232	13.09	1____.09	13.0____	1____.____9
A–233	3.22	3.____4	3.2____	3.____4

FRACTIONS – BETWEEN

Write three different fractions that are between the two given fractions.

Example	$\frac{1}{7}$	$\frac{1}{3}$	$\frac{1}{6}$	$\frac{1}{5}$	$\frac{1}{4}$
A–234	$\frac{2}{9}$	$\frac{6}{9}$	_____	_____	_____
A–235	$\frac{1}{6}$	$\frac{10}{12}$	_____	_____	_____
A–236	$\frac{2}{8}$	$\frac{3}{4}$	_____	_____	_____
A–237	$\frac{1}{5}$	$\frac{8}{10}$	_____	_____	_____
A–238	$\frac{1}{2}$	$\frac{5}{6}$	_____	_____	_____
A–239	$\frac{1}{4}$	$\frac{1}{2}$	_____	_____	_____

DECIMAL NUMBERS – BETWEEN

Write three different decimal numbers that are between the two given numbers.

Example	12.49	12.53	**12.50**	**12.51**	**12.52**
A–240	9.98	10.06	_____	_____	_____
A–241	0.49	0.55	_____	_____	_____
A–242	1.4	1.9	_____	_____	_____
A–243	2.108	2.112	_____	_____	_____
A–244	0.4	0.49	_____	_____	_____
A–245	1.5	1.7	_____	_____	_____

ESTIMATING DECIMALS

Circle the number nearest in value to the number in the box.

Example	2.9 →	1	③	30	2	20
A–246	3.4 →	3	30	4	40	2
A–247	0.6 →	0	2	20	1	10
A–248	9.8 →	9	90	8	80	10
A–249	1.2 →	0	1	10	2	12
A–250	6.6 →	6	60	7	70	10
A–251	19.8 →	18	180	19	20	10

ESTIMATING DECIMALS

Circle the number nearest in value to the number in the box.

Example	0.18 ➤	0.0	0.3	1.0	(0.2)	2.0
A–252	4.75 ➤	4.0	4.8	5.0	5.8	5.7
A–253	9.09 ➤	10.0	9.0	9.1	10.1	9.9
A–254	8.91 ➤	9.0	9.1	8.0	8.9	9.9
A–255	1.24 ➤	1.4	0.9	10.0	1.0	1.1
A–256	0.99 ➤	0.1	1.9	10.0	1.5	1.1
A–257	19.49 ➤	18.0	18.5	19.0	18.4	19.4

ESTIMATING FRACTIONS

The number line shows the location of tenths.

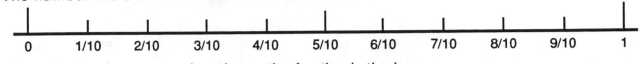

Circle the fraction nearest in value to the fraction in the box.

Example $\boxed{\dfrac{1}{3}} \longrightarrow$ $\dfrac{1}{10}$ $\boxed{\dfrac{3}{10}}$ $\dfrac{5}{10}$ $\dfrac{7}{10}$ $\dfrac{9}{10}$

A–258 $\boxed{\dfrac{5}{12}} \longrightarrow$ $\dfrac{1}{10}$ $\dfrac{2}{10}$ $\dfrac{3}{10}$ $\dfrac{4}{10}$ $\dfrac{6}{10}$

A–259 $\boxed{\dfrac{2}{3}} \longrightarrow$ $\dfrac{3}{10}$ $\dfrac{5}{10}$ $\dfrac{7}{10}$ $\dfrac{8}{10}$ $\dfrac{9}{10}$

A–260 $\boxed{\dfrac{3}{4}} \longrightarrow$ $\dfrac{3}{10}$ $\dfrac{4}{10}$ $\dfrac{5}{10}$ $\dfrac{6}{10}$ $\dfrac{8}{10}$

A–261 $\boxed{\dfrac{4}{5}} \longrightarrow$ $\dfrac{5}{10}$ $\dfrac{6}{10}$ $\dfrac{7}{10}$ $\dfrac{8}{10}$ $\dfrac{9}{10}$

A–262 $\boxed{\dfrac{1}{8}} \longrightarrow$ $\dfrac{1}{10}$ $\dfrac{3}{10}$ $\dfrac{4}{10}$ $\dfrac{6}{10}$ $\dfrac{8}{10}$

ESTIMATING FRACTIONS

The number line shows the location of some decimal numbers.

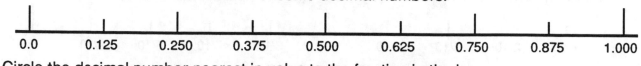

Circle the decimal number nearest in value to the fraction in the box.

Example $\dfrac{2}{3}$ → 0.250   (0.625)   0.875   0.375

A–263 $\dfrac{1}{4}$ → 0.125   0.375   0.250   0.875

A–264 $\dfrac{1}{5}$ → 0.250   0.875   0.125   0.375

A–265 $\dfrac{3}{8}$ → 0.125   0.375   0.625   0.875

A–266 $\dfrac{9}{10}$ → 0.875   0.125   0.625   0.375

A–267 $\dfrac{8}{10}$ → 0.250   0.625   0.875   0.750

ESTIMATING DECIMAL NUMBERS

Circle the decimal number which best estimates the number of shaded rectangles.

Example

1.7   3.8   (4.3)   4.7

A–268

0.4   2.5   5.2   2.8

A–269

3.0   0.5   3.5   4.0

A–270

3.5   0.6   4.3   5.5

A–271

1.8   0.5   1.2   1.0

ESTIMATING FRACTIONS

Circle the fraction which best estimates the number of shaded rectangles.

Example

$2\frac{1}{2}$ $3\frac{3}{4}$ $\boxed{2\frac{1}{4}}$ 2

A–272

$6\frac{7}{8}$ $7\frac{1}{8}$ $\frac{1}{8}$ $7\frac{7}{8}$

A–273

5 $\frac{1}{6}$ 1 $1\frac{1}{4}$

A–274

$\frac{7}{18}$ 3 $\frac{11}{2}$ $\frac{7}{2}$

A–275

$\frac{3}{4}$ $\frac{1}{4}$ $\frac{9}{4}$ $\frac{3}{10}$

ESTIMATING FRACTIONS

Compare the number of shaded rectangles to the total number of rectangles in each exercise.

Circle the fraction which best estimates the fractional part of the total number of rectangles that is shaded.

Example

$$\frac{11}{16} \qquad 2\frac{1}{2} \qquad \frac{3}{8} \qquad \boxed{\left(\frac{5}{16}\right)}$$

A–276

$$2\frac{1}{2} \qquad \frac{5}{10} \qquad \frac{5}{8} \qquad \frac{3}{5}$$

A–277

$$\frac{1}{3} \qquad 1 \qquad \frac{1}{2} \qquad \frac{2}{3}$$

A–278

$$5\frac{1}{2} \qquad \frac{11}{20} \qquad \frac{9}{20} \qquad \frac{3}{5}$$

A–279

$$\frac{2}{3} \qquad \frac{1}{3} \qquad \frac{1}{2} \qquad 2$$

ESTIMATING FRACTIONS

Circle the fraction which best estimates the part of the rectangle that is shaded.

Example

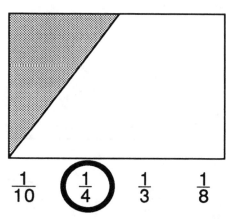

$\frac{1}{10}$ $\left(\frac{1}{4}\right)$ $\frac{1}{3}$ $\frac{1}{8}$

A–280

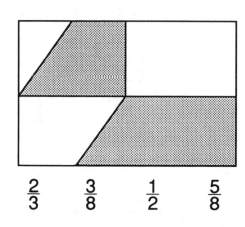

$\frac{2}{3}$ $\frac{3}{8}$ $\frac{1}{2}$ $\frac{5}{8}$

A–281

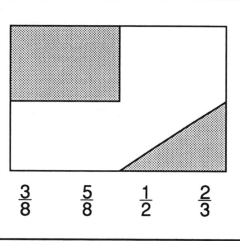

$\frac{3}{8}$ $\frac{5}{8}$ $\frac{1}{2}$ $\frac{2}{3}$

A–282

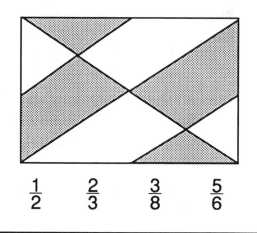

$\frac{1}{2}$ $\frac{2}{3}$ $\frac{3}{8}$ $\frac{5}{6}$

A–283

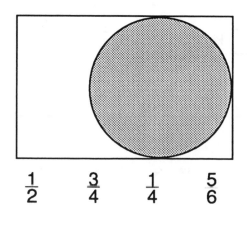

$\frac{1}{2}$ $\frac{3}{4}$ $\frac{1}{4}$ $\frac{5}{6}$

A–284

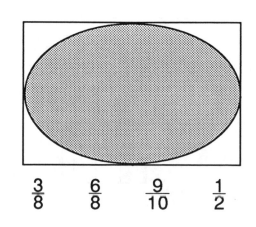

$\frac{3}{8}$ $\frac{6}{8}$ $\frac{9}{10}$ $\frac{1}{2}$

       P.O. BOX 448, PACIFIC GROVE, CA 93950

EQUIVALENT FRACTIONS

Circle all the fractions that tell what part of the figure is shaded.

Example

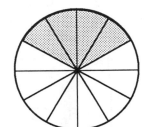

a. $\frac{4}{8}$ b. $\boxed{\frac{4}{12}}$

c. $\frac{4}{6}$ d. $\boxed{\frac{1}{3}}$

A–285

a. $\frac{2}{4}$ b. $\frac{1}{3}$

c. $\frac{2}{6}$ d. $\frac{2}{3}$

A–286

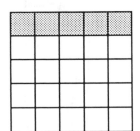

a. $\frac{1}{4}$ b. $\frac{5}{25}$

c. $\frac{5}{20}$ d. $\frac{1}{5}$

A–287

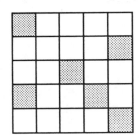

a. $\frac{6}{19}$ b. $\frac{6}{25}$

c. $\frac{1}{5}$ d. $\frac{60}{100}$

A–288

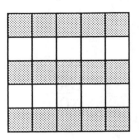

a. $\frac{3}{5}$ b. $\frac{2}{3}$

c. $\frac{20}{25}$ d. $\frac{15}{25}$

A–289

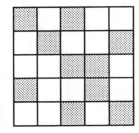

a. $\frac{10}{15}$ b. $\frac{10}{25}$

c. $\frac{2}{5}$ d. $\frac{40}{100}$

9/11/08

EQUIVALENT FRACTIONS

In each row circle all the fractions that are equivalent to the fraction in the box.

Example $\boxed{\dfrac{1}{4}}$ → $\dfrac{1}{8}$ $\dfrac{2}{4}$ $\boxed{\dfrac{2}{8}}$ $\dfrac{1}{2}$ $\boxed{\dfrac{5}{20}}$

A–290 $\boxed{\dfrac{2}{3}}$ → $\dfrac{2}{6}$ $\dfrac{6}{9}$ $\dfrac{4}{9}$ $\dfrac{4}{6}$ $\dfrac{6}{12}$

A–291 $\boxed{\dfrac{5}{6}}$ → $\dfrac{5}{10}$ $\dfrac{5}{12}$ $\dfrac{10}{12}$ $\dfrac{3}{6}$ $\dfrac{15}{24}$

A–292 $\boxed{\dfrac{6}{8}}$ → $\dfrac{6}{12}$ $\dfrac{9}{12}$ $\dfrac{3}{4}$ $\dfrac{12}{24}$ $\dfrac{12}{16}$

A–293 $\boxed{\dfrac{2}{10}}$ → $\dfrac{2}{5}$ $\dfrac{1}{5}$ $\dfrac{1}{10}$ $\dfrac{3}{20}$ $\dfrac{5}{25}$

A–294 $\boxed{\dfrac{3}{10}}$ → $\dfrac{3}{20}$ $\dfrac{6}{10}$ $\dfrac{6}{50}$ $\dfrac{9}{30}$ $\dfrac{30}{100}$

EQUIVALENT FRACTIONS

Each set contains four equivalent fractions.
Place an **X** on all the fractions that are not equivalent to those in the set.

Example

$\{\dfrac{4}{6}, \dfrac{6}{9}, \dfrac{12}{18}, \dfrac{16}{24}\}$

a. $\dfrac{10}{15}$ b. $\dfrac{9}{12}$

c. $\dfrac{6}{12}$ d. $\dfrac{2}{3}$

A–295

$\{\dfrac{4}{5}, \dfrac{12}{15}, \dfrac{20}{25}, \dfrac{24}{30}\}$

a. $\dfrac{8}{10}$ b. $\dfrac{8}{20}$

c. $\dfrac{15}{20}$ d. $\dfrac{28}{35}$

A–296

$\{\dfrac{5}{8}, \dfrac{20}{32}, \dfrac{15}{24}, \dfrac{25}{40}\}$

a. $\dfrac{30}{48}$ b. $\dfrac{25}{64}$

c. $\dfrac{5}{16}$ d. $\dfrac{10}{16}$

A–297

$\{\dfrac{8}{10}, \dfrac{24}{30}, \dfrac{12}{15}, \dfrac{40}{50}\}$

a. $\dfrac{4}{5}$ b. $\dfrac{4}{10}$

c. $\dfrac{16}{20}$ d. $\dfrac{20}{25}$

A–298

$\{\dfrac{5}{10}, \dfrac{10}{20}, \dfrac{4}{8}, \dfrac{15}{30}\}$

a. $\dfrac{3}{4}$ b. $\dfrac{6}{12}$

c. $\dfrac{10}{15}$ d. $\dfrac{1}{2}$

     P.O. BOX 448, PACIFIC GROVE, CA 93950

DECIMAL NUMBERS

Circle the decimal number that tells what part of the figure is shaded.

Example

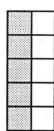

a. 0.1   b. 0.2

c. 0.5   d. 0.4

A–299

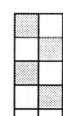

a. 0.4   b. 0.3

c. 0.2   d. 0.6

A–300

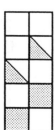

a. 0.7   b. 0.5

c. 0.2   d. 0.3

A–301

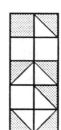

a. 0.3   b. 0.7

c. 0.4   d. 0.6

A–302

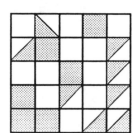

a. 0.60   b. 0.20

c. 0.40   d. 0.14

A–303

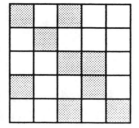

a. 0.90   b. 0.18

c. 0.36   d. 0.64

DECIMAL NUMBERS

Each large square represents one unit.
Shade a portion of the figure to match the decimal number.

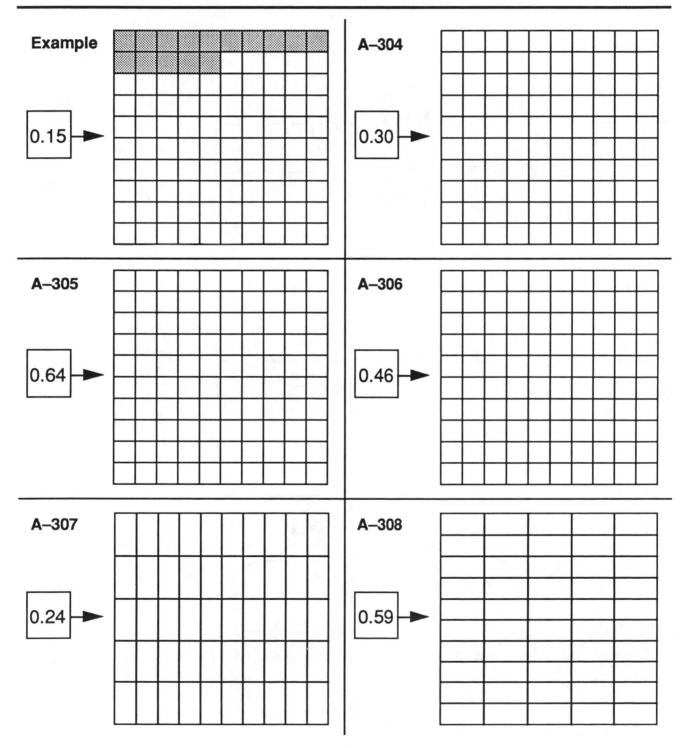

FRACTIONS AND DECIMAL NUMBERS

Circle all the decimal numbers and fractions that tell what part of the figure is shaded.

Example

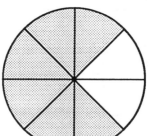

a. $\dfrac{4}{6}$ b. $\left(\dfrac{2}{5}\right)$

c. $\left(0.4\right)$ d. $\left(\dfrac{8}{20}\right)$

A–309

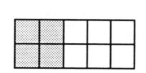

a. $\dfrac{1}{2}$ b. $\dfrac{4}{10}$

c. $\dfrac{5}{10}$ d. 0.5

A–310

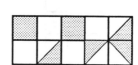

a. $\dfrac{4}{10}$ b. 0.4

c. $\dfrac{2}{5}$ d. 0.04

A–311

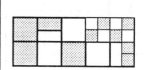

a. $\dfrac{11}{100}$ b. 0.5

c. $\dfrac{3}{10}$ d. $\dfrac{1}{2}$

A–312

a. 0.8 b. 0.75

c. $\dfrac{6}{8}$ d. $\dfrac{3}{4}$

A–313

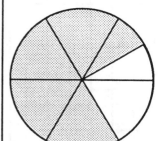
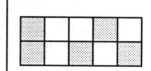

a. $\dfrac{2}{3}$ b. $\dfrac{9}{12}$

c. 0.75 d. $\dfrac{3}{4}$

          P.O. BOX 448, PACIFIC GROVE, CA 93950

FRACTIONS AND DECIMAL NUMBERS

The figure in each exercise represents one unit.
Shade a portion of the figure to match the number in the box.

Example

0.3

A–314

$\dfrac{5}{16}$

A–315

0.75

A–316

$\dfrac{5}{8}$

A–317

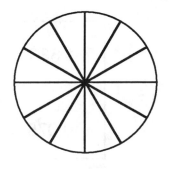

0.25

A–318

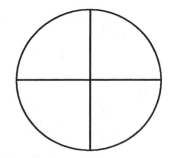

$\dfrac{5}{6}$

                   P.O. BOX 448, PACIFIC GROVE, CA 93950

FRACTIONS AND DECIMAL NUMBERS

Circle the decimal number that is equal to the fraction.

Example

$\frac{3}{4}$

7.5	1.33
0.075	(0.75)

A–319

$\frac{5}{8}$

0.0625	0.625
1.60	6.25

A–320

$\frac{3}{2}$

0.15	0.015
0.666	1.5

A–321

$\frac{4}{16}$

0.025	4.00
0.25	2.5

A–322

$2\frac{1}{5}$

0.454	2.2
0.022	0.22

A–323

$\frac{9}{12}$

1.333	7.5
0.075	0.75

FRACTIONS AND DECIMAL NUMBERS

Circle all the fractions that are equal to the decimal number.

Example

0.5

$\dfrac{1}{3}$ $\dfrac{4}{20}$ $\dfrac{4}{7}$

$\boxed{\dfrac{1}{2}}$ $\dfrac{5}{25}$ $\boxed{\dfrac{5}{10}}$

A–324

0.75

$\dfrac{7}{10}$ $\dfrac{3}{4}$ $\dfrac{5}{10}$

$\dfrac{6}{8}$ $\dfrac{1}{2}$ $\dfrac{75}{100}$

A–325

0.35

$\dfrac{3}{10}$ $\dfrac{35}{100}$ $\dfrac{5}{100}$

$\dfrac{14}{40}$ $\dfrac{7}{20}$ $\dfrac{35}{10}$

A–326

0.875

$\dfrac{7}{8}$ $\dfrac{5}{100}$ $\dfrac{85}{100}$

$\dfrac{15}{16}$ $\dfrac{85}{10}$ $\dfrac{875}{1000}$

A–327

3.2

$\dfrac{32}{10}$ $3\dfrac{1}{5}$ $\dfrac{320}{100}$

$\dfrac{32}{100}$ $3\dfrac{2}{10}$ $3\dfrac{2}{5}$

A–328

1.25

$1\dfrac{1}{4}$ $\dfrac{125}{100}$ $1\dfrac{1}{2}$

$1\dfrac{25}{100}$ $\dfrac{3}{2}$ $\dfrac{5}{4}$

61   P.O. BOX 448, PACIFIC GROVE, CA 93950

FRACTIONS AND DECIMAL NUMBERS

Circle all the values that are equal to the number in the box.

Example	$\frac{3}{4}$	(0.75)	7.5			0.075
A–329	$\frac{5}{8}$	$\frac{10}{15}$	$\frac{14}{16}$	6.25	0.625	0.0625
A–330	0.45	$\frac{9}{20}$	$\frac{4}{10}$	$\frac{45}{100}$	$\frac{45}{10}$	4.50
A–331	4.6	$\frac{46}{10}$	4.60	$\frac{46}{100}$	$4\frac{6}{10}$	0.46
A–332	$\frac{9}{5}$	0.18	$1\frac{4}{5}$	$1\frac{8}{10}$	1.8	18.0
A–333	0.375	$\frac{375}{1000}$	3.75	$\frac{3}{8}$	$\frac{5}{16}$	0.3750
A–334	$2\frac{3}{20}$	$\frac{43}{20}$	21.5	2.15	$\frac{23}{20}$	0.215
A–335	$\frac{195}{100}$	1.95	$\frac{195}{10}$	$1\frac{9}{20}$	$1\frac{95}{100}$	0.195

CONSTRUCTING FIGURES

Eight points are labeled on each geoboard design.
Draw the figure that is the union of the segments listed.

Example $\overline{GI}, \overline{IC}, \overline{BC}, \overline{GB}$ **B–1** $\overline{BC}, \overline{GH}, \overline{BG}, \overline{HC}$

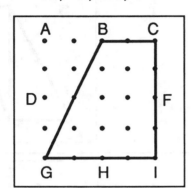

B–2 $\overline{HC}, \overline{CA}, \overline{HG}, \overline{GA}$ **B–3** $\overline{HC}, \overline{IH}, \overline{CI}$

B–4 $\overline{GI}, \overline{BC}, \overline{GB}, \overline{HC}, \overline{CI}$ **B–5** $\overline{AC}, \overline{CI}, \overline{IG}, \overline{AG}, \overline{BG}, \overline{CH}$

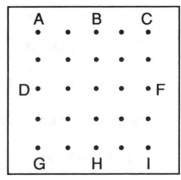

CONSTRUCTING FIGURES

Draw the figure that is the union of Figures 1, 2, and 3.
Name any triangles in the completed figure that are not already listed.

Example
    Figure 1: triangle GHB

    Figure 2: triangle CIH

    Figure 3: quadrilateral BCIH

    Name the triangles: _____**Triangle CBH**_____

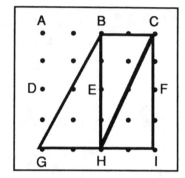

B–6
    Figure 1: quadrilateral GICB

    Figure 2: triangle GIC

    Figure 3: triangle GHC

    Name the triangles: _____

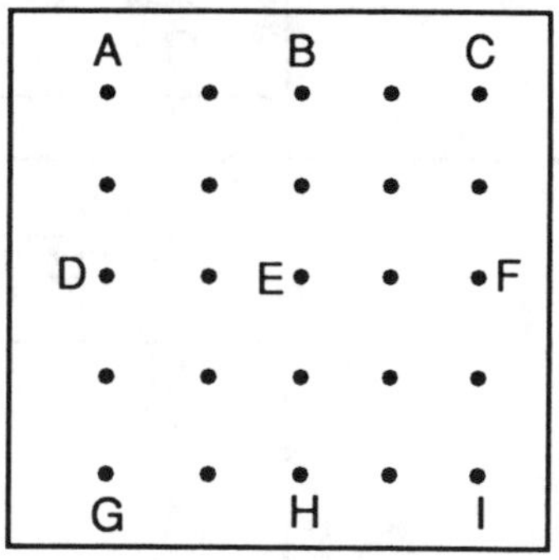

B–7
    Figure 1: triangle ACI

    Figure 2: triangle GAE

    Figure 3: triangle ACE

    Name the triangles: _____

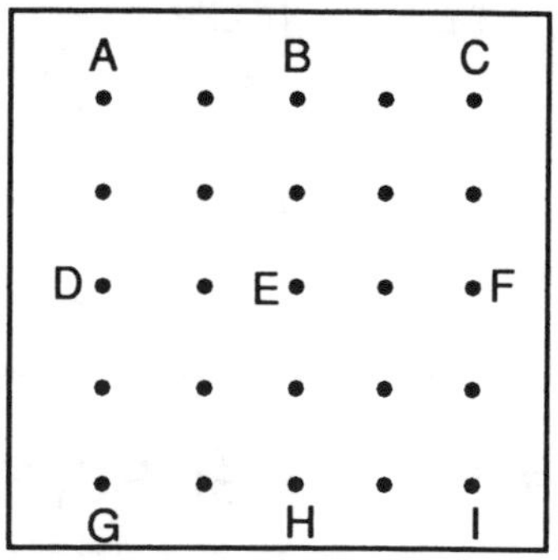

B–8
    Figure 1: triangle GAC

    Figure 2: triangle IAC

    Figure 3: triangle GIA

    Name the triangles: _____

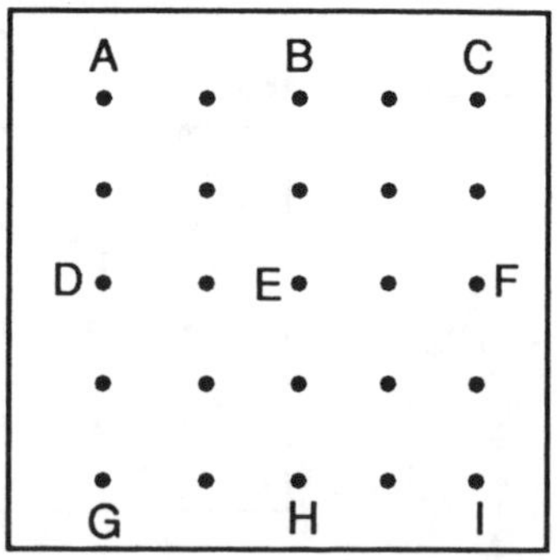

COMPARING LENGTHS

Circle the letter of each statement that is true.

Example

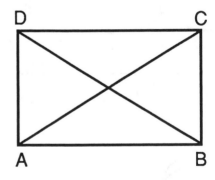

Figure DAC is a right triangle.

a. $\overline{DC}$ is longer than $\overline{AD}$.   b. $\overline{AB}$ is shorter than $\overline{DB}$.

c. $\overline{DB}$ is shorter than $\overline{AD}$.   d. $\overline{DC}$ is longer than $\overline{BD}$.

e. $\overline{BC}$ is shorter than $\overline{AC}$.   f. $\overline{AC}$ is shorter than $\overline{AB}$.

B–9

Figure ABCD is a rectangle.

a. $\overline{AD}$ is congruent to $\overline{BC}$.   b. $\overline{AC}$ is longer than $\overline{BD}$.

c. $\overline{AB}$ is shorter than $\overline{BC}$.   d. $\overline{AB}$ is shorter than $\overline{BD}$.

e. $\overline{AC}$ is shorter than $\overline{BC}$.   f. $\overline{AB}$ is congruent to $\overline{DC}$.

B–10

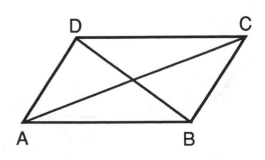

Figure ABCD is a parallelogram.

a. $\overline{AD}$ is longer than $\overline{AB}$.   b. $\overline{BD}$ is longer than $\overline{BC}$.

c. $\overline{AB}$ is shorter than $\overline{AC}$.   d. $\overline{AD}$ is congruent to $\overline{BC}$.

e. $\overline{AB}$ is shorter than $\overline{DC}$.   f. $\overline{AC}$ is congruent to $\overline{BD}$.

COMPARING PATHS

Use X's to indicate the shortest path from A to B.

Example

B–11

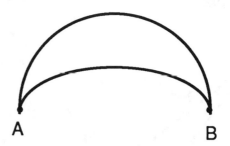

B–12

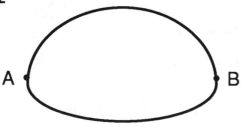

B–13

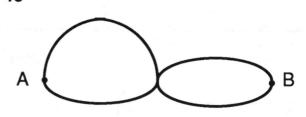

B–14

B–15

B–16

B–17

COMPARING LENGTHS

The center of each circle is "O."
Circle the letter in front of each statement that is true.

Example

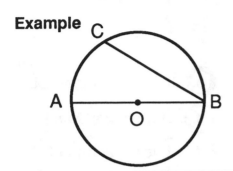

a. $\overline{AB}$ is longer than $\overline{CB}$.   b. $\overline{BC}$ is shorter than $\overarc{BC}$.

c. $\overline{OB}$ is longer than $\overline{CB}$.   d. $\overarc{AC}$ is longer than $\overarc{BC}$.

e. $\overline{AO}$ is congruent to $\overline{OB}$.   f. $\overline{AB}$ is equal to $\overarc{AB}$.

B–18

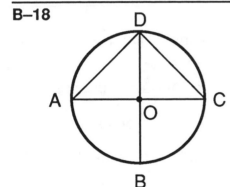

$\overline{AC}$ and $\overline{BD}$ are perpendicular line segments.

a. $\overline{CD}$ is congruent to $\overarc{CD}$.   b. $\overline{AC}$ is congruent to $\overline{BD}$.

c. $\overline{AD}$ is congruent to $\overline{DC}$.   d. $\overarc{AD}$ is shorter than $\overarc{DC}$.

e. $\overline{AD}$ is longer than $\overarc{AD}$.   f. $\overline{AO}$ is congruent to $\overline{OD}$.

B–19

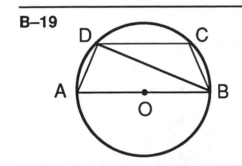

ABCD is an isosceles trapezoid.

a. $\overline{AB}$ is shorter than $\overline{BD}$.   b. $\overline{DC}$ is shorter than $\overarc{DC}$.

c. $\overline{DC}$ is congruent to $\overline{AB}$.   d. $\overline{AD}$ is congruent to $\overline{CB}$.

e. $\overarc{AD}$ is shorter than $\overarc{CB}$.   f. $\overarc{AD}$ is congruent to $\overarc{DC}$.

B–20

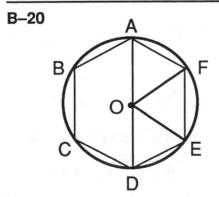

The six points are equally spaced around the circle.

a. $\overline{OD}$ is shorter than $\overline{OF}$.   b. $\overline{AD}$ is shorter than $\overline{BC}$.

c. $\overline{AB}$ is congruent to $\overline{CD}$.   d. $\overarc{AB}$ is congruent to $\overarc{CD}$.

e. $\overline{AO}$ is longer than $\overline{OE}$.   f. $\overline{CD}$ is shorter than $\overarc{AB}$.

COMPARING LENGTHS

The center of each circle is "O."
Circle the letter in front of each statement that is true.

Example

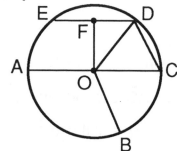

$\overline{AC}$ is parallel to $\overline{ED}$.

(a.) $\overline{OD}$ is congruent to $\overline{OB}$.   (b.) $\overline{OF}$ is shorter than $\overline{OD}$.

c. $\overline{AO}$ is congruent to $\overline{OF}$.   (d.) $\overline{ED}$ is shorter than $\overparen{ED}$.

(e.) $\overparen{AE}$ is congruent to $\overparen{DC}$.   f. $\overparen{AE}$ is longer than $\overparen{DC}$.

B–21

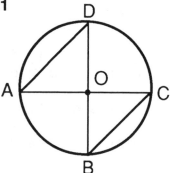

$\overline{AC}$ and $\overline{BD}$ are perpendicular line segments.

a. $\overline{AD}$ is congruent to $\overline{BC}$.   b. $\overline{AO}$ is congruent to $\overline{AD}$.

c. $\overparen{AD}$ is shorter than $\overparen{BC}$.   d. $\overline{BD}$ is longer than $\overline{AC}$.

e. $\overparen{BC}$ is longer than $\overline{AD}$.   f. $\overparen{DC}$ is shorter than $\overparen{AB}$.

B–22

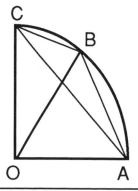

$\overparen{AC}$ is $\frac{1}{4}$ of a circle with the center at "O."

a. $\overline{OC}$ is shorter than $\overline{AC}$.   b. $\overparen{AC}$ is longer than $\overline{AC}$.

c. $\overline{AB}$ is congruent to $\overline{BC}$.   d. $\overline{AB}$ is congruent to $\overparen{BC}$.

e. $\overline{AC}$ is shorter than $\overparen{AB}$.   f. $\overline{OB}$ is longer than $\overline{OC}$.

B–23

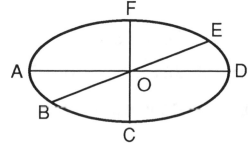

The curved figure is an ellipse.

a. $\overline{OF}$ is longer than $\overline{AO}$.   b. $\overline{OF}$ is congruent to $\overline{OE}$.

c. $\overline{AD}$ is shorter than $\overline{FC}$.   d. $\overline{AD}$ is longer than $\overline{BE}$.

e. $\overline{BO}$ is shorter than $\overline{OD}$.   f. $\overline{BO}$ is congruent to $\overline{OF}$.

COMPARING CHORDS

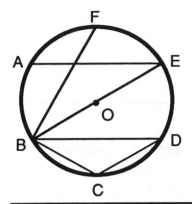

The center of the circle is "O."
The six other points are equally spaced around the circle.
Six chords connect these points.

Example	Name the longest chord in the circle.	$\overline{BE}$
B–24	Name the shortest chord in the circle.	
B–25	Name a diameter of the circle.	
B–26	Name two radii of the circle.	
B–27	Name a chord the same length as $\overline{BC}$.	
B–28	Name a chord the same length as $\overline{AE}$.	
B–29	Name a chord shorter than the path from B to C to D.	
B–30	Name a path longer than the path from F to B to D.	

CONSTRUCTING FIGURES

The six points are equally spaced around the circle.
Draw each figure described using the given six points.

Example

A diameter containing point A

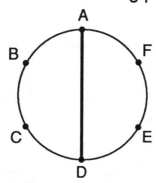

B–31

An equilateral triangle

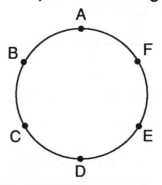

B–32

The longest path using only the points F, B, and C

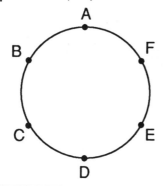

B–33

A rectangle

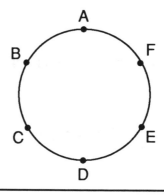

B–34

The longest path using only the points B, C, D, and F

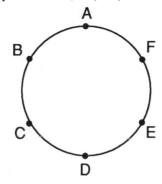

B–35

A scalene triangle

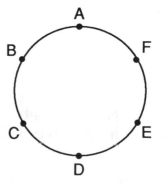

COMPARING ANGLES

Circle the letter in front of each statement that is true.

Example

$\overline{AB}$ and $\overline{DO}$ are perpendicular line segments.

(a.) ∠DOB is congruent to ∠AOD.

(b.) ∠COB is less than ∠DOB.

c. ∠COB is greater than ∠AOD.

(d.) ∠AOC is greater than ∠DOB.

e. ∠DOC is greater than ∠AOD.

B–36

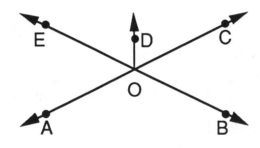

a. ∠COB is congruent to ∠EOA.

b. ∠EOC is less than ∠DOC.

c. ∠AOB is greater than ∠EOD.

d. ∠COB is less than ∠AOB.

e. ∠AOD is less than ∠DOC.

B–37

$\overline{AD}$ and $\overline{BE}$ are perpendicular line segments.

a. ∠COB is greater than ∠DOB.

b. ∠EOD is congruent to ∠DOB.

c. ∠EOF is greater than ∠FOA.

d. ∠AOF is less than ∠DOE.

e. ∠EOC is congruent to ∠BOF.

COMPARING ANGLES

Circle the letter in front of each statement that is true.

Example   Figure ABCD is a rectangle.

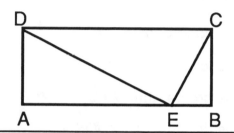

        ⓐ ∠DAE is congruent to ∠EBC.

        b. ∠ADE is congruent to ∠ECB.

        ⓒ ∠ADC is greater than ∠ADE.

        d. ∠AED is congruent to ∠CEB.

B–38   Figure ABCD is a rectangle and Figure BEO is a right triangle.

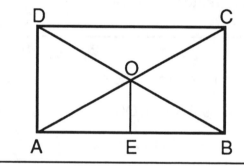

        a. ∠DOC is congruent to ∠COB.

        b. ∠AOD is congruent to ∠COB.

        c. ∠OAE is congruent to ∠OBE.

        d. ∠AEO is less than ∠EBC.

B–39   Figure ABCD is a trapezoid and Figure DAB is a right triangle.

        a. ∠BCD is less than ∠CDA.

        b. ∠DOA is less than ∠COB.

        c. ∠DAB is congruent to ∠ABC.

        d. ∠ABC is greater than ∠CAB.

B–40   Figure CAB is a right triangle.

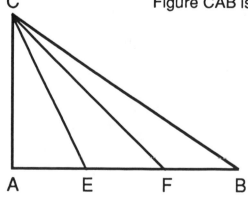

        a. ∠CEA is greater than ∠CFA.

        b. ∠CEF is less than ∠CAE.

        c. ∠CEF is less than ∠CFB.

        d. ∠ACF is greater than ∠ACE.

ISOMETRIC GRIDS

Each array of dots forms an isometric grid.
Connect dots to construct each of the polygons.

Example   An equilateral triangle

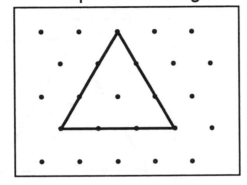

B–41   A right triangle

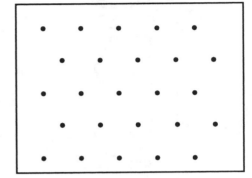

B–42   A regular hexagon

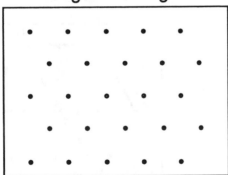

B–43   A rectangle

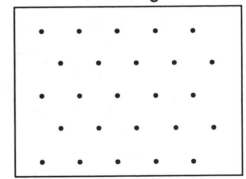

B–44   A trapezoid

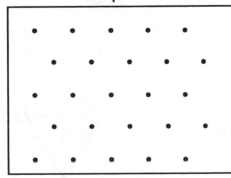

B–45   A parallelogram

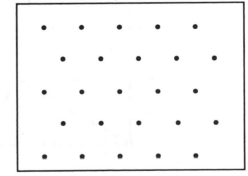

         P.O. BOX 448, PACIFIC GROVE, CA 93950

COMPARING ANGLES

Each figure below is shown on an isometric grid.
Circle both angles if they are congruent.
If they are not congruent, circle the greater angle.

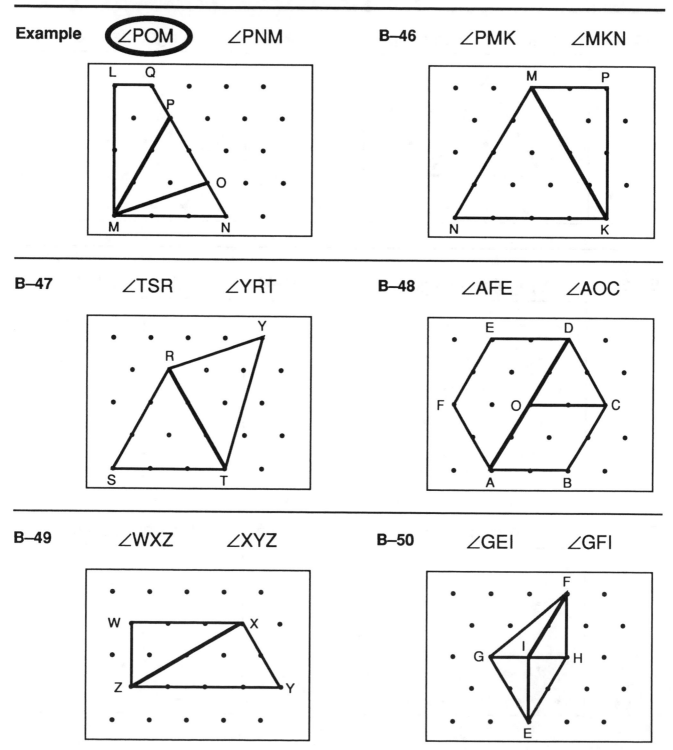

Example   ⟨(∠POM)⟩   ∠PNM

B–46   ∠PMK   ∠MKN

B–47   ∠TSR   ∠YRT

B–48   ∠AFE   ∠AOC

B–49   ∠WXZ   ∠XYZ

B–50   ∠GEI   ∠GFI

       P.O. BOX 448, PACIFIC GROVE, CA 93950

CONSTRUCTING ANGLES

The quadrilateral ABCD is drawn on the isometric grid. Construct each of the following angles.

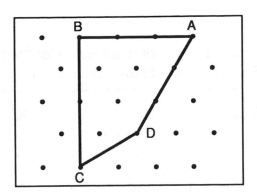

Example   ∠RST, which is the same size as ∠DAB

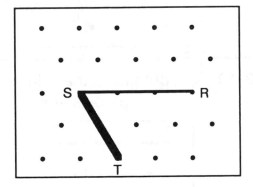

B–51   ∠PQR, which is twice the size of ∠BAD

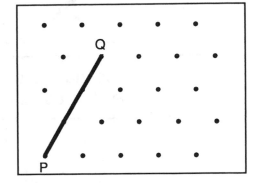

B–52   ∠KLM, which is the same size as ∠ABC

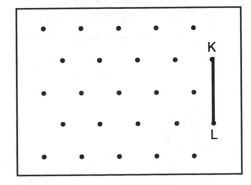

B–53   ∠FGH, which is half the size of ∠BAD

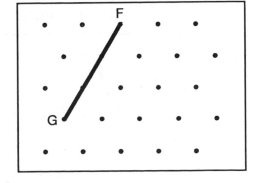

CONSTRUCTING POLYGONS

Each array of dots forms an isometric grid.
Construct the figures described.

Example A trapezoid with $\overline{XY}$ as
one of the parallel sides

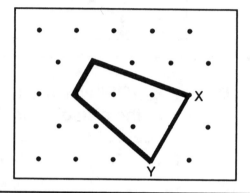

B–54   An equilateral triangle
with $\overline{PQ}$ as a side

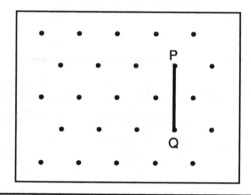

B–55 An isosceles triangle with $\overline{RS}$
as the shortest side

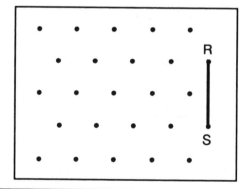

B–56 An equilateral triangle with $\overline{AB}$
as one side

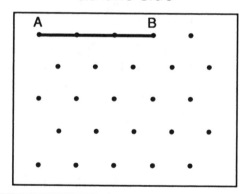

B–57 A scalene triangle with $\overline{MN}$
as one side

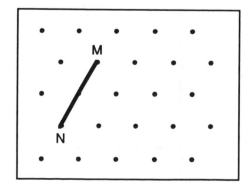

B–58   A right triangle with $\overline{CD}$
as one leg

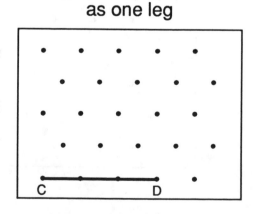

                                   P.O. BOX 448, PACIFIC GROVE, CA 93950

CONSTRUCTING POLYGONS

Each array of dots forms an isometric grid. Using triangle ABC, construct polygons that satisfy each condition.

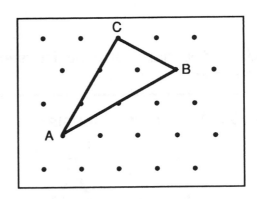

Example Triangle RST so that the measure of ∠R is twice that of ∠A	**B–59** Triange DEF, which is the same size and shape as triangle ABC

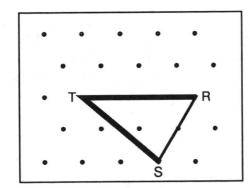

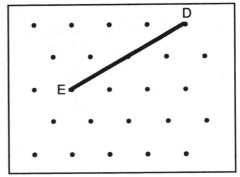

B–60 Triangle LMN so that the measure of ∠L is four times greater than that of ∠A	**B–61** Isosceles triangle PQR so that the measure of ∠Q is the same as ∠B

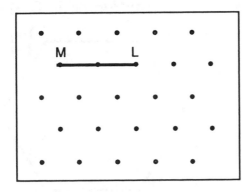

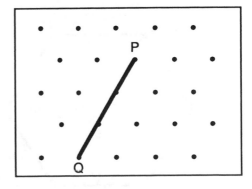

DECOMPOSING POLYGONS

Using diagonals that do not intersect inside the polygon, separate each polygon into the figures listed.

Example   Three triangles

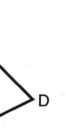

B–62   Three triangles different from those in the Example

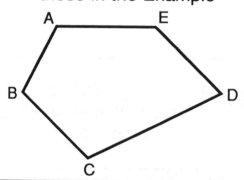

B–63   A quadrilateral and a triangle

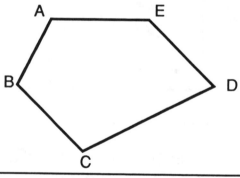

B–64   A quadrilateral and a triangle different from those constructed in B–63

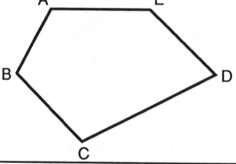

B–65   A quadrilateral and two triangles

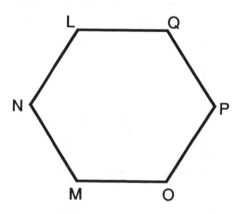

B–66   A quadrilateral and two triangles different from those constructed in B–65

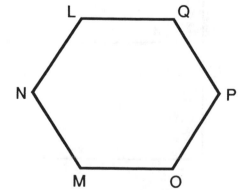

       P.O. BOX 448, PACIFIC GROVE, CA 93950

DECOMPOSING POLYGONS

Five numbered figures appear on the geoboard design.
Decompose each polygon into either three or four of these figures.
Number the pieces to match the given figures.

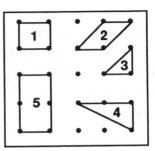

Example

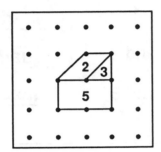

B–67

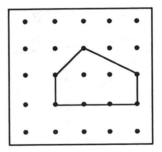

B–68

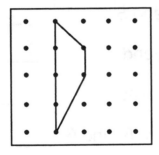

B–69

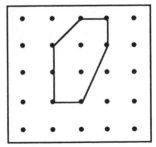

B–70

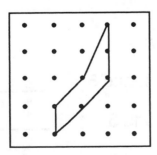

B–71

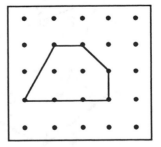

LOCATING POLYGONS

Each polygon has been subdivided into smaller figures.
Each region is identified with a number.
Name the polygon that is formed by combining the indicated regions.

Example

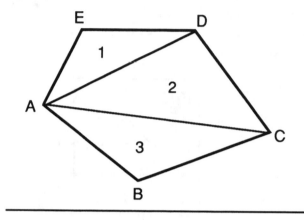

Regions	
1	**triangle**
1 and 2	**quadrilateral**
2 and 3	**quadrilateral**

B–72

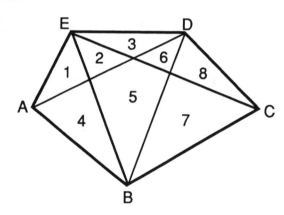

Regions	
1 and 2	_____
4 and 5	_____
4, 5, and 7	_____
3, 6, and 8	_____
1, 2, 3, 4, 5, and 6	_____

B–73

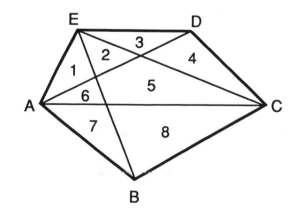

Regions	
5 and 6	_____
5 and 8	_____
2, 3, 4, and 5	_____
4 and 5	_____
2 and 3	_____

LOCATING POLYGONS

Each polygon has been subdivided into smaller regions.
Each region is identified with a number.

Example

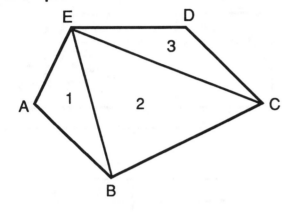

Find two quadrilaterals that can be formed by combining regions.
Name the regions.

1 and 2
_____

2 and 3
_____

B–74

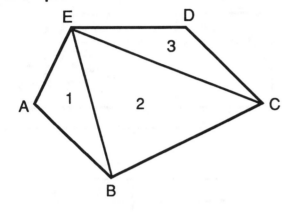

Find four quadrilaterals that can be formed by combining two or more regions.
Name the regions .

_____   _____

_____   _____

B–75

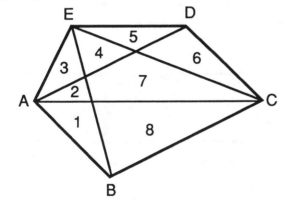

Find four quadrilaterals that can be formed by combining two or more regions.
Name the regions .

_____   _____

_____   _____

MATCHING SHAPES

Select figure a or b or c to complete the shading of the given figure.

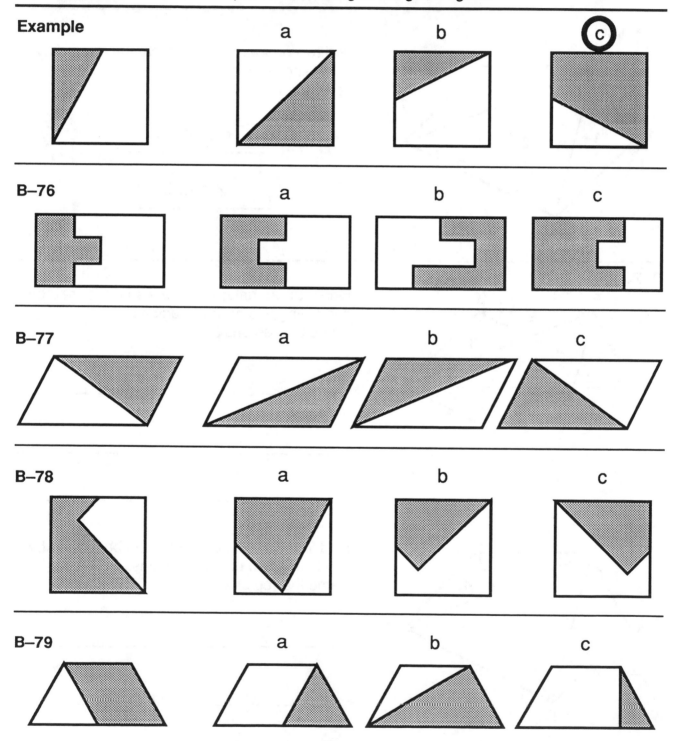

CONGRUENT FIGURES

Compare Figure 1 and Figure 2.

Figure 1

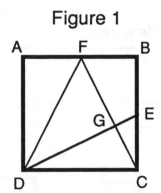

Figure 2

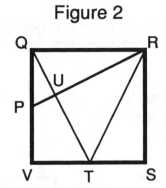

Name a shape in Figure 2 that is congruent to the shape in Figure 1.

Example	Figure 1: △DFC	Figure 2:	△**RTQ**
B–80	Figure 1: △ECD	Figure 2:	_____
B–81	Figure 1: △FGD	Figure 2:	_____
B–82	Figure 1: $\overline{GD}$	Figure 2:	_____
B–83	Figure 1: Quadrilateral ABED	Figure 2:	_____
B–84	Figure 1: Quadrilateral FDEB	Figure 2:	_____

83   P.O. BOX 448, PACIFIC GROVE, CA 93950

PROPERTIES OF POLYGONS

Place an X inside each polygon that is described by the statement.

Example

A polygon with four congruent sides or four congruent angles.

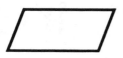 

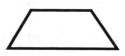

B–85

A polygon that is not a quadrilateral and has at least one right angle.

 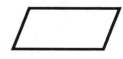

B–86

A polygon that has all sides congruent or all angles congruent.

 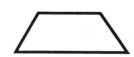

B–87

A polygon that is a parallelogram and is not a rectangle.

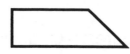 

PROPERTIES OF POLYGONS

Write the letter of each polygon that is described by the statement.

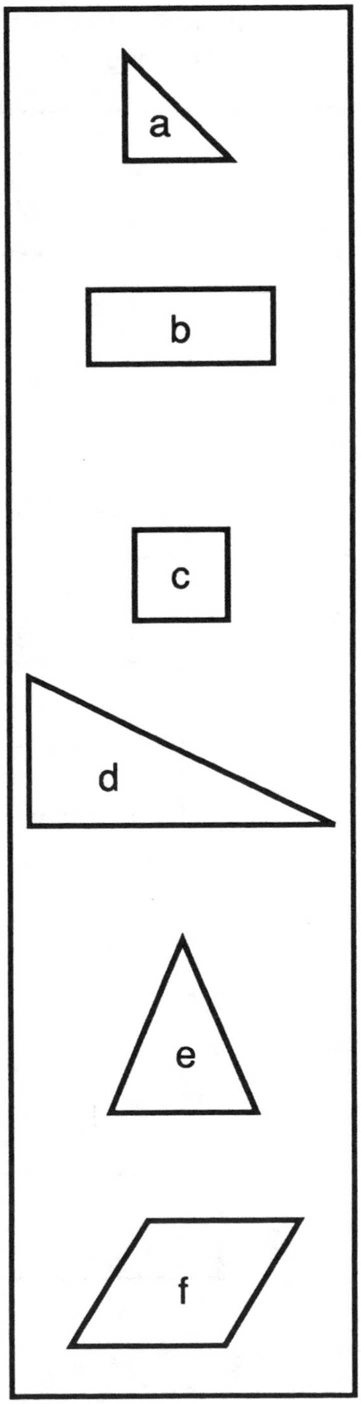

Example

The polygon is a parallelogram and has four congruent sides.

_____ **c and f** _____

B–88

The polygon is a triangle and has two congruent sides.

_____

B–89

The polygon is a rectangle and has all sides congruent.

_____

B–90

The polygon is not a parallelogram and has one right angle.

_____

B–91

The polygon is a right triangle and has two congruent sides.

_____

B–92

The polygon is a rhombus and has a right angle.

_____

PROPERTIES OF POLYGONS

Describe the properties of each polygon using the list below.
Write the numbers of the properties below each polygon.

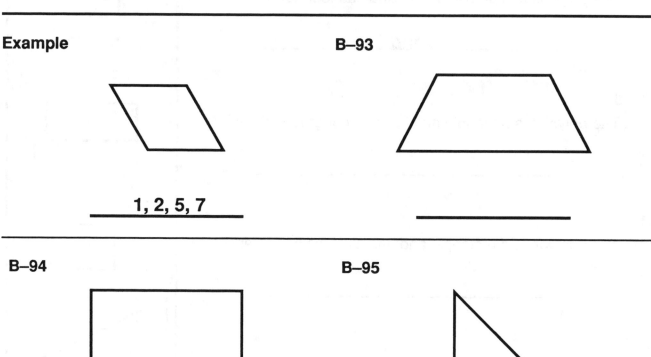

SIDES	ANGLES	PARALLEL
1. all congruent	4. all congruent	7. opposite sides
2. at least two congruent	5. at least two congruent	8. exactly two sides
3. none congruent	6. at least one right	9. no sides

Example   **B–93**

1, 2, 5, 7

B–94   **B–95**

B–96   **B–97**

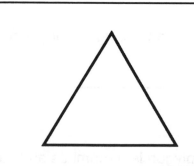

        86   P.O. BOX 448, PACIFIC GROVE, CA 93950

PROPERTIES OF POLYGONS

Draw a polygon that has the properties described.

Example

A polygon that is a parallelogram and has a right angle

B–98

A polygon that is a quadrilateral and has two parallel sides

B–99

A polygon that is a right triangle and has two congruent sides

B–100

A polygon that is a parallelogram and has four congruent sides

B–101

A polygon that is a quadrilateral and has two sets of parallel sides

B–102

A polygon that is a triangle and has exactly two congruent sides

CLASSIFYING POLYGONS

Circle the letter in front of each word that makes the following statement true.

"Pictured is a set of _____."

Underline the word which best describes the set.

Example

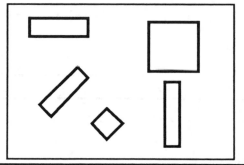

   (a.) polygons   (b.) rectangles
   (c.) quadrilaterals   d. squares
   (e.) parallelograms   f. trapezoids
   g. triangles   h. rhombuses
   i. regular polygons

B–103

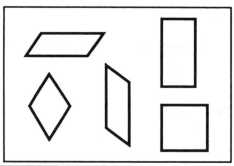

   a. polygons   b. rectangles
   c. quadrilaterals   d. squares
   e. parallelograms   f. trapezoids
   g. triangles   h. rhombuses
   i. regular polygons

B–104

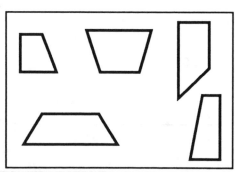

   a. polygons   b. rectangles
   c. quadrilaterals   d. squares
   e. parallelograms   f. trapezoids
   g. triangles   h. rhombuses
   i. regular polygons

B–105

   a. polygons   b. rectangles
   c. quadrilaterals   d. squares
   e. parallelograms   f. trapezoids
   g. triangles   h. rhombuses
   i. regular polygons

 P.O. BOX 448, PACIFIC GROVE, CA 93950

PROPERTIES OF POLYGONS

Each polygon belongs in one of the regions in the diagram.
Place the number of the region inside each polygon.

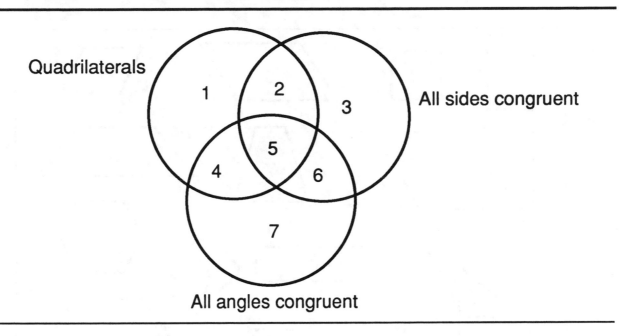

Quadrilaterals

1 2 3 All sides congruent

5

4 6

7

All angles congruent

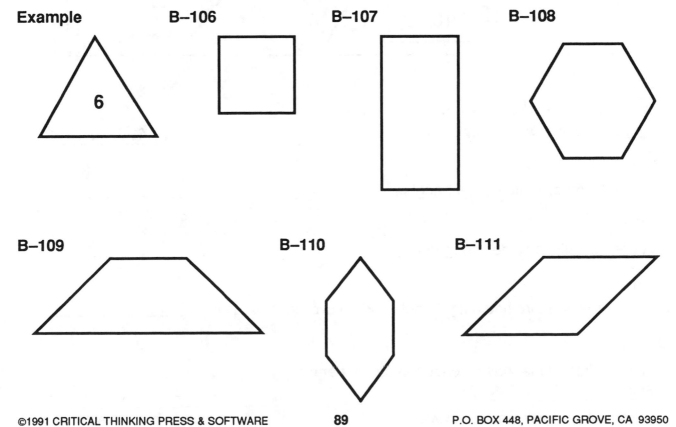

Example   **B–106**   **B–107**   **B–108**

6

B–109   **B–110**   **B–111**

CLASSIFYING POLYGONS

List the numbers of all polygons that fit the following descriptions.

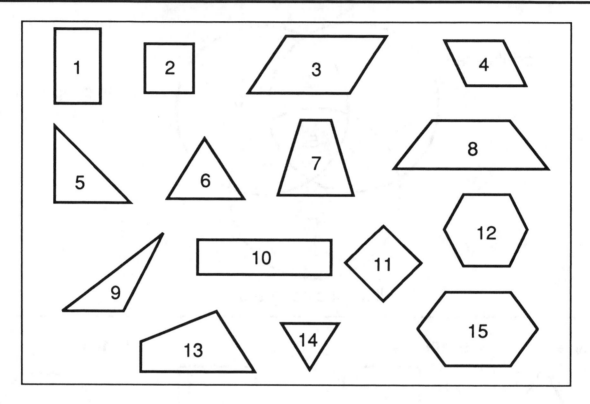

Example

A polygon with at least one pair of parallel sides and an
angle greater than a right angle   **3, 4, 7, 8, 12, 15**

B–112

A parallelogram with no right angles   _____

B–113

A polygon with all sides congruent   _____

B–114

A quadrilateral that has a right angle and no two sides parallel   _____

B–115

A quadrilateral that has at least one pair of parallel
sides and is not a rectangle   _____

DESCRIBING SETS OF POLYGONS

Write a description for the set of polygons chosen from those below.

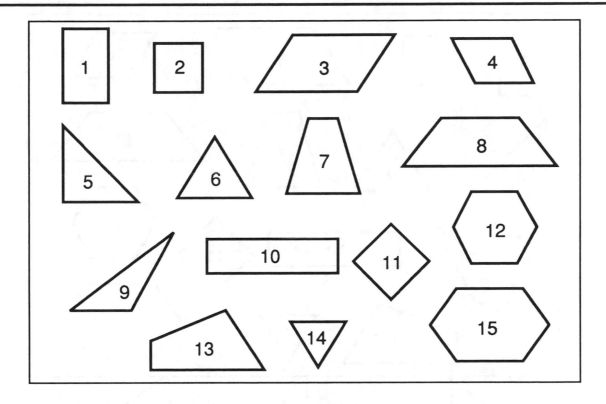

Example	Polygons: 1, 2, 10, 11	**Quadrilaterals with all right angles**
		(or rectangles)

B–116   Polygons: 5, 6, 14 _____

_____

B–117   Polygons: 1, 2, 5, 10, 11, 13 _____

_____

B–118   Polygons: 12, 15 _____

_____

B–119   Polygons: 2, 4, 11 _____

_____

DIVIDING A SET INTO SUBSETS

Divide the set below into three disjoint subsets.
Describe each subset and list the numbers of the polygons that belong to each set.

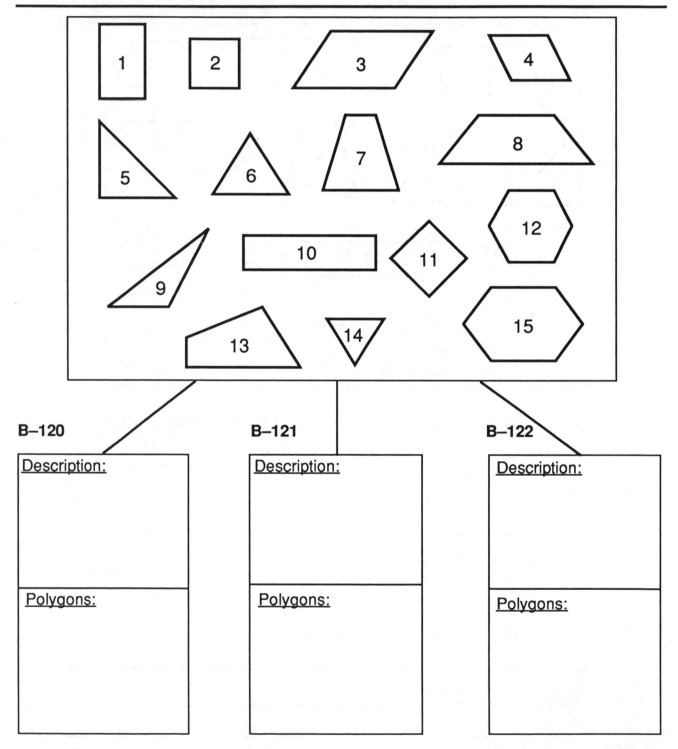

B–120

Description:
Polygons:

B–121

Description:
Polygons:

B–122

Description:
Polygons:

PROPERTIES OF POLYGONS

Each square represents a set of polygons.
Place an X in each region that could be the location of the polygon described.

Example

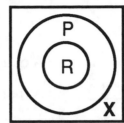

A polygon that is not
a parallelogram

B–123

A parallelogram that
is not a rectangle

**All rectangles
are parallelograms.**

B–124

A parallelogram that
is a rectangle

B–125

A polygon that is
not a rectangle

B–126

A polygon that is
a paralleolgram

**All squares
are rhombuses.**

B–127

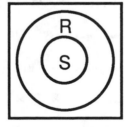

A rhombus that is
a square

B–128

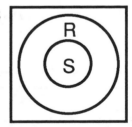

A polygon that is
not a rhombus

B–129

A rhombus that is
not a square

B–130

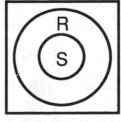

A polygon that is
a rhombus

B–131

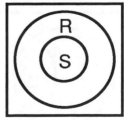

A polygon that is
not a square

93   P.O. BOX 448, PACIFIC GROVE, CA 93950

PROPERTIES OF POLYGONS

Each rectangle represents a set of polygons.
Write the number of the region into which each polygon should be placed.

Example

Some quadrilaterals (Q)
have all sides congruent(C).

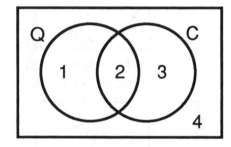

__2__ a. A quadrilateral that is a square

__2__ b. A rhombus that is not a square

__1__ c. A rectangle that is not a square

__4__ d. A hexagon with sides that are not congruent

__3__ e. An equilateral triangle

__1__ f. A parallelogram that is not a rectangle

B–132

Some right triangles (R)
are isosceles triangles (I).

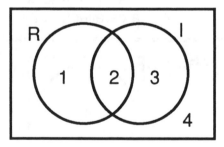

_____ a. A quadrilateral that is a square

_____ b. A right triangle with no congruent sides

_____ c. An isosceles triangle with no right angles

_____ d. An isosceles triangle with one right angle

_____ e. An equilateral triangle

_____ f. A scalene triangle with no right angles

B–133

Some parallelograms (P)
have all angles congruent (C).

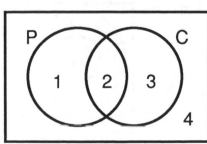

_____ a. A quadrilateral that is a square

_____ b. A quadrilateral that is a trapezoid

_____ c. A rectangle that is not a square

_____ d. A rhombus that is not a square

_____ e. An equilateral triangle

_____ f. A parallelogram that is not a rhombus

SIMILAR FIGURES

Similar figures have the same shape.
Draw a figure on the dot paper that is similar to the given figure.
Make the figure as large as possible.

Example

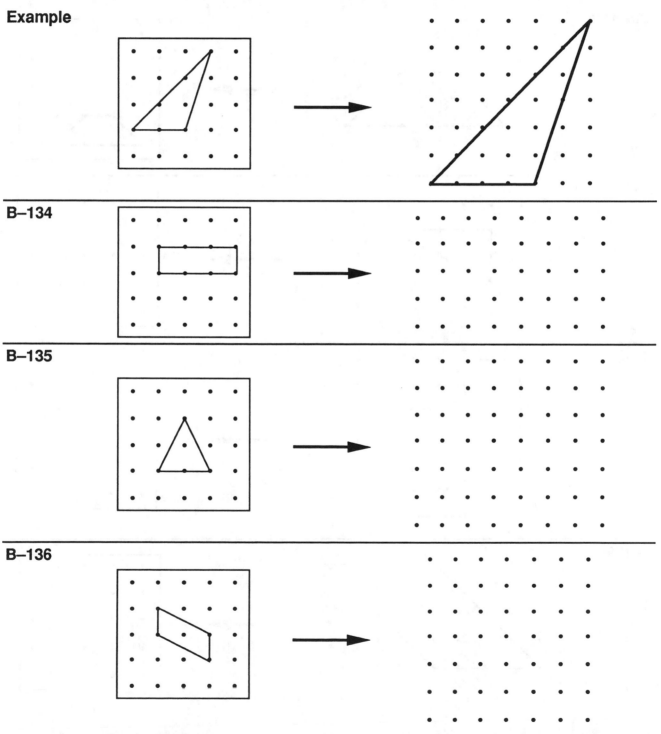

B–134

B–135

B–136

SIMILAR FIGURES

Similar figures have the same shape.
Connect dots on the geoboard design to make a figure similar to the given figure.
Make the figure as small as possible.

Example

B–137

B–138

B–139

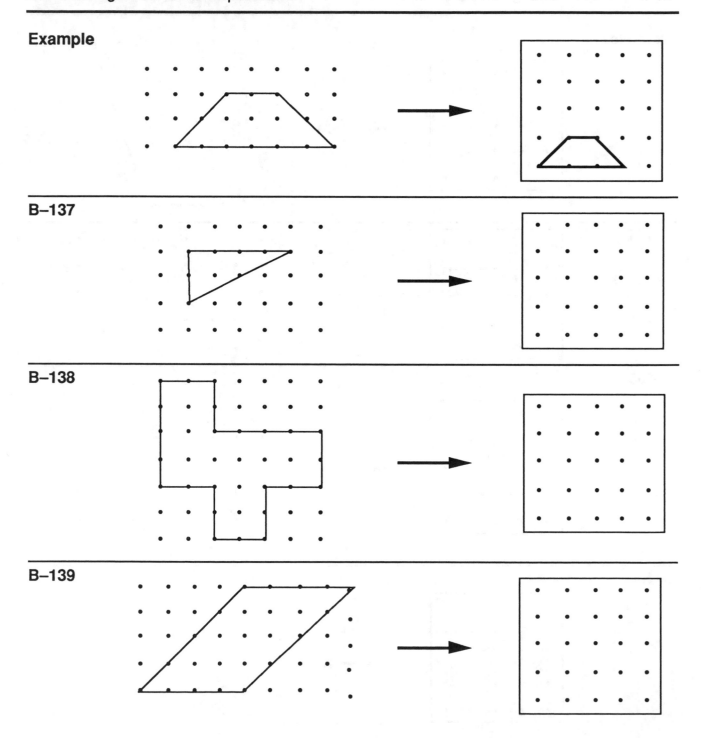

                   P.O. BOX 448, PACIFIC GROVE, CA 93950

TRANSLATIONS

A figure is pictured before a translation.
Draw the figure after the translation indicated.

Example

Translate the figure

four units to the right.

B–140

Translate the figure

five units to the left.

B–141

Translate the figure

one unit down and

six units to the right.

B–142

Translate the figure

one unit up and

three units to the left.

REFLECTIONS

Use the line AB as the line of reflection.
Draw the given figure after a reflection across line AB.

Example   **B–143**

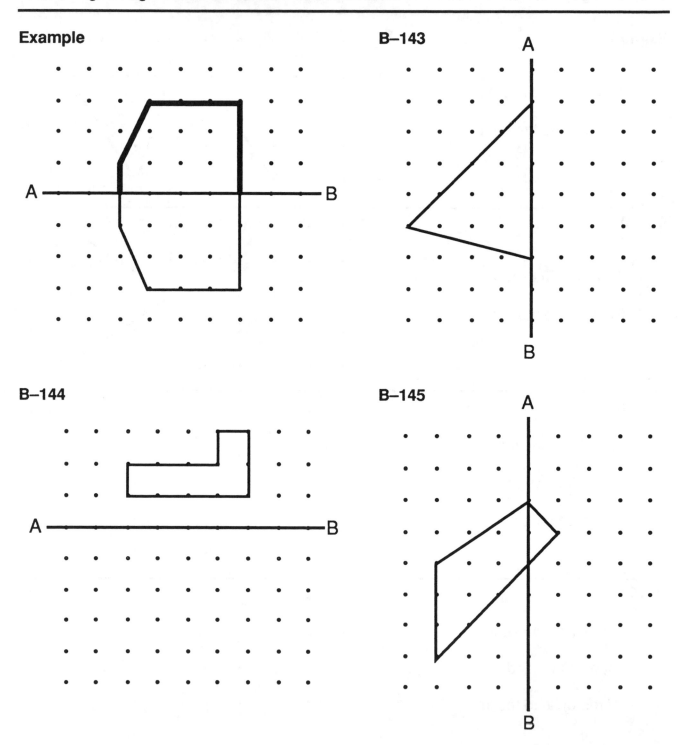

B–144

B–145

REFLECTIONS

Use the line AB as the line of reflection.
Draw the given figure after a reflection across line AB.

Example   **B–146**

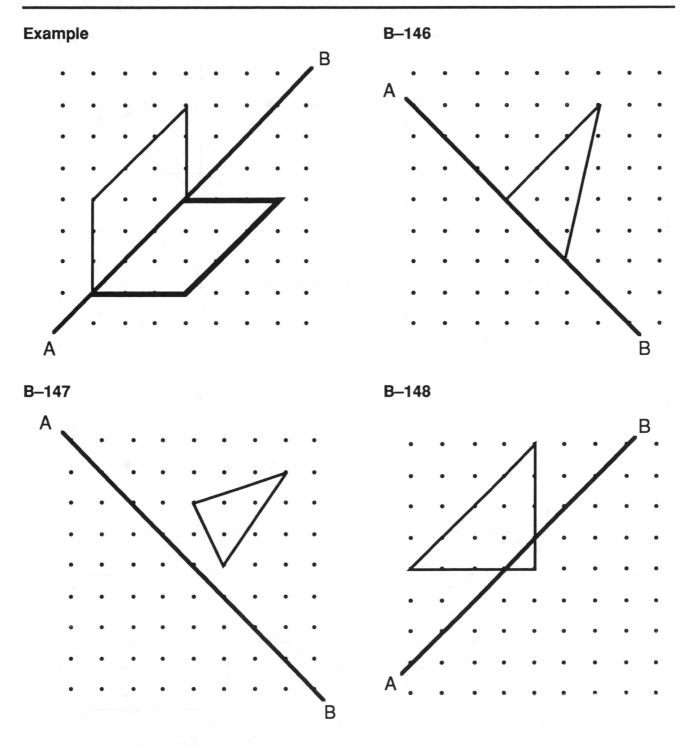

B–147   **B–148**

ROTATIONS

Rotate each figure a quarter turn around the center dot on the geoboard.
Draw the rotated figure and label the points to match the given figure.

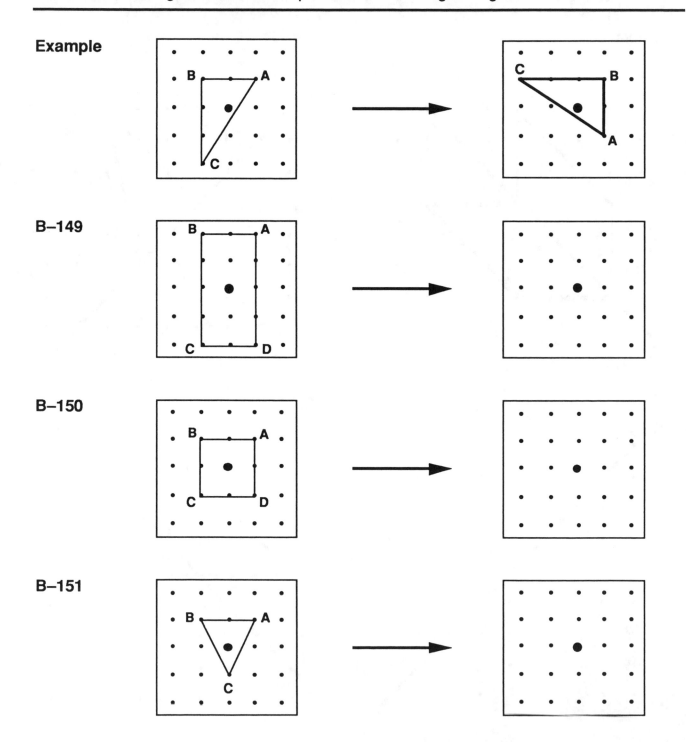

Example

B–149

B–150

B–151

ROTATIONS

Rotate each figure a half turn around the center dot on the geoboard.
Draw the rotated figure and label the points to match the given figure.

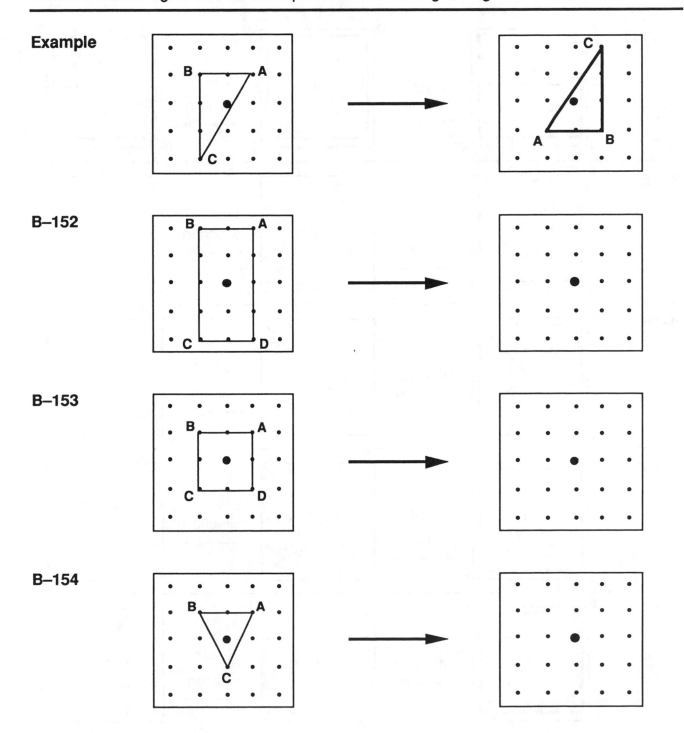

Example

B–152

B–153

B–154

CONSTRUCTING FIGURES

The dotted line is the line of reflection and the center dot is the center of rotation.
Draw each figure after the indicated reflections or clockwise rotations.
Label the figures that you draw.

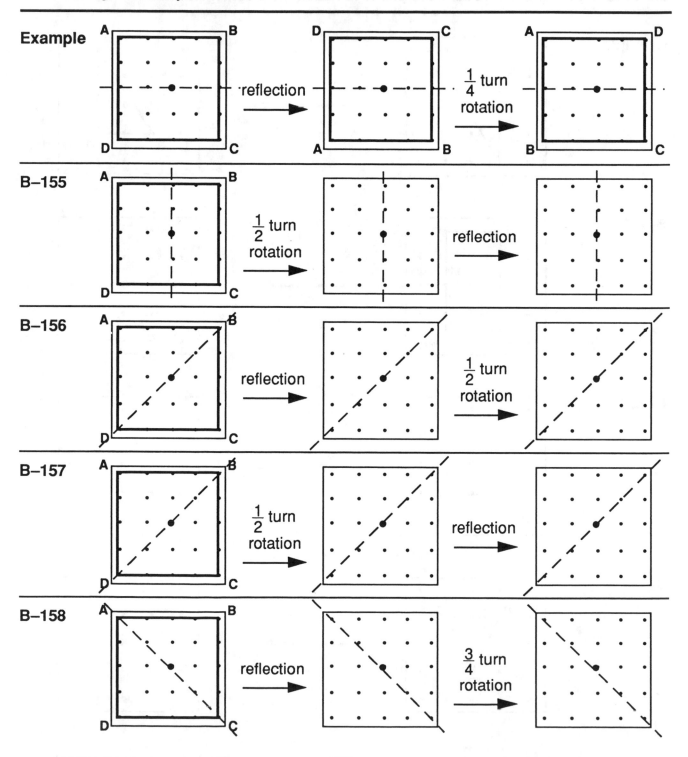

REFLECTIONS AND ROTATIONS

Name a single motion that transforms Figure A into Figure B.
For rotations identify the amount of rotation in a clockwise direction.
For reflections indicate the line of reflection.

Example FIGURE A FIGURE B MOTION

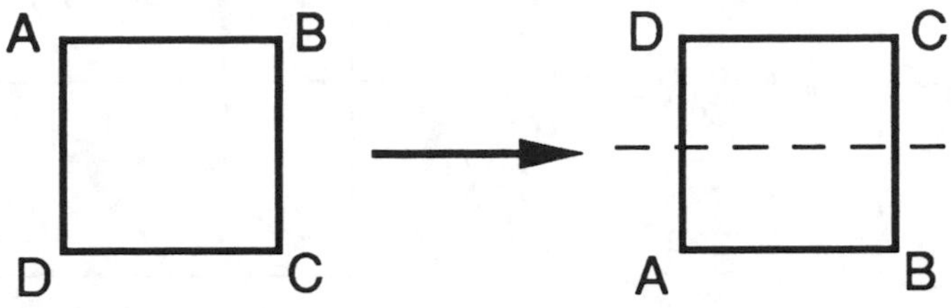

reflection

horizontal line

B–159

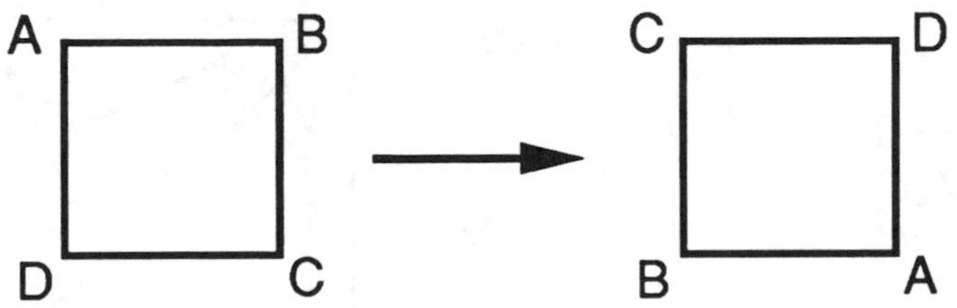

____

____

B–160

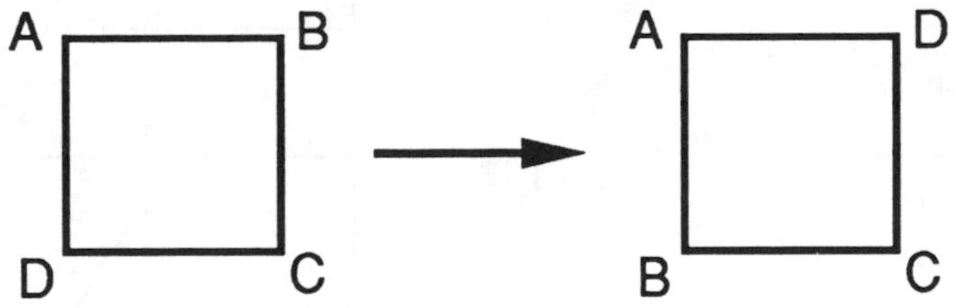

____

____

B–161

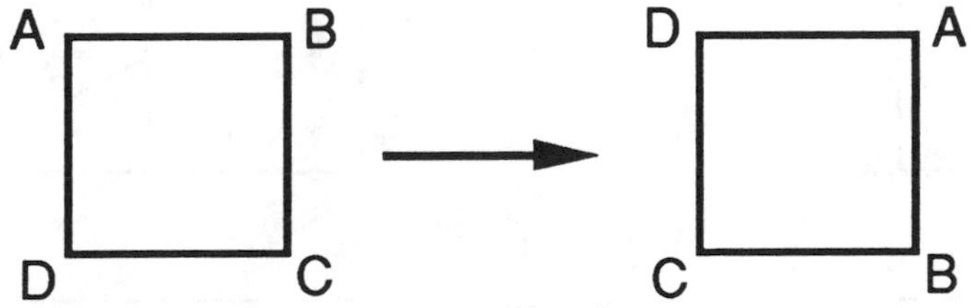

____

____

B–162

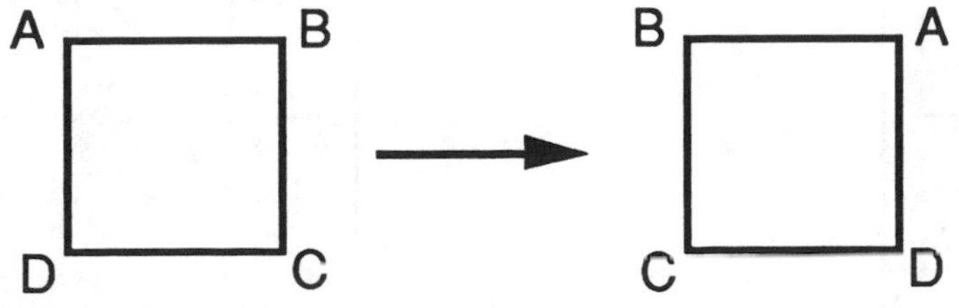

____

____

  P.O. BOX 448, PACIFIC GROVE, CA 93950

LINE SYMMETRY

Half of a symmetric figure is drawn.
The dotted line is the line of symmetry.
Draw the other half of the figure.

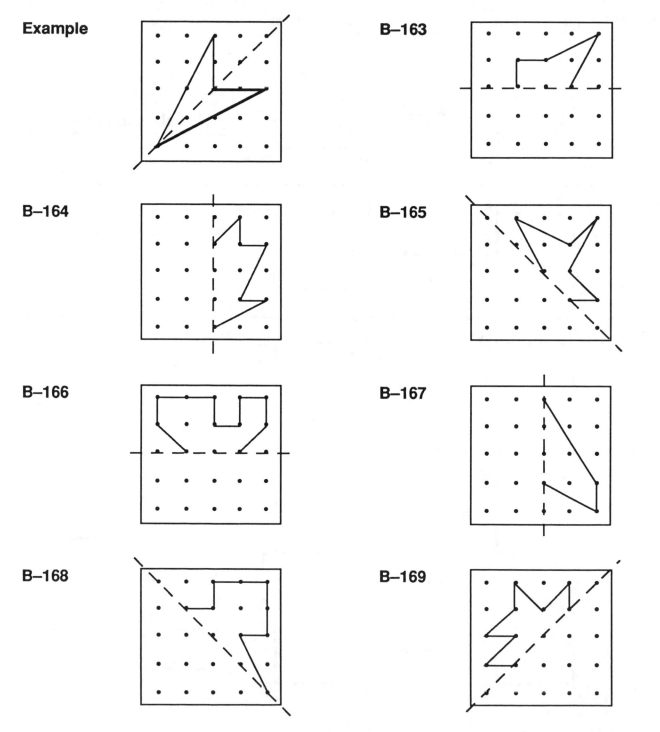

Example

B–163

B–164

B–165

B–166

B–167

B–168

B–169

LINE SYMMETRY

Draw all possible lines of symmetry for each figure.
Write the number of lines of symmetry in the box below the figure.
Write a "0" in the box if the figure does not have line symmetry.

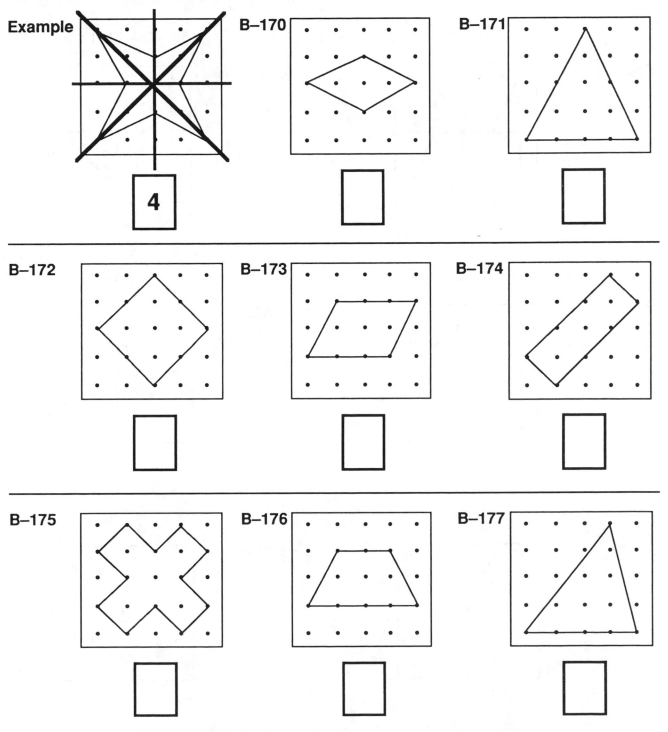

ROTATIONAL SYMMETRY

Use the center dot as the point of rotation.
Reproduce the given figure as often as possible using the turn listed for the figure.

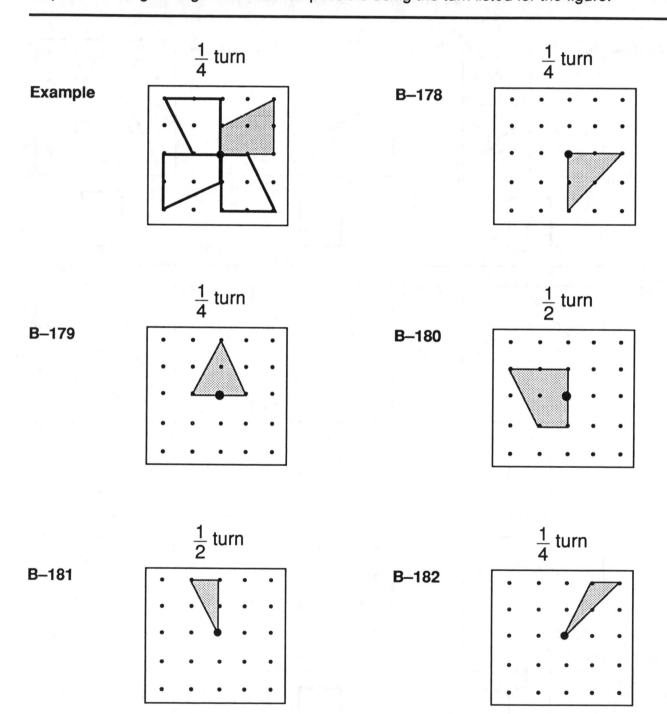

ROTATIONAL SYMMETRY

Each figure has rotational symmetry with the center dot as the point of rotation.
In the box, write the smallest turn that illustrates this symmetry.

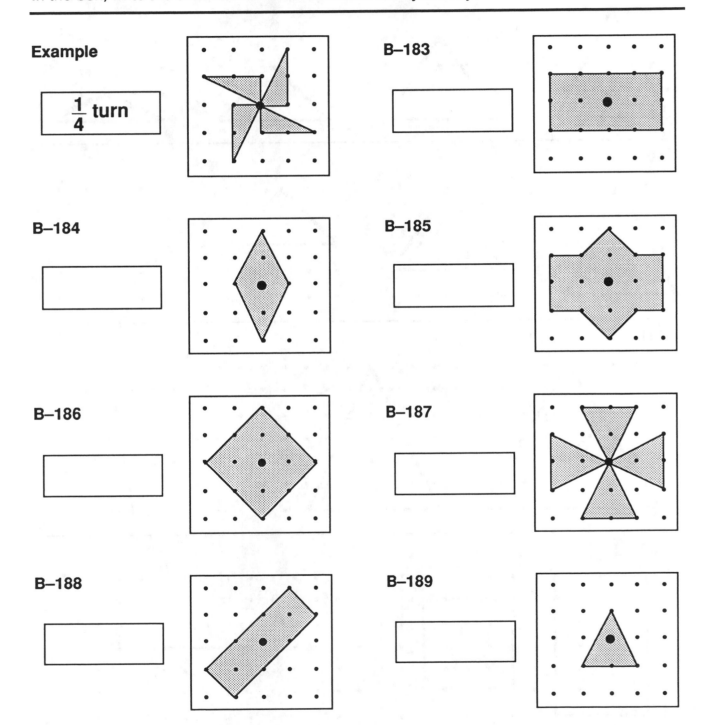

Example

$\frac{1}{4}$ turn

B–183

B–184

B–185

B–186

B–187

B–188

B–189

107   P.O. BOX 448, PACIFIC GROVE, CA 93950

SHRINKING POLYGONS

The polygons in each sequence are shrinking.
Draw the missing polygon in each sequence

Example

B–190

B–191

B–192

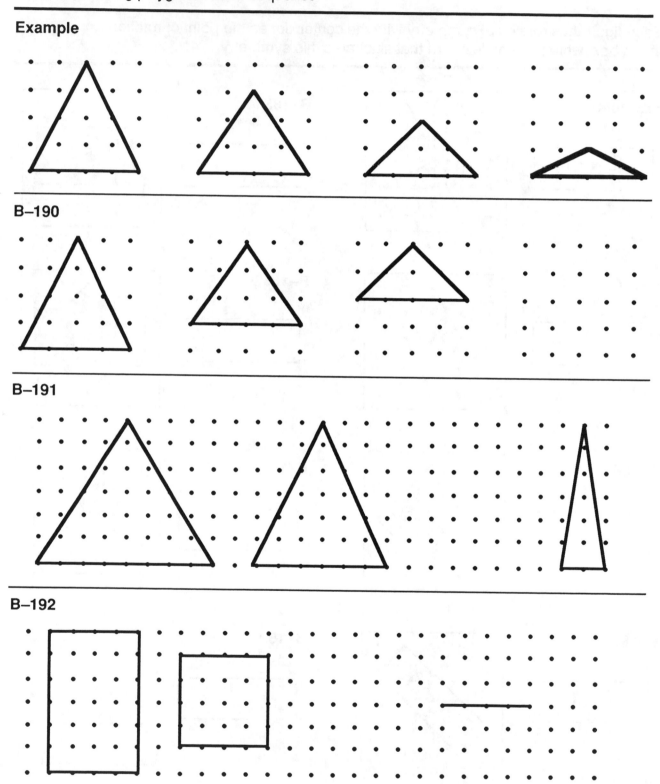

STRETCHING POLYGONS

The polygons in each sequence are stretching.
Draw the missing polygon in each sequence

Example

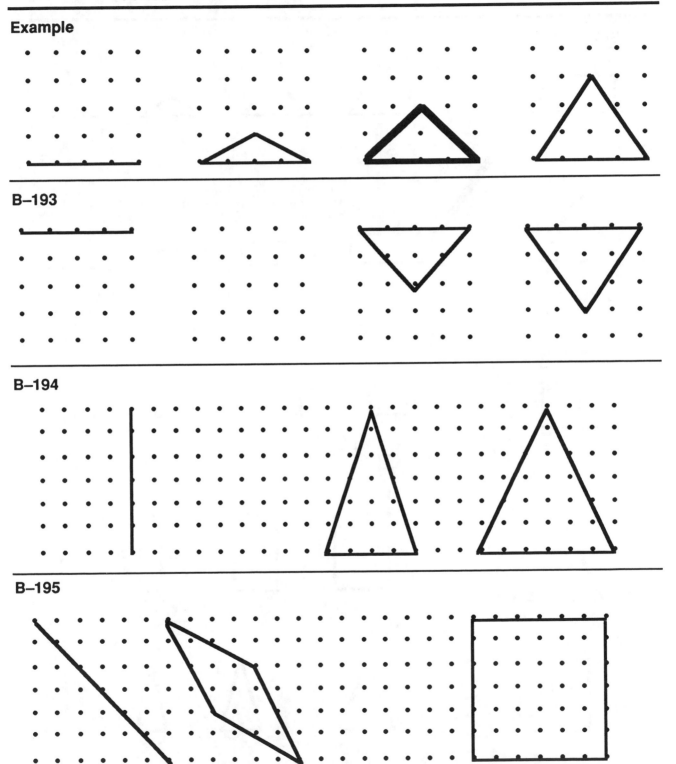

B–193

B–194

B–195

ROTATING POLYGONS

As each polygon is turned around the dotted line, its shadow changes shape. Match each polygon with its sequence of shadows.

Example

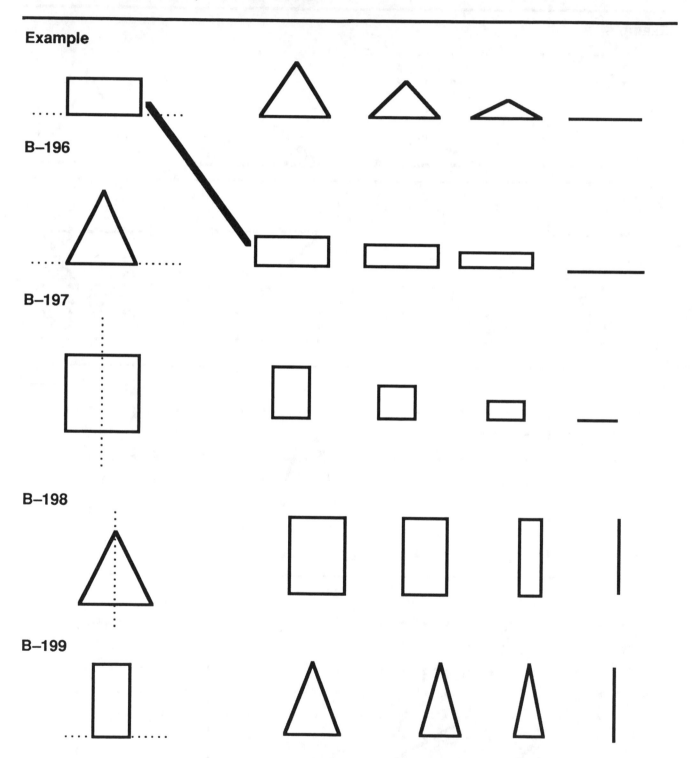

B–196

B–197

B–198

B–199

ROTATING POLYGONS

As each figure is turned around the dotted line, its shadow changes shape.
Match the figure with its sequence of shadows.

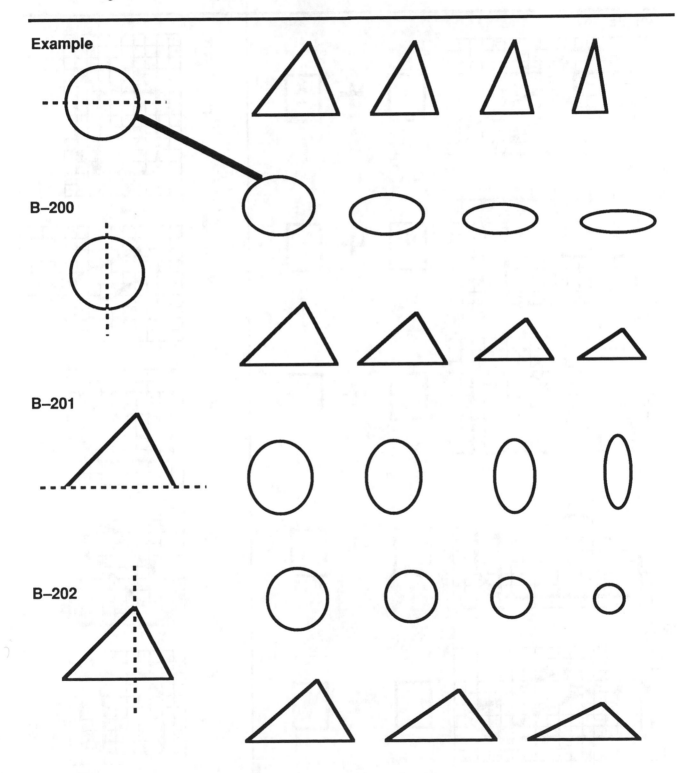

Example

B–200

B–201

B–202

DECOMPOSING SOLIDS

Each given solid can be separated into two different solids.
Write the numbers of these two solids in the boxes.

Example

B–203 | 1 | + | 2 |

B–204 | | + | |

B–205 | | + | |

B–206 | | + | |

| | + | |

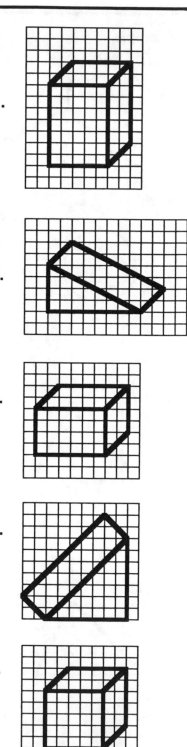

1.

2.

3.

4.

5.

COMPOSITION OF SOLIDS

Find the solid that can be formed by combining the two given solids.
Write its number in the box.

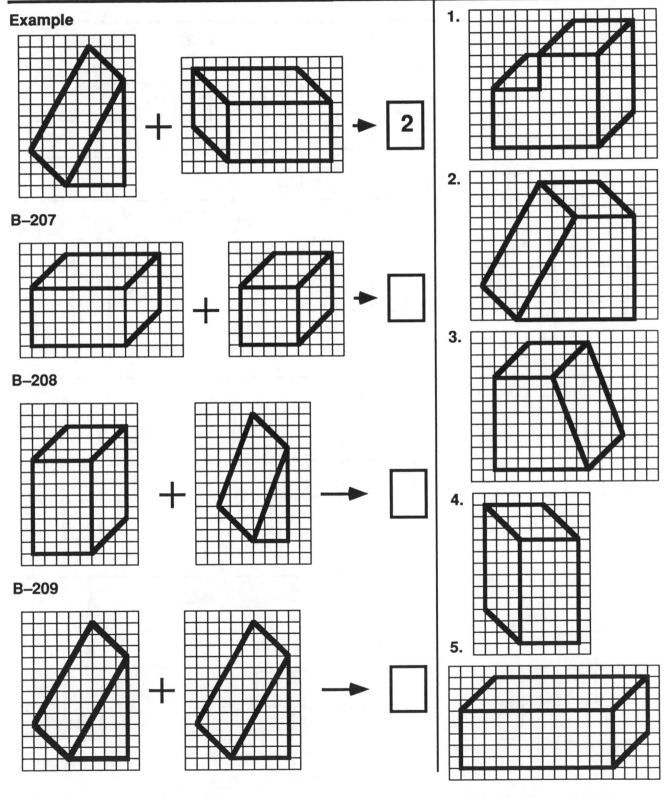

Example

B–207

B–208

B–209

1.

2.

3.

4.

5.

113   P.O. BOX 448, PACIFIC GROVE, CA 93950

MAKING SOLIDS BY FOLDING

When folded along the connecting lines, each pattern of squares will form a cube.
The letter "B" in a square marks the bottom of the cube.
Place a "T" in a square to mark the top of each cube

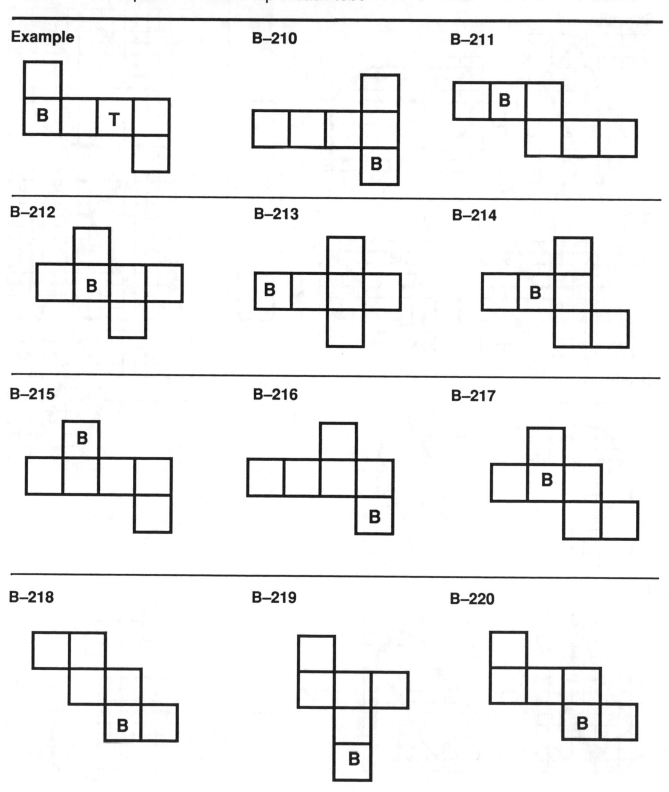

Example   **B–210**   **B–211**

B–212   **B–213**   **B–214**

B–215   **B–216**   **B–217**

B–218   **B–219**   **B–220**

MAKING SOLIDS BY FOLDING

When folded, each pattern forms a rectangular solid.
"B" marks the base of the solid formed, and the other 5 faces are numbered.
Number the faces of each solid to correspond to the numbers on the pattern.

Example

B–221

B–222

B–223

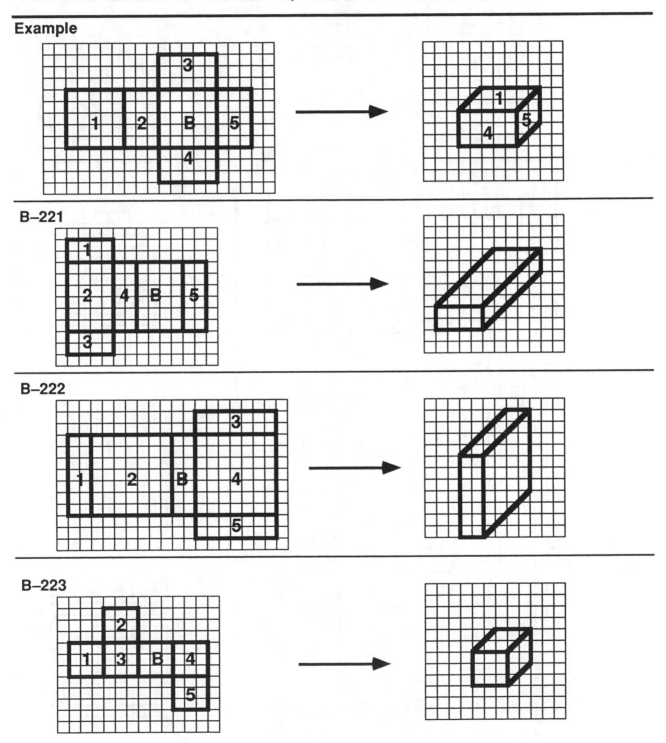

MAKING SOLIDS BY FOLDING

When folded, each pattern forms a solid.
Draw lines connecing each pattern to its corresponding solid.

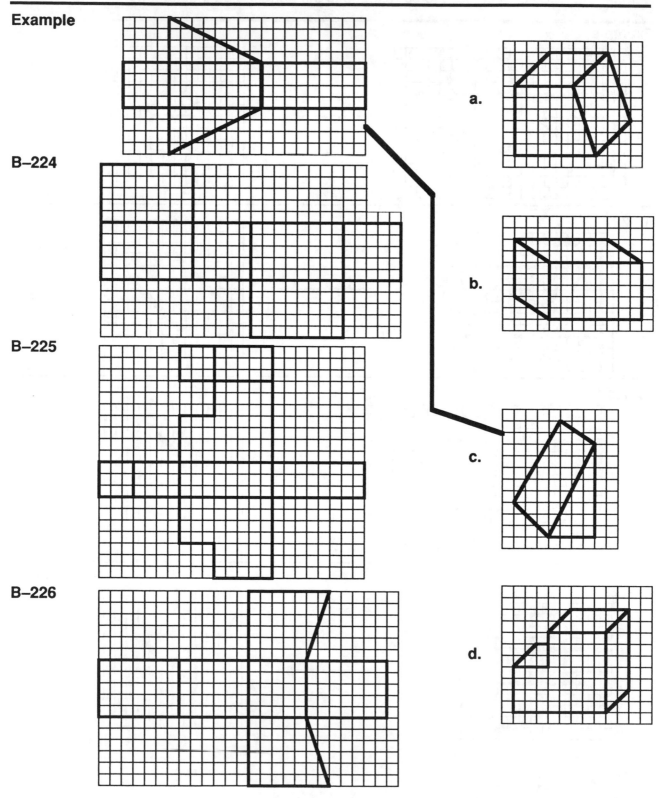

Example

B–224

B–225

B–226

a.

b.

c.

d.

SEPARATING REGIONS

The two circles in the diagram at right partition the box into 3 separate regions.
Each region has been numbered.
Number each region in the boxes below, and write the number of separate regions above the box.

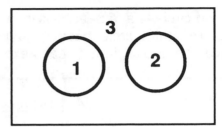

Example _4_

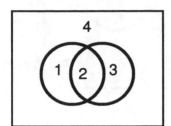

B–227 _____

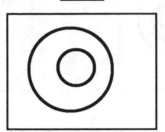

B–228 _____

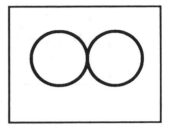

B–229 _____

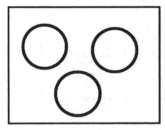

B–230 _____

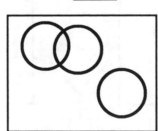

B–231 _____

B–232 _____

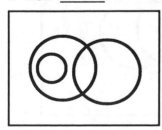

B–233 _____

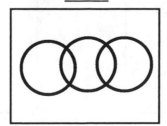

B–234 _____

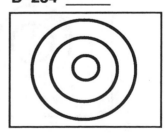

SEPARATING REGIONS

Two circles have been drawn in each box.
Draw a third circle that will partition the box into the number of regions indicated.
Number the regions in each exercise.

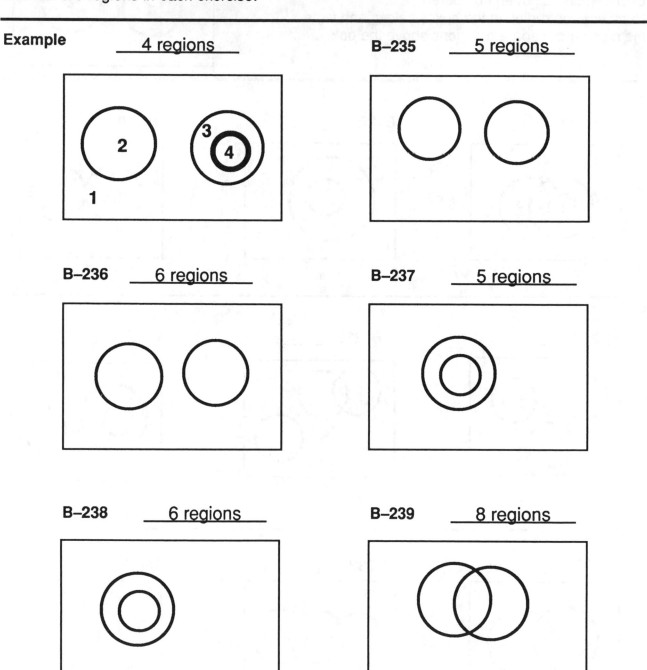

Example ___4 regions___

B–235 ___5 regions___

B–236 ___6 regions___

B–237 ___5 regions___

B–238 ___6 regions___

B–239 ___8 regions___

118   P.O. BOX 448, PACIFIC GROVE, CA 93950

SEPARATING REGIONS

Four circles partition each box into separate regions.
Number each region in the box, and write the number of separate regions above the box.

Example   7

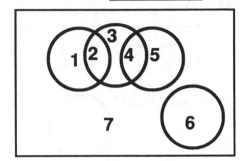

B–240   _____

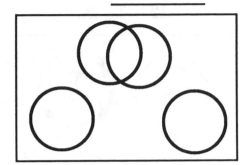

B–241   _____

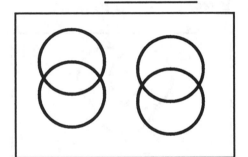

B–242   _____

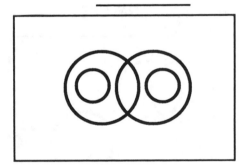

B–243   _____

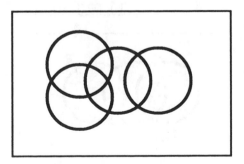

B–244   _____

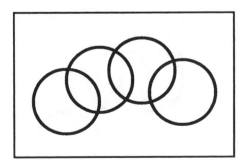

SEPARATING REGIONS

Three circles have been drawn in each box.
Draw a fourth circle that will partition the box into the number of regions indicated.
Number the regions in each exercise.

Example ___5 regions___

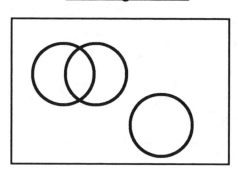

B–245 ___6 regions___

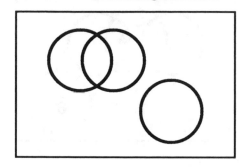

B–246 ___7 regions___

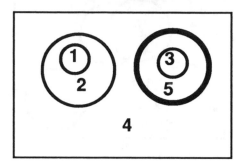

B–247 ___10 regions___

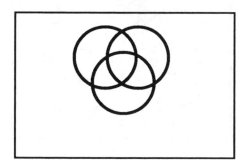

B–248 ___9 regions___

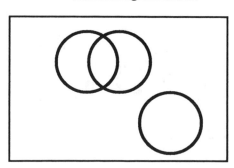

B–249 ___11 regions___

120   P.O. BOX 448, PACIFIC GROVE, CA 93950

TRACING NETWORKS

The points in each network are labeled.
Beginning at point A, determine whether it is possible to
trace the network using each line exactly once.
Number the lines to indicate the path followed.

Example

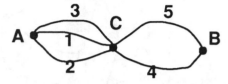

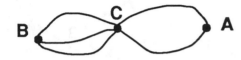

Is it possible? **YES**   Is it possible? **NO**

B–250

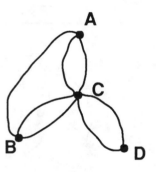

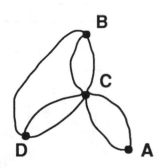

Is it possible? _____   Is it possible? _____

B–251

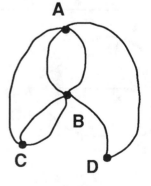

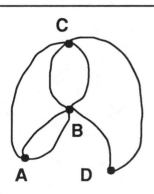

Is it possible? _____   Is it possible? _____

TRACING NETWORKS

The points in each network are labeled.
Determine whether it is possible to begin at one of the points and
trace the network using each line exactly once.
If it is possible, name the beginning point and end point, and
number the lines to indicate the path followed.

Example

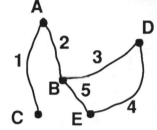

Is it possible? **YES**

Starting Point **C**   End Point **B**

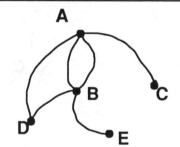

Is it possible? **NO**

Starting Point ____   End Point ____

B–252

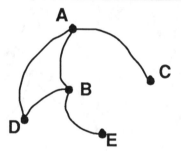

Is it possible? _____

Starting Point ____   End Point ____

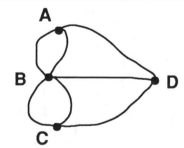

Is it possible? _____

Starting Point ____   End Point ____

B–253

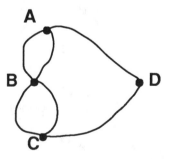

Is it possible? _____

Starting Point ____   End Point ____

Is it possible? _____

Starting Point ____   End Point ____

DRAWING PATHS

Each figure represents the floor plan of a building, and the openings represent doorways.
Each room is labelled with the letter B, C, or D, and the outside is labelled with the letter A.
Determine if a path can be drawn from A, passing through each door exactly once.
If it is possible, draw the path.

Example

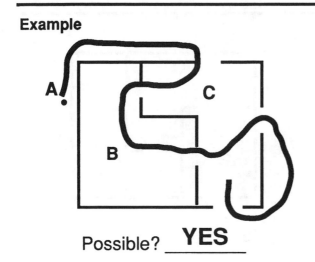

Possible? **YES**

B–254

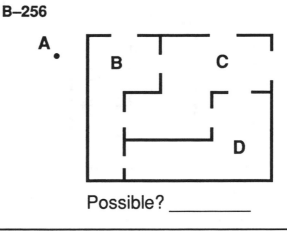

Possible? _____

B–255

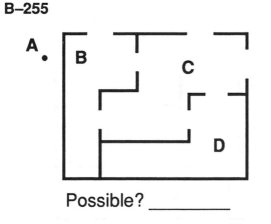

Possible? _____

B–256

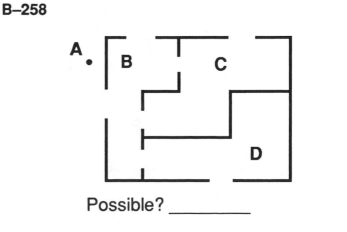

Possible? _____

B–257

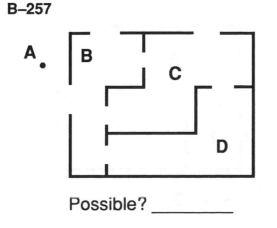

Possible? _____

B–258

Possible? _____

DRAWING PATHS

Each figure represents the floor plan of a building, and the openings represent doorways.
Each room is labelled with the letter B, C, D, or E, and the outside is labelled with the letter A.
Determine if a path can be drawn, passing through each door exactly once.
If it is possible, draw the path.

Example

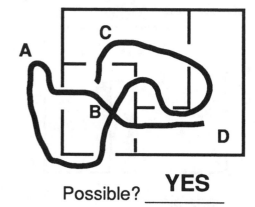

Possible? **YES**

B–259

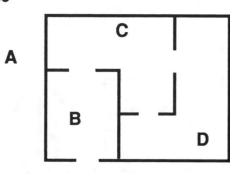

Possible? _____

B–260

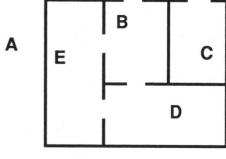

Possible? _____

B–261

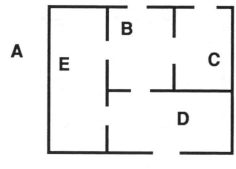

Possible? _____

B–262

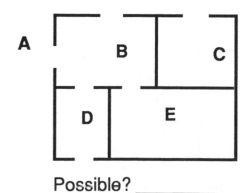

Possible? _____

B–263

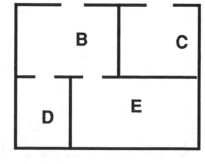

Possible? _____

---

124   P.O. BOX 448, PACIFIC GROVE, CA 93950

COUNTING ARRAYS

Find the number of columns and rows in each array of cubes.
Circle all of the expressions that tell how many cubes are in each array.

Example

Number of Rows = ___4___

Number of Columns = ___3___

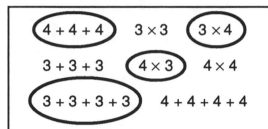

(4 + 4 + 4)	3 × 3	(3 × 4)
3 + 3 + 3	(4 × 3)	4 × 4
(3 + 3 + 3 + 3)		4 + 4 + 4 + 4

C–1

Number of Rows = _____

Number of Columns = _____

4 + 4 + 4 + 4	5 × 5	4 × 5
5 + 5 + 5 + 5	5 × 4	4 × 4
5 + 5 + 5 + 5 + 5	4 + 4 + 4 + 4 + 4	

C–2

Number of Rows = _____

Number of Columns = _____

6 + 6 + 6 + 6	5 × 6	5 × 5
6 + 6 + 6 + 6 + 6	6 × 6	
5 + 5 + 5 + 5 + 5 + 5	6 × 5	

C–3

Number of Rows = _____

Number of Columns = _____

8 + 8 + 8 + 8	4 × 8	3 × 8
8 + 8 + 8	8 × 4	8 × 8
4 + 4 + 4 + 4 + 4 + 4 + 4 + 4		

125   P.O. BOX 448, PACIFIC GROVE, CA 93950

COUNTING ARRAYS

Circle the letters of the expressions that tell how many cubes are in the pair of arrays.

Example

a. $(4 \times 3) + (4 \times 5)$ ⟵ circled

b. $5 \times (4 + 3)$

c. $(3 \times 3) + (4 \times 4)$

d. $4 \times (3 + 5)$ ⟵ circled

C–4

a. $(5 \times 3) + (3 \times 5)$

b. $5 \times (6 + 3)$

c. $(6 \times 5) + (6 \times 3)$

d. $(5 \times 6) + (5 \times 3)$

C–5

a. $(7 \times 4) + (7 \times 6)$

b. $7 \times (4 + 7)$

c. $7 \times (4 + 6)$

d. $(4 \times 6) + (5 \times 7)$

C–6

a. $(4 \times 4) + (6 \times 6)$

b. $(4 \times 6) + (4 \times 6)$

c. $4 \times (6 + 6)$

d. $6 \times (4 + 4)$

COMPUTING ARRAYS

Each circle represents a set of objects.
The number in each circle tells how many objects are in the set.
Circle all the expressions that tell the total number of objects in each exercise.

Example   (7) (7) (7)
               (7) (7) (7)

a. $7 + 7 + 7$ b. $7 \times (3 + 3)$

c. 7×3 d. $7 + 7 + 7 + 7 + 7 + 7$

e. 7×7 f. 7×6

C–7   (5) (5) (5)
           (5) (5) (5)

a. $5 + 5 + 5$ b. $5 \times (2 + 3)$

c. $5 \times (3 + 3)$ d. $5 + 5 + 5 + 5 + 5 + 5$

e. 5×6 f. 5×3

C–8   (4) (4) (4) (4)
           (4) (4)

a. $7 + 7 + 7$ b. $4 \times (4 + 2)$

c. $4 \times (3 + 2)$ d. $(4 \times 4) + 2$

e. 4×6 f. $4 + 4 + 4 + 4 + 4 + 4$

C–9   (2) (2) (2) (2) (2)
           (2) (2) (2)

a. $2 \times (5 + 3)$ b. $8 \times (5 + 3)$

c. $2 \times (6 + 2)$ d. 8×2

e. 5×2 f. 2×8

C–10   (9) (9) (9) (9) (9)
            (9) (9) (9) (9)

a. $9 \times (5 + 4)$ b. 9×4

c. 9×9 d. $9 \times (8 + 1)$

e. 9×5 f. $9 \times (4 + 3)$

COMPUTING ARRAYS

Each circle represents a set of objects.
The number in each circle tells how many objects are in the set.
Circle all the expressions that tell the total number of objects in each exercise.

Example ③ ③ ③ ③
③ ③ ③

a. 3×8 b. $3 \times (4 + 3)$ (circled)

c. $3 \times (5 + 3)$ d. $(3 \times 4) + (3 \times 3)$ (circled)

e. $3 \times (6 + 1)$ (circled)   f. $4 \times (3 + 4)$

C–11 ⑥ ⑥ ⑥ ⑥
⑥ ⑥ ⑥

a. $6 \times (4 + 3)$ b. $(6 \times 6) + (6 \times 1)$

c. 6×8 d. $6 \times (4 + 4)$

e. $(6 \times 4) + (6 \times 3)$ f. $6 \times (6 + 1)$

C–12 ⑧ ⑧ ⑧ ⑧ ⑧
⑧ ⑧ ⑧

a. 8×8 b. 8×5

c. $8 \times (6 + 2)$ d. $8 \times (5 + 3)$

e. $(8 \times 6) + (8 \times 2)$ f. $8 \times (6 + 3)$

C–13 ⑤ ⑤ ⑤ ⑤
⑤ ⑤ ⑤ ⑤

a. 5×5 b. $(5 \times 4) + (5 \times 4)$

c. $5 \times (4 + 2)$ d. $5 \times (4 + 4)$

e. $5 \times (3 + 5)$ f. $5 \times (6 + 2)$

C–14 ④ ④ ④ ④ ④
④ ④ ④ ④ ④

a. $4 \times (6 + 4)$ b. $4 \times (6 + 6)$

c. $4 \times (5 + 5)$ d. $(4 \times 6) + (4 \times 4)$

e. $2 \times (4 + 5)$ f. $(4 \times 5) + (4 \times 5)$

P. O. BOX 448, PACIFIC GROVE, CA 93950

MULTIPLYING FRACTIONS

In each exercise rectangles are subdivided into equal parts.
Circle the number sentence that tells how many rectangles can be made
with the shaded subdivisions.

Example

  a. $\dfrac{1}{3} \times 1 = \dfrac{1}{3}$ b. $\dfrac{1}{3} \times 3 = 1$

  (c.) $\dfrac{1}{3} \times 6 = 2$ d. $\dfrac{2}{3} \times 6 = 4$

C–15

  a. $\dfrac{1}{2} \times 4 = 2$ b. $\dfrac{1}{4} \times 4 = 1$

  c. $\dfrac{3}{4} \times 4 = 3$ d. $\dfrac{1}{4} \times 1 = \dfrac{1}{4}$

C–16

  a. $\dfrac{1}{3} \times 3 = 1$ b. $\dfrac{2}{3} \times 1 = \dfrac{2}{3}$

  c. $\dfrac{1}{3} \times 2 = \dfrac{2}{3}$ d. $\dfrac{2}{3} \times 3 = 2$

C–17

  a. $\dfrac{2}{5} \times 5 = 2$ b. $\dfrac{3}{5} \times 5 = 3$

  c. $\dfrac{2}{5} \times 1 = \dfrac{2}{5}$ d. $\dfrac{1}{5} \times 5 = 1$

C–18

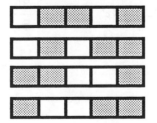

  a. $\dfrac{2}{5} \times 4 = 1\dfrac{3}{5}$ b. $\dfrac{1}{5} \times 4 = \dfrac{4}{5}$

  c. $\dfrac{3}{5} \times 4 = 2\dfrac{2}{5}$ d. $\dfrac{3}{5} \times 3 = 1\dfrac{4}{5}$

              P.O. BOX 448, PACIFIC GROVE, CA 93950

MULTIPLYING FRACTIONS

Circle the number sentences that describe the fractional part of the rectangle that is shaded.

Example

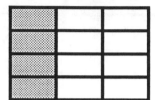

(a.) $\dfrac{1}{3} \times 1 = \dfrac{1}{3}$ b. $\dfrac{2}{3} \times 1 = \dfrac{2}{3}$

(c.) $\dfrac{4}{12} \times 1 = \dfrac{4}{12}$ d. $\dfrac{4}{12} \times 12 = 4$

C–19

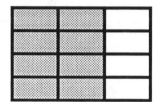

a. $\dfrac{2}{3} \times 12 = 8$ b. $\dfrac{1}{3} \times 1 = \dfrac{1}{3}$

c. $\dfrac{3}{4} \times 1 = \dfrac{3}{4}$ d. $\dfrac{2}{3} \times 1 = \dfrac{2}{3}$

C–20

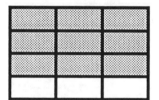

a. $\dfrac{3}{4} \times 1 = \dfrac{3}{4}$ b. $\dfrac{1}{4} \times 1 = \dfrac{1}{4}$

c. $\dfrac{9}{12} \times 1 = \dfrac{9}{12}$ d. $\dfrac{9}{12} \times 12 = 9$

C–21

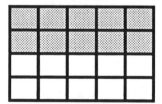

a. $\dfrac{10}{20} \times 20 = 10$ b. $\dfrac{2}{5} \times 1 = \dfrac{2}{5}$

c. $\dfrac{2}{4} \times 1 = \dfrac{2}{4}$ d. $\dfrac{1}{2} \times 1 = \dfrac{1}{2}$

C–22

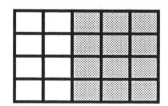

a. $\dfrac{12}{20} \times 20 = 12$ b. $\dfrac{3}{5} \times 1 = \dfrac{3}{5}$

c. $\dfrac{2}{5} \times 1 = \dfrac{2}{5}$ d. $\dfrac{12}{20} \times 1 = \dfrac{12}{20}$

MULTIPLYING FRACTIONS

Shade in a fractional part of the rectangle to match the number sentence.

Example

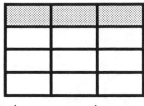

$$\frac{1}{4} \times 1 = \frac{1}{4}$$

C–23

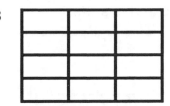

$$\frac{2}{3} \times 1 = \frac{2}{3}$$

C–24

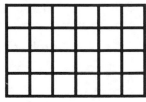

$$\frac{6}{24} \times 1 = \frac{6}{24}$$

C–25

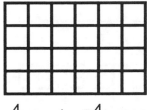

$$\frac{4}{6} \times 1 = \frac{4}{6}$$

C–26

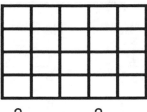

$$\frac{2}{5} \times 1 = \frac{2}{5}$$

C–27

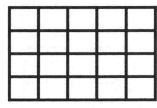

$$\frac{3}{4} \times 1 = \frac{3}{4}$$

C–28

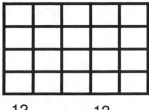

$$\frac{12}{20} \times 1 = \frac{12}{20}$$

C–29

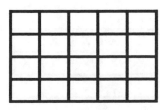

$$\frac{5}{20} \times 1 = \frac{5}{20}$$

         P.O. BOX 448, PACIFIC GROVE, CA 93950

MULTIPLYING FRACTIONS

Circle the fraction that matches the fractional part of each rectangle that is shaded.
Circle the fraction that matches the fractional part of the rectangle containing "Xs."
Circle the number sentence that tells the fractional part of the rectangle
that is shaded and has "Xs."

Example

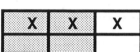

Shaded	"Xs"	Number sentence
$\frac{1}{2}$	$\boxed{\frac{1}{2}}$	$\boxed{\frac{1}{2} \times \frac{2}{3} = \frac{2}{6}}$
$\boxed{\frac{2}{3}}$	$\frac{1}{3}$	$\frac{2}{6} \times \frac{1}{3} = \frac{2}{18}$
$\frac{3}{6}$	$\frac{2}{6}$	$\frac{3}{6} \times \frac{2}{6} = \frac{6}{36}$

C–30

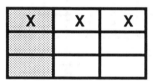

Shaded	"Xs"	Number sentence
$\frac{1}{9}$	$\frac{1}{9}$	$\frac{1}{9} \times \frac{1}{3} = \frac{1}{27}$
$\frac{2}{3}$	$\frac{1}{3}$	$\frac{2}{3} \times \frac{2}{3} = \frac{4}{9}$
$\frac{1}{3}$	$\frac{2}{3}$	$\frac{1}{3} \times \frac{1}{3} = \frac{1}{9}$

C–31

Shaded	"Xs"	Number sentence
$\frac{2}{4}$	$\frac{2}{4}$	$\frac{1}{3} \times \frac{2}{6} = \frac{1}{18}$
$\frac{2}{6}$	$\frac{2}{3}$	$\frac{2}{6} \times \frac{2}{4} = \frac{4}{24}$
$\frac{1}{3}$	$\frac{2}{6}$	$\frac{1}{2} \times \frac{2}{3} = \frac{2}{6}$

C–32

Shaded	"Xs"	Number sentence
$\frac{3}{4}$	$\frac{1}{2}$	$\frac{3}{4} \times \frac{2}{3} = \frac{6}{12}$
$\frac{3}{5}$	$\frac{4}{10}$	$\frac{3}{5} \times \frac{4}{10} = \frac{12}{50}$
$\frac{3}{9}$	$\frac{2}{3}$	$\frac{2}{3} \times \frac{3}{5} = \frac{6}{15}$

P. O. BOX 448, PACIFIC GROVE, CA 93950

MULTIPLYING FRACTIONS

Circle the letter of the number sentence that tells the fractional part of the rectangle that is shaded and has "Xs."

Example

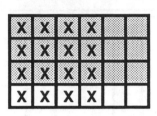

a. $\dfrac{2}{4} \times \dfrac{1}{3} = \dfrac{2}{12}$

b. $\dfrac{4}{12} \times \dfrac{2}{12} = \dfrac{8}{24}$

ⓒ c. $\dfrac{2}{4} \times \dfrac{2}{3} = \dfrac{4}{12}$

C–33

a. $\dfrac{4}{6} \times \dfrac{3}{4} = \dfrac{12}{24}$

b. $\dfrac{2}{12} \times \dfrac{3}{12} = \dfrac{6}{24}$

c. $\dfrac{1}{4} \times \dfrac{2}{6} = \dfrac{2}{24}$

C–34

a. $\dfrac{1}{4} \times \dfrac{3}{5} = \dfrac{3}{20}$

b. $\dfrac{2}{5} \times \dfrac{1}{4} = \dfrac{2}{20}$

c. $\dfrac{3}{4} \times \dfrac{2}{5} = \dfrac{6}{20}$

C–35

a. $\dfrac{2}{4} \times \dfrac{1}{5} = \dfrac{2}{20}$

b. $\dfrac{4}{5} \times \dfrac{3}{4} = \dfrac{12}{20}$

c. $\dfrac{2}{4} \times \dfrac{4}{5} = \dfrac{8}{20}$

C–36

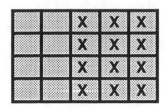

a. $\dfrac{3}{5} \times 1 = \dfrac{12}{20}$

b. $\dfrac{3}{4} \times 1 = \dfrac{15}{20}$

c. $\dfrac{2}{5} \times 1 = \dfrac{5}{20}$

---

    133   P.O. BOX 448, PACIFIC GROVE, CA 93950

MULTIPLYING FRACTIONS

Shade in a fractional part of the rectangle to match the first fraction.
Put "Xs" in a fractional part of the rectangle to match the second fraction.
Use the rectangle to complete the number sentence.

Example

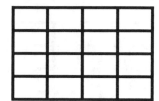

$$\frac{3}{5} \times \frac{3}{4} = \frac{9}{20}$$

C–37

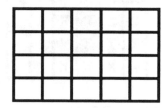

$$\frac{3}{4} \times \frac{1}{4} = \underline{\quad\quad}$$

C–38

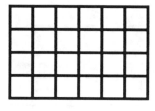

$$\frac{3}{6} \times \frac{1}{4} = \underline{\quad\quad}$$

C–39

$$\frac{1}{4} \times \frac{2}{5} = \underline{\quad\quad}$$

C–40

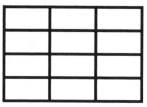

$$\frac{1}{3} \times \frac{2}{4} = \underline{\quad\quad}$$

C–41

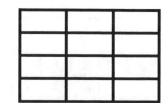

$$\frac{1}{4} \times \frac{1}{4} = \underline{\quad\quad}$$

C–42

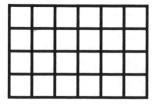

$$\frac{5}{6} \times \frac{4}{4} = \underline{\quad\quad}$$

C–43

$$\frac{4}{4} \times \frac{2}{3} = \underline{\quad\quad}$$

                         P. O. BOX 448, PACIFIC GROVE, CA 93950

MODELS FOR DIVISION

The number in each circle tells the number of objects in that circle.
Circle the model that illustrates the solution to each question.
In the box, write a number sentence that describes the model.

Example   A taxi service sends 6 vans to transport 24 people to a meeting.
How many people should ride in each van?

$$24 \div 6 = 4$$

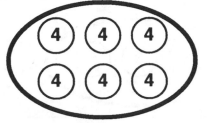

C–44   A bottled water distributor is able to pack 6 jugs of water in each box.
How many boxes will be needed to package 2 dozen jugs of water?

C–45   A local newspaper purchases 24 tons of paper.
If its trucks can carry 6 tons of paper, how many trips
are needed to deliver the paper to its printing plant?

C–46   A butcher wants to divide 24 pounds of hamburger into 6 packages.
How many pounds should be placed in each package?

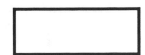

MODELS FOR DIVISION

The number in each circle tells the number of objects in that circle.
Circle the model that illustrates the solution to each question.
In the box, write a number sentence that describes the model.

Example A cake recipe requires 8 eggs.
If a chef has 2 dozen eggs, how many cakes can she make?

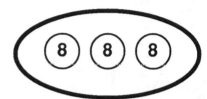 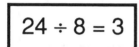 

C–47 Each student needs 4 cubes to make a pattern.
If the teacher has a set of 20 cubes, how many students can make the pattern?

C–48 A chef wants to make 8 omelets from 2 dozen eggs.
How many eggs can he put in each omelet?

C–49 A teacher wants to divide a set of 20 cubes between 4 students.
How many cubes will each student receive?

C–50 Cassette tapes are on sale for $5.00 per tape. How many tapes
could be purchased with $30.00?

COMPUTATIONS WITH PARENTHESES

Circle the answer to each computation.

		a.	b.	c.	d.
Example	$(24 \div 4) + 2 =$	3	4	⑧	10
C–51	$24 \div (4 + 2) =$	3	4	8	10
C–52	$(24 - 4) \times 2 =$	16	18	24	40
C–53	$24 - (4 \times 2) =$	16	18	24	40
C–54	$24 + (4 + 2) =$	14	30	32	96
C–55	$(24 + 4) + 2 =$	14	30	32	96
C–56	$(24 - 4) - 2 =$	18	20	22	26
C–57	$24 - (4 - 2) =$	18	20	22	26
C–58	$(24 \div 4) \div 2 =$	3	4	12	14
C–59	$24 \div (4 \div 2) =$	3	4	12	14
C–60	$(24 \times 4) \times 2 =$	172	176	183	192
C–61	$24 \times (4 \times 2) =$	172	176	183	192

COMPUTATIONS WITH PARENTHESES

Insert parentheses to make each statement true.

Example

$$24 + (4 \div 2) = 26$$

C–62

$$24 + 4 \times 2 = 56$$

C–63

$$24 \times 4 - 2 = 94$$

C–64

$$24 \div 4 - 2 = 12$$

C–65

$$24 \times 4 \div 2 = 48$$

C–66

$$6 = 12 \div 4 - 2$$

C–67

$$27 = 28 - 4 - 3$$

C–68

$$4 = 28 \div 4 + 3$$

C–69

$$3 + 4 \times 2 = 8 + 3$$

C–70

$$12 \div 2 = 5 \times 0 + 6$$

C–71

$$3 + 4 \times 2 = 18 \div 2 + 5$$

C–72

$$12 - 8 - 4 = 16 \div 4 \div 2$$

COMPLETING COMPUTATIONS

Use the numbers in the set below to complete each computation.
In each exercise use a different number in each box.

| 0 | 1 | 2 | 3 |
| 4 | 6 | 8 | 12 |

Example

$(12 \div \boxed{4}) - 2 = 1$

C–73

$6 = 12 \div (4 - \boxed{})$

C–74

$(3 \times \boxed{}) \div \boxed{} = 2$

C–75

$(\boxed{} \div 3) - 4 = \boxed{}$

C–76

$\boxed{} = 8 - (\boxed{} + 1)$

C–77

$(\boxed{} - 6) \times 3 = 9 \times \boxed{}$

C–78

$\boxed{} - (\boxed{} - \boxed{}) = 6$

C–79

$3 \times \boxed{} = (\boxed{} + 6) \times \boxed{}$

THE DISTRIBUTIVE PROPERTY

Place a number in each box to make the number sentence true.

Example

$(\boxed{5} \times 3) + (5 \times 7) = 50$

C–80

$7 \times (3 + \boxed{}) = 63$

C–81

$9 \times (\boxed{} + 3) = 45$

C–82

$(3 \times 5) + (3 \times \boxed{}) = 39$

C–83

$\boxed{} \times (3 + 7) = 50$

C–84

$(7 \times 3) + (7 \times \boxed{}) = 63$

C–85

$(2 \times \boxed{}) + (2 \times 7) = 16$

C–86

$2 \times (\boxed{} + 7) = 16$

C–87

$3 \times (5 + \boxed{}) = 39$

C–88

$(9 \times \boxed{}) + (9 \times 3) = 45$

WHOLE NUMBER DIVISION

In the division example on the right the <u>divisor</u> is 5,
the <u>dividend</u> is 17, the <u>quotient</u> is 3, and the <u>remainder</u> is 2.

The division can be checked by the following computation:

$$(5 \times 3) + 2 = 17.$$

$$5\overline{)17}$$
$$\,3$$
$$15$$
$$\,\,2$$

Fill in the blanks in the following exercises.

Example

Divisor = ☐ 2

Dividend = 7

Quotient = 3

Remainder = 1

C–89

Divisor = 5

Dividend = 39

Quotient = ☐

Remainder = ☐

C–90

Divisor = 6

Dividend = ☐

Quotient = 9

Remainder = 3

C–91

Divisor = ☐

Dividend = 85

Quotient = 8

Remainder = 5

C–92

Divisor = ☐

Dividend = 100

Quotient = 33

Remainder = 1

C–93

Divisor = ☐

Dividend = 17

Quotient = ☐

Remainder = 2

EXPANDED NOTATION

Place a single digit in each blank to make the computation match the set.
In the box, write the number in standard form.
Refer to the chart below.

 = 100   = 10   = 1

Example

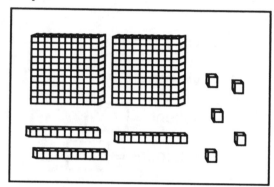

(_2_ × 100) + (_3_ × 10) + (_5_)

235

C–94

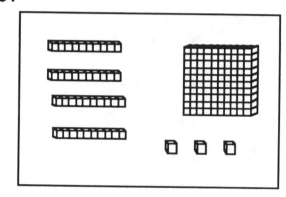

(___ × 100) + (___ × 10) + (___)

C–95

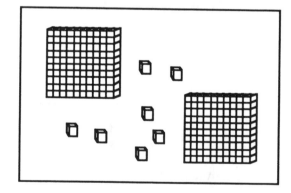

(___ × 100) + (___ × 10) + (___)

C–96

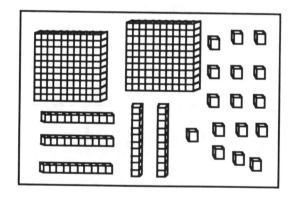

(___ × 100) + (___ × 10) + (___)

P. O. BOX 448, PACIFIC GROVE, CA 93950

EXPANDED NOTATION

The following numbers are associated with the shapes pictured below.

◯ = 25   ▢ = 10   △ = 5

Circle the number represented by each computation.

---

		a.	b.	c.
Example	$(3 \times ◯) + (2 \times ▢) + (1 \times △) + 2 =$	87	92	(102)
C–97	$(2 \times ◯) + (4 \times ▢) + (0 \times △) + 4 =$	74	94	99
C–98	$(4 \times ▢) + (4 \times △) + 9 =$	69	119	129
C–99	$(0 \times ◯) + (1 \times △) + 1 =$	6	31	36
C–100	$(5 \times ◯) + (5 \times △) + 9 =$	144	159	184
C–101	$(8 \times ◯) + (13 \times ▢) + (4 \times △) + 12 =$	242	317	362

EXPANDED NOTATION

Place a single digit in each blank to make the statement true.
Refer to the chart below.

$\bigcirc$ = 100 $\bigcirc$ = 25 $\square$ = 10 $\triangle$ = 5

Example

($\underline{1}$ × $\bigcirc$) + ($\underline{2}$ × $\bigcirc$) + ($\underline{1}$ × $\square$) + ($\underline{1}$ × $\triangle$) + $\underline{3}$ = 168

C–102

(__ × $\bigcirc$) + (__ × $\bigcirc$) + (__ × $\square$) + (__ × $\triangle$) + ___ = 342

C–103

(__ × $\bigcirc$) + (__ × $\bigcirc$) + (__ × $\square$) + (__ × $\triangle$) + ___ = 103

C–104

(__ × $\bigcirc$) + (__ × $\bigcirc$) + (__ × $\square$) + (__ × $\triangle$) + ___ = 590

C–105

(__ × $\bigcirc$) + (__ × $\bigcirc$) + (__ × $\square$) + (__ × $\triangle$) + ___ = 191

C–106

(__ × $\bigcirc$) + (__ × $\bigcirc$) + (__ × $\square$) + (__ × $\triangle$) + ___ = 85

C–107

(__ × $\bigcirc$) + (__ × $\bigcirc$) + (__ × $\square$) + (__ × $\triangle$) + ___ = 999

EXPANDED NOTATION

Circle the number represented by each computation.
Refer to the chart below.

$$10^3 = 1,000 \qquad 10^2 = 100 \qquad 10^1 = 10$$

		a.	b.	c.
Example	$(5 \times 10^3) + (0 \times 10^2) + (8 \times 10^1) + 2 =$	582	(5,082)	5,182
C–108	$(8 \times 10^3) + (7 \times 10^2) + (1 \times 10^1) + 9 =$	7,819	8,710	8,719
C–109	$(7 \times 10^3) + (4 \times 10^2) + (9 \times 10^1) + 0 =$	749	4,790	7,490
C–110	$(0 \times 10^3) + (7 \times 10^2) + (8 \times 10^1) + 9 =$	789	1,789	7,809
C–111	$(9 \times 10^3) + (2 \times 10^2) + (8 \times 10^1) + 12 =$	9,282	9,292	92,812
C–112	$(7 \times 10^3) + (9 \times 10^2) + (9 \times 10^1) + 10 =$	7,910	8,000	79,910

EXPANDED NOTATION

Place a single digit in each blank to make the statement true.
Refer to the chart below.

$10^4 = 10,000$	$10^3 = 1,000$	$10^2 = 100$	$10^1 = 10$

Example

$$(\underline{1} \times 10^4) + (\underline{2} \times 10^3) + (\underline{0} \times 10^2) + (\underline{9} \times 10^1) + \underline{5} = 12,095$$

C–113

$$(\underline{} \times 10^4) + (\underline{} \times 10^3) + (\underline{} \times 10^2) + (\underline{} \times 10^1) + \underline{} = 9,880$$

C–114

$$(\underline{} \times 10^4) + (\underline{} \times 10^3) + (\underline{} \times 10^2) + (\underline{} \times 10^1) + \underline{} = 10,100$$

C–115

$$(\underline{} \times 10^4) + (\underline{} \times 10^3) + (\underline{} \times 10^2) + (\underline{} \times 10^1) + \underline{} = 798$$

C–116

$$(\underline{} \times 10^4) + (\underline{} \times 10^3) + (\underline{} \times 10^2) + (\underline{} \times 10^1) + \underline{} = 7,980$$

C–117

$$(\underline{} \times 10^4) + (\underline{} \times 10^3) + (\underline{} \times 10^2) + (\underline{} \times 10^1) + \underline{} = 1,010$$

EXPANDED DECIMAL NOTATION

Place a single digit in each blank to make the computation match the set.
In the box, write the number in decimal form. Refer to the chart below.

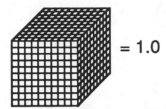 = 1.0   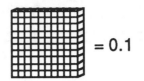 = 0.1 | = 0.01   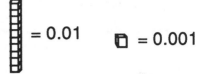 = 0.001

Example

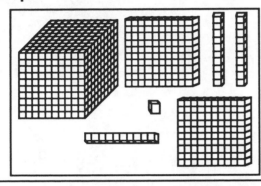

($\underline{1} \times 1.0$) + ($\underline{2} \times 0.1$) + ($\underline{3} \times 0.01$) + ($\underline{1} \times 0.001$)

1.231

C–118

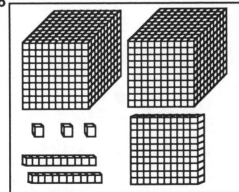

($\underline{} \times 1.0$) + ($\underline{} \times 0.1$) + ($\underline{} \times 0.01$) + ($\underline{} \times 0.001$)

C–119

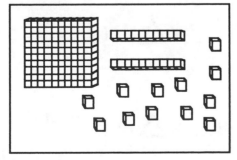

($\underline{} \times 1.0$) + ($\underline{} \times 0.1$) + ($\underline{} \times 0.01$) + ($\underline{} \times 0.001$)

EXPANDED DECIMAL NOTATION

Place a single digit in each blank to make the statement true.
Refer to the chart below.

⬭ = 1.00	◯ = 0.25	▢ = 0.10	△ = 0.05	▮ = 0.01

Example

(_4_ × ⬭) + (_3_ × ◯) + (_2_ × ▢) + (_0_ × △) + (_2_ × ▮) = 4.97

C–120

(__ × ⬭) + (__ × ◯) + (__ × ▢) + (__ × △) + (__ × ▮) = 7.94

C–121

(__ × ⬭) + (__ × ◯) + (__ × ▢) + (__ × △) + (__ × ▮) = 9.98

C–122

(__ × ⬭) + (__ × ◯) + (__ × ▢) + (__ × △) + (__ × ▮) = 6.50

C–123

(__ × ⬭) + (__ × ◯) + (__ × ▢) + (__ × △) + (__ × ▮) = 1.10

C–124

(__ × ⬭) + (__ × ◯) + (__ × ▢) + (__ × △) + (__ × ▮) = 0.41

C–125

(__ × ⬭) + (__ × ◯) + (__ × ▢) + (__ × △) + (__ × ▮) = 0.87

MAKING CHANGE

Each exercise states the cost of an item and the amount paid by the customer.
Place a single digit in each box to indicate the customer's change.

Example

Cost = $2.85

Paid = $5.00

Dollars	Quarters	Dimes	Nickels	Pennies
2	0	1	1	0

C–126

Cost = $14.60

Paid = $20.00

Dollars	Quarters	Dimes	Nickels	Pennies

C–127

Cost = $0.63

Paid = $1.00

Dollars	Quarters	Dimes	Nickels	Pennies

C–128

Cost = $5.98

Paid = $10.00

Dollars	Quarters	Dimes	Nickels	Pennies

C–129

Cost = $2.25

Paid = $5.25

Dollars	Quarters	Dimes	Nickels	Pennies

C–130

Cost = $5.89

Paid = $6.04

Dollars	Quarters	Dimes	Nickels	Pennies

         P.O. BOX 448, PACIFIC GROVE, CA 93950

FRACTIONAL PARTS

A fractional part of each figure is shaded.
In the box, write the fraction that indicates the shaded part of the figure.
In the circle, write the fraction that indicates the unshaded part of the figure.
Write each fraction in lowest terms.

Example

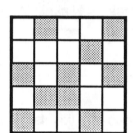

$$\boxed{\frac{2}{5}} + \left(\frac{3}{5}\right) = 1$$

C–131

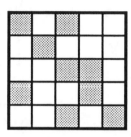

$$\square + \bigcirc = 1$$

C–132

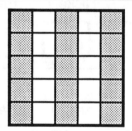

$$\square + \bigcirc = 1$$

C–133

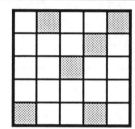

$$\square + \bigcirc = 1$$

C–134

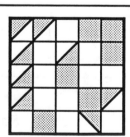

$$\square + \bigcirc = 1$$

C–135

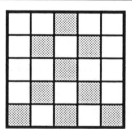

$$\square + \bigcirc = 1$$

                             P. O. BOX 448, PACIFIC GROVE, CA 93950

MIXED NUMBERS

In the box, write a mixed number which estimates the number of shaded rectangles.
In the circle, write the number of unshaed rectangles.

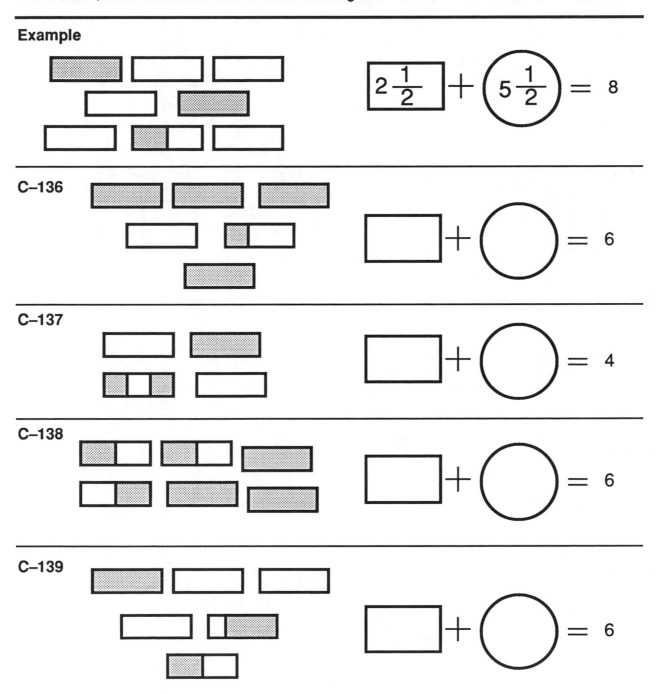

Example

$2\frac{1}{2}$ + $5\frac{1}{2}$ = 8

C–136

+ = 6

C–137

+ = 4

C–138

+ = 6

C–139

+ = 6

MISSING ADDENDS

In each box, write the fraction or mixed number that completes the number sentence.
Reduce each fraction to lowest terms.

Example

$$2\frac{1}{4} + \boxed{6\frac{3}{4}} = 9$$

C–140

$$\boxed{} + \frac{3}{5} = 1$$

C–141

$$\boxed{} + 4\frac{5}{12} = 6$$

C–142

$$6\frac{7}{8} + \boxed{} = 9$$

C–143

$$2 = \frac{1}{8} + \boxed{} + \frac{1}{2}$$

C–144

$$\frac{2}{3} + \boxed{} + \frac{1}{9} = 1$$

C–145

$$3\frac{1}{5} + \boxed{} = 10\frac{4}{5}$$

C–146

$$2\frac{1}{2} = 2\frac{1}{4} + \boxed{}$$

C–147

$$\boxed{} + 2\frac{1}{2} = 4\frac{1}{4}$$

C–148

$$6\frac{3}{4} + \boxed{} = 8\frac{1}{4}$$

                   P. O. BOX 448, PACIFIC GROVE, CA 93950

DECIMAL NUMBERS

Each grid below represents one unit.
In the box, write the decimal that indicates the shaded portion of the grid.
In the oval, write the decimal that indicates the unshaded portion.

Example

C–149

0.26 + 0.74 = 1

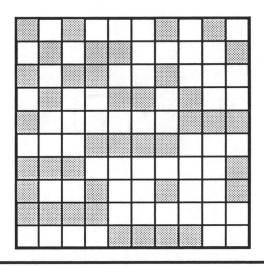

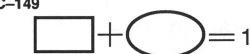

C–150

C–151

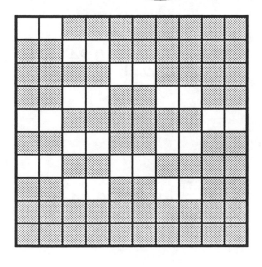

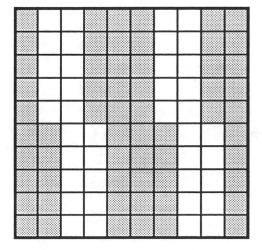

MISSING ADDENDS

In each box, write a decimal number that completes the number sentence.

Example

$0.81 + \boxed{0.19} = 1.0$

C–152

$\boxed{} + 0.7 = 1.0$

C–153

$1.0 = 0.36 + \boxed{}$

C–154

$0.07 + \boxed{} = 1.0$

C–155

$0.24 + \boxed{} + 0.15 = 1.0$

C–156

$0.64 + 0.36 = \boxed{}$

C–157

$\boxed{} + 0.36 = 2.0$

C–158

$0.15 + \boxed{} + 0.24 = 3.0$

C–159

$0.7 + \boxed{} = 3.9$

C–160

$\boxed{} + 0.68 = 2.04$

SUMMING DECIMAL NUMBERS

A number, N, is pictured on a Japanese Abacus.
The location of the decimal point is not shown.
Based upon the statement below the abacus, write two possible values for N in the blanks.
Write the sum of these two values in the box.

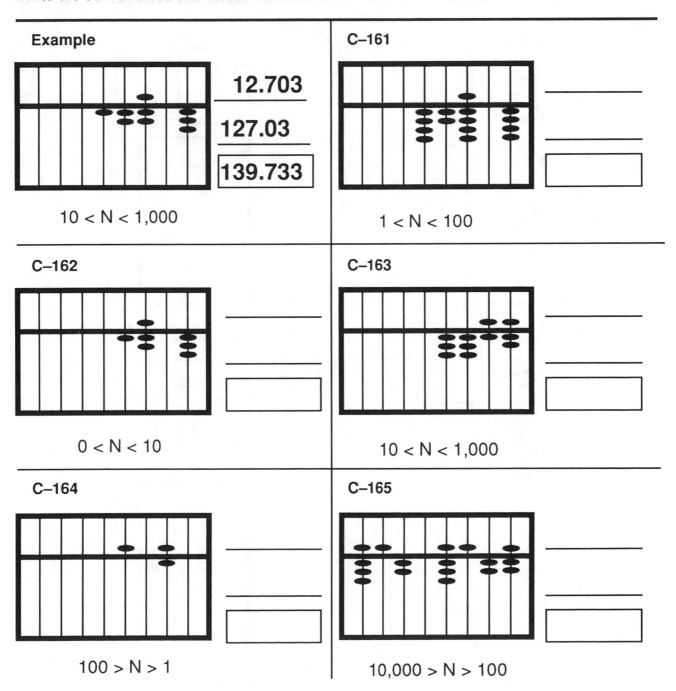

Example

12.703
127.03
139.733

10 < N < 1,000

C–161

1 < N < 100

C–162

0 < N < 10

C–163

10 < N < 1,000

C–164

100 > N > 1

C–165

10,000 > N > 100

SUMMING DECIMAL NUMBERS

Two numerals and a decimal point are written on 3 cards.
Write all the possible arrangements of these cards in the box.
Then write the sum of these decimal numbers.

Example

Cards

| 8 | 7 | . |

| 87. |
| 78. |
| 8.7 |
| 7.8 |
| .78 |
| .87 |

Sum = ___183.15___

C–166

Cards

| 9 | 4 | . |

Sum = _____

C–167

Cards

| 5 | 6 | . |

Sum = _____

C–168

Cards

| 3 | 3 | . |

Sum = _____

ILLUSTRATING NUMBER PROPERTIES

Using only whole numbers, write a numerical example to illustrate each statement below.

Example   A number times itself is greater than 5 times the number.

$$7 \times 7 > 5 \times 7$$

C–169   The sum of two different odd numbers is an even number.

C–170   The difference of two numbers is 18.

C–171   The product of two odd numbers is an odd number.

C–172   The sum of two prime numbers is a prime number.

C–173   The sum of two numbers is 12 and one of the numbers is twice as large as the other.

C–174   A number times itself is equal to the same number.

USING NUMBER PROPERTIES

N represents a whole number.
Find all possible values of N described in each exercise below.

Example

Properties of N

N is odd.
N > 3.
N < 12.
3 does not divide N.
N does not divide 5.

Possible Values of N

7, 11

C–175

Properties of N

N < 10.
2 does not divide N.
3 does not divide N.
N is not prime.

Possible Values of N

C–176

Properties of N

N is a two-digit number.
N < 40.
9 divides the sum of the two digits.

Possible Values of N

C–177

Properties of N

N < 40.
N is a multiple of 3.
N is odd.
9 does not divide N.

Possible Values of N

C–178

Properties of N

N > 10.
N < 40.
N is prime.
The sum of the digits of N is less than 10.

Possible Values of N

C–179

Properties of N

N is even.
N < 50.
N is a multiple of 3.
9 divides the sum of its digits.

Possible Values of N

DISCOVERING NUMBER PROPERTIES

In each exercise below, N represents a whole number.
Check all the properties of N that are always true.

Example

If N is between 0 and 10,
then N – 1 is

    ____even
    ____odd
    ____not zero
    ✓ less than N
    ✓ less than 10

C–180

If N > 5, then 2 × N is

    ____even
    ____odd
    ____not zero
    ____greater than N
    ____greater than 10

C–181

If N is even, then N + N is

    ____even
    ____odd
    ____not zero
    ____greater than N

C–182

If N is odd, then N + 2 is

    ____even
    ____odd
    ____not zero
    ____greater than N
    ____greater than 3

C–183

If N is even, then 3 × N is

    ____even
    ____odd
    ____not zero
    ____greater than N
    ____divisible by 2
    ____divisible by 3
    ____divisible by 6

C–184

If N is odd, then 3 × N is

    ____even
    ____odd
    ____not zero
    ____greater than N
    ____divisible by 2
    ____divisible by 3
    ____not a prime number

DIVISIBLITY OF NUMBERS

Put a box around all the numbers greater than 2 that are divisible by 2.
Circle all the numbers greater than 3 that are divisible by 3.

1	2	3	4	5	6	7	8	9	10
11	12	13	14	15	16	17	18	19	20
21	22	23	24	25	26	27	28	29	30
31	32	33	34	35	36	37	38	39	40
41	42	43	44	45	46	47	48	49	50
51	52	53	54	55	56	57	58	59	60
61	62	63	64	65	66	67	68	69	70
71	72	73	74	75	76	77	78	79	80
81	82	83	84	85	86	87	88	89	90
91	92	93	94	95	96	97	98	99	100

C–185 What numbers in the list are divisible by 4? _____

_____

C–186 What numbers in the list can be divided by both 2 and 3? _____

_____

C–187 What numbers in the list are divisible by 9? _____

_____

DIVISIBLITY OF NUMBERS

Put a box around all the numbers greater than 5 that are divisible by 5.
Circle all the numbers greater than 7 that are divisible by 7.

1	2	3	4	5	6	7	8	9	[10]
11	12	13	(14)	15	16	17	18	19	20
21	22	23	24	25	26	27	28	29	30
31	32	33	34	35	36	37	38	39	40
41	42	43	44	45	46	47	48	49	50
51	52	53	54	55	56	57	58	59	60
61	62	63	64	65	66	67	68	69	70
71	72	73	74	75	76	77	78	79	80
81	82	83	84	85	86	87	88	89	90
91	92	93	94	95	96	97	98	99	100

C–188 What numbers in the list are divisible by 10?

C–189 What numbers in the list can be divided by both 5 and 7?

C–190 List all the prime numbers that are less than 100.

CONSTRUCTING RECTANGLES

Two different rectangles can be constructed with a set of 6 tiles.
The two models below show the possible arrangements of the tiles

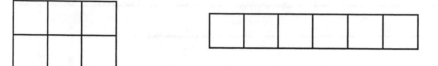

Example	Determine how many different rectangles can be constructed with 3 tiles. Then write the dimensions of the rectangles.

$$1 \times 3$$

C–191	Write the dimensions of the different rectangles that can be constructed with 4 tiles.

C–192	Write the dimensions of the different rectangles that can be constructed with 12 tiles.

C–193	Find the smallest set of tiles that would be needed to construct 4 different rectangles. Then write the dimensions of each rectangle.

C–194	Write the dimensions of the different rectangles that can be constructed using the number of tiles indicated.

a. 2 _____   e. 7 _____

b. 10 _____   f. 21 _____

c. 45 _____   g. 30 _____

d. 34 _____   h. 41 _____

CONSTRUCTING RECTANGLES

The numbers in the chart below have been sorted by the number of possible
rectangles that can be constructed from a set of tiles.
Use the information in the chart to complete the exercises.

Number of Rectangles

ONE	TWO	THREE	FOUR	FIVE	SIX
2	4	16	24	48	60
3	6	20	30	80	72
5	8	28	42		
11	9	50	54		
17	14	68	56		
19	21	76	64		
37	25	81			
53	49				

Example   Write the dimensions of the rectangles that can be made with the following
number of tiles.

$$2 = \underline{1 \times 2} \qquad\qquad 11 = \underline{1 \times 11}$$

$$17 = \underline{1 \times 17} \qquad\qquad 37 = \underline{1 \times 37}$$

C–195   Write the dimensions of the rectangles that can be constructed with the
following number of tiles.

$$4 = \underline{\hspace{4cm}} \qquad\qquad 9 = \underline{\hspace{4cm}}$$

$$25 = \underline{\hspace{4cm}} \qquad\qquad 49 = \underline{\hspace{4cm}}$$

C–196   Write the dimensions of the rectangles that can be constructed with the
following number of tiles.

$$20 = \underline{\hspace{5cm}} \qquad\qquad 50 = \underline{\hspace{5cm}}$$

$$30 = \underline{\hspace{5cm}} \qquad\qquad 42 = \underline{\hspace{5cm}}$$

$$48 = \underline{\hspace{5cm}} \qquad\qquad 60 = \underline{\hspace{5cm}}$$

C–197   List 3 numbers less than 100 which are not in the chart that can be used to
construct two different rectangles.

FACTOR TREES

A factor tree is suggested for the number in each exercise.
Use the tree to write the number as a product of prime numbers.

Example

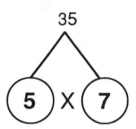

35
5 X 7

C–198

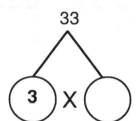

33
3 X

C–199

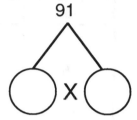

91
X

C–200

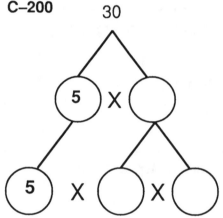

30
5 X
5 X X

C–201

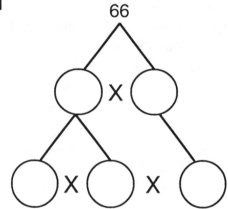

66
X
X X

C–202

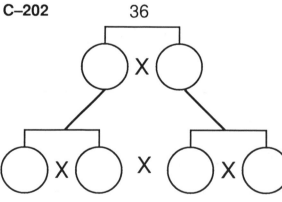

36
X
X X X

C–203

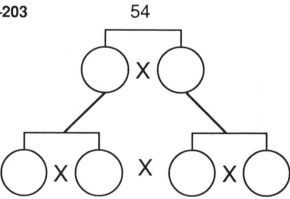

54
X
X X X

P. O. BOX 448, PACIFIC GROVE, CA 93950

FOLLOWING A FLOWCHART

Using a pair of dice, follow the flowchart below.

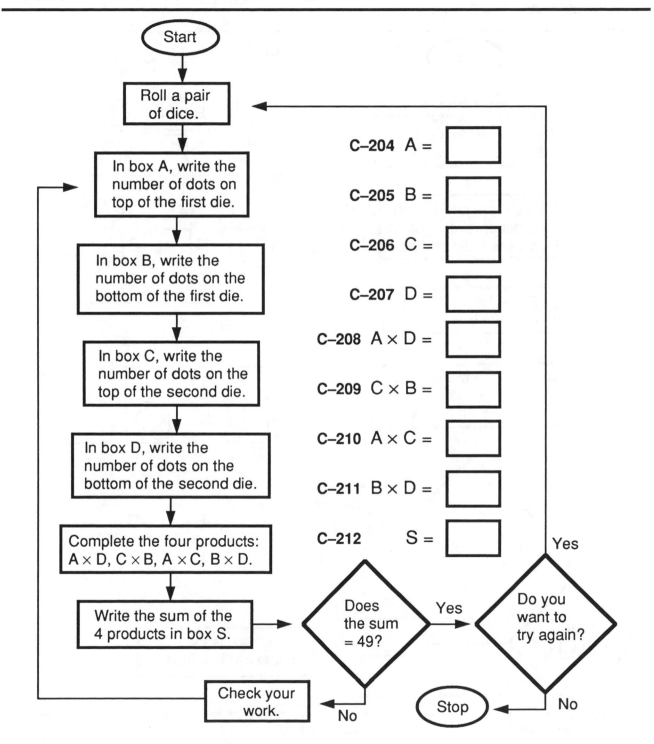

FOLLOWING A FLOWCHART

Follow the flowchart below using the fractions in the exercises.
Write the final answer in the circle.

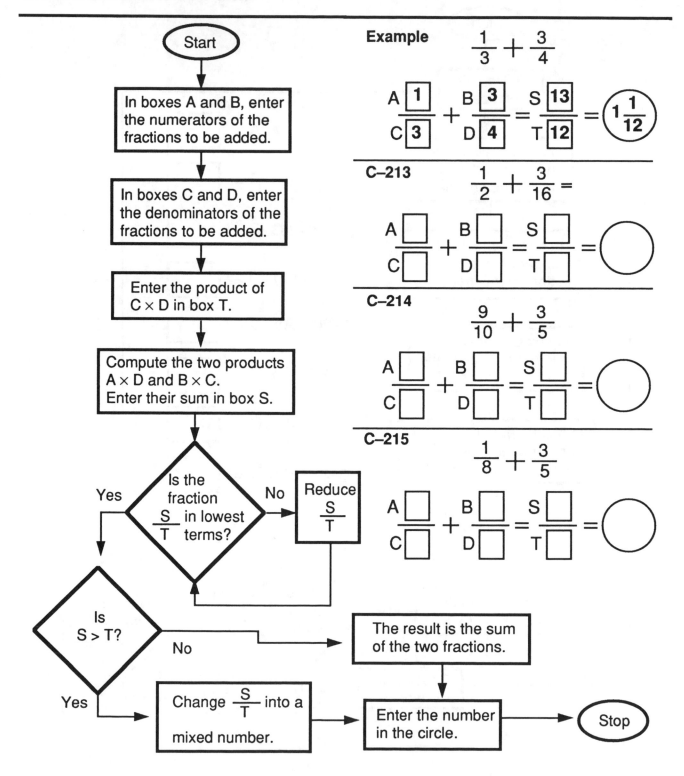

Example $\dfrac{1}{3} + \dfrac{3}{4}$

A $\boxed{1}$ B $\boxed{3}$ S $\boxed{13}$ $= \left(1\dfrac{1}{12}\right)$
C $\boxed{3}$ D $\boxed{4}$ T $\boxed{12}$

C–213 $\dfrac{1}{2} + \dfrac{3}{16} =$

C–214 $\dfrac{9}{10} + \dfrac{3}{5}$

C–215 $\dfrac{1}{8} + \dfrac{3}{5}$

Start

In boxes A and B, enter the numerators of the fractions to be added.

In boxes C and D, enter the denominators of the fractions to be added.

Enter the product of C × D in box T.

Compute the two products A × D and B × C. Enter their sum in box S.

Is the fraction $\dfrac{S}{T}$ in lowest terms?

Yes / No

Reduce $\dfrac{S}{T}$

Is S > T?

No

Yes

The result is the sum of the two fractions.

Change $\dfrac{S}{T}$ into a mixed number.

Enter the number in the circle.

Stop

COMPLETING A FLOWCHART

You wish to divide two fractions.
Complete the flowchart below to accomplish this task.
Test the completed flowchart using the fractions in the exercises.

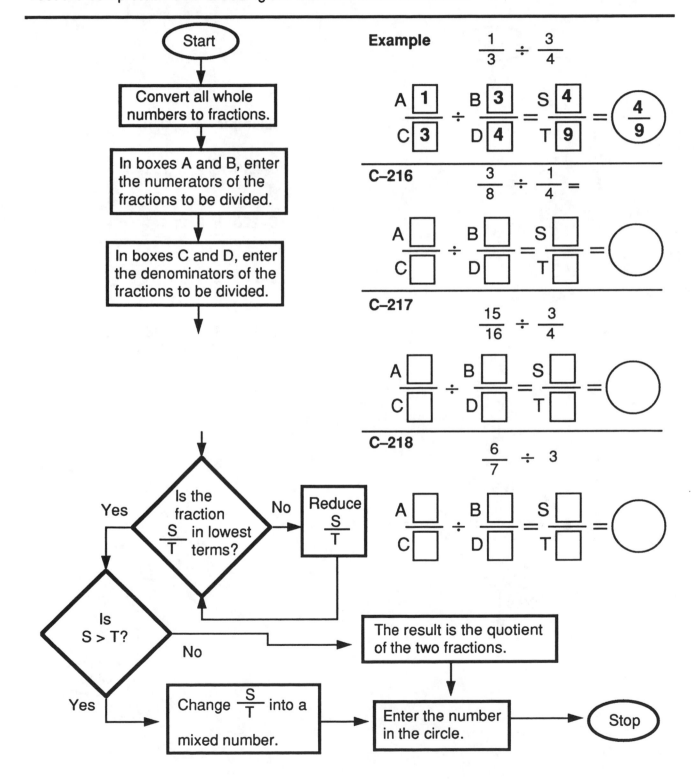

COMPLETING A FLOWCHART

You wish to average a list of whole numbers and express the answer to the nearest tenth.
Complete the flowchart to accomplish this task.
Then test your flowchart using the list of numbers in each exercise.

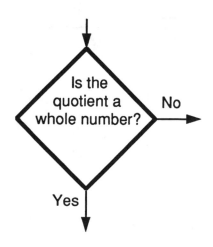

Example 4, 6, 3, 8

C–219 3, 2, 5, 7, 1, 0

C–220 5, 2, 2, 6, 4

C–221 9, 17, 5

C–222 100, 90, 88, 85, 80, 78, 60, 50, 15

P. O. BOX 448, PACIFIC GROVE, CA 93950

CONSTRUCTING A FLOWCHART

A well-known number game is described below.
Construct a flowchart for the game.
Then test your flowchart using the numbers in the exercises.

1. Write down a 3-digit number, making sure that the unit's digit and the hundred's digit differ by at least 2.

2. Reverse the digits and write down the resulting number.

3. Compute the difference of these two numbers and write it down.

4. Reverse the digits of this new number and add the result to the previous number.

5. The sum should always be 1089.

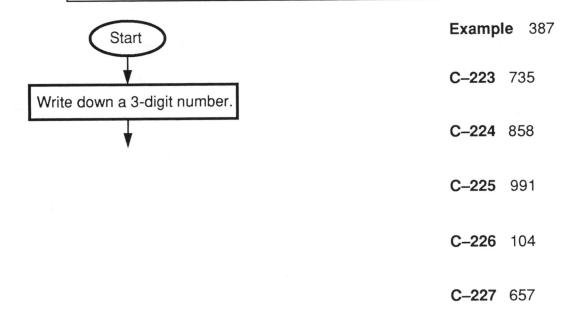

Example 387

C–223 735

C–224 858

C–225 991

C–226 104

C–227 657

     P.O. BOX 448, PACIFIC GROVE, CA 93950

CONSTRUCTING A FLOWCHART

The formula for the relationship between Fahrenheit and
Centigrade temperature is given below.
Construct a flowchart to convert Fahrenheit temperature to Centigrade temperature.
Then test your flowchart using the Fahrenheit temperatures in the exercises.

$$C = \frac{5}{9} \times (F - 32)$$

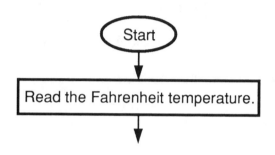

Start

Read the Fahrenheit temperature.

Example 212° F = $\underline{100}$° C

C–228 32° F   = _____ ° C

C–229 98.6° F = _____ ° C

C–230 68° F   = _____ ° C

C–231 90° F   = _____ ° C

Stop

PROBLEM SOLVING

A record store recently had a sale on tape cassettes. Tapes priced at $4.99 were reduced to $3.69, $6.99 tapes were reduced to $4.99, and $5.99 tapes were reduced to $4.99. Circle the computation that tells how much each person spent on tapes.

Example   Jim purchased 3 tapes that normally sell for $5.99.

$3 \times \$5.99$ 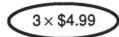 $\left(3 \times \$4.99\right)$ $3 \times \$3.69$

C–232   Sally purchased 4 tapes that normally sell for $4.99

$4 \times \$4.99$ $4 \times \$5.99$ $4 \times \$3.69$

C–233   Hector purchased 3 tapes that normally sell for $5.99 and 4 tapes that normally sell for $4.99.

$(3 \times \$4.99) + (4 \times \$3.69)$ $(3 \times \$5.99) + (4 \times \$4.99)$

$7 \times \$4.99$ $(4 \times \$4.99) + (3 \times \$3.69)$

C–234   Sam bought 4 tapes that normally sell for $6.99 and 2 tapes that normally sell for $4.99.

$(4 \times \$4.99) + (2 \times \$4.99)$ $(4 \times \$5.99) + (2 \times \$3.69)$

$(4 \times \$4.99) + (2 \times \$3.69)$ $6 \times \$4.99$

C–235   Juanita bought 3 tapes that normally sell for $6.99, 2 tapes that normally sell for $5.99, and 1 tape that normally sells for $4.99.

$(3 \times \$4.99) + (3 \times \$4.99)$ $(3 \times \$5.99) + (2 \times \$4.99) + \$3.69$

$(5 \times \$4.99) + \$3.69$ $(3 \times \$4.99) + (2 \times \$4.99) + \$3.69$

---

171   P.O. BOX 448, PACIFIC GROVE, CA 93950

PROBLEM SOLVING

A record store recently had a sale on tape cassettes. Tapes priced at $4.99 were reduced to $3.69, $6.99 tapes were reduced to $4.99, and $5.99 tapes were reduced to $4.99.
Fill in the blanks in each computation and find the solution to the problem.

Example

Jim purchased 3 tapes that normally sell for $6.99.
How much money did he save?

$$3 \times (\underline{\$6.99} - \underline{\$4.99}) = \underline{\$6.00}$$

C–236

Hector purchased 2 tapes that normally sell for $5.99.
How much money did he spend?

$$\underline{\hspace{2cm}} \times (\$5.99 - \underline{\hspace{2cm}}) = \underline{\hspace{2cm}}$$

C–237

Juanita purchased 3 tapes that normally sell for $4.99 and
1 tape that normally sells for $6.99.
How much money did she spend?

$$3 \times (\underline{\hspace{2cm}} - \underline{\hspace{2cm}}) + (\underline{\hspace{2cm}} - \underline{\hspace{2cm}}) = \underline{\hspace{2cm}}$$

C–238

Mary bought 2 tapes that normally sell for $6.99
and 3 tapes that normally sell for $5.99.
How much money did she save?

$$2 \times (\underline{\hspace{2cm}} - \$4.99) + \underline{\hspace{2cm}} \times (\underline{\hspace{2cm}} - \$4.99) = \underline{\hspace{2cm}}$$

$$2 \times (\underline{\hspace{2cm}}) + 3 \times (\underline{\hspace{2cm}}) = \underline{\hspace{2cm}}$$

C–239

Sally bought 3 tapes.
What is the most money that she could have saved on the tapes?

$$3 \times (\underline{\hspace{2cm}} - \underline{\hspace{2cm}}) = \underline{\hspace{2cm}}$$

PROBLEM SOLVING

Circle the letter of the expression that describes the amount of money spent for each purchase. Then complete the computation to answer each question.

Example
The hardware store sells quarts of paint for $4.95 and gallon cans of paint for $16.95. Juanita purchased 2 quarts of white paint, 3 quarts of blue paint, and a gallon of red paint. How much did she pay for the paint?

a. (1 × $4.95) + (2 × $16.95)   b. (3 × $4.95) + (3 × $16.95)

ⓒ (5 × $4.95) + (1 × $16.95)   d. (5 × $16.95) + (1 × $4.95)

ANSWER: $ 41.70

C–240
The supermarket is selling limes at 3/59¢ and lemons at 4/69¢. How much money does John need to buy 6 limes and a dozen lemons?

a. (6 × 59¢) + (12 × 69¢)   b. (2 × 69¢) + (3 × 69¢)

c. (2 × 59¢) + (4 × 69¢)   d. (2 × 59¢) + (3 × 69¢)

ANSWER:_____

C–241
The supermarket sells cans of vegetables at 2/99¢ and cans of fruit at 3/99¢.
Jim bought 2 cans of corn, 1 can of beans, 3 cans of peas, 2 cans of peaches, 1 can of pears, 2 cans of applesauce, and a can of plums. How much money did Jim spend?

a. 12 × 99¢   b. (6 × 99¢) + (6 × 99¢)

c. (3 × 99¢) + (2 × 99¢)   d. 5 × 99¢

ANSWER:_____

C–242
The supermarket sells oranges at $1.09 per dozen.
Sue purchased 1/2 dozen oranges on Wednesday and another 1/2 dozen oranges on Friday. How much did she pay for the dozen oranges?

a. (2 × $1.09)   b. ($1.09 ÷ 2) + ($1.09 ÷ 2)

c. (1 × $1.09)   d. 2 × ($1.09 ÷ 2)

ANSWER:_____

PROBLEM SOLVING

Circle the letter of the expression that describes the amount of money spent for each purchase. Then complete the computation to answer each question.

C–243

The sale price on socks in the department store was 2 pairs for $5.99. Jose decided to buy 5 pairs of socks. How much money did he spend?

a. $5 \times \$5.99$

b. $(2 \times \$5.99) + \$2.99$

c. $(2 \times \$5.99) + (\$5.99 \div 2)$

d. $(3 \times \$5.99)$

ANSWER:_____

C–244

A garden and nursery center is selling 3 bags of lawn fertilizer for $23.89. Each bag will fertilize 5,000 square feet. Jill bought enough fertilizer for 24,354 square feet. How much did she pay for the fertilizer?

a. $5 \times \$23.89$

c. $3 \times \$23.89$

b. $(3 \times \$23.89) + (\$23.89 \div 3)$

d. $\$23.89 + 2 \times (\$23.89 \div 3)$

ANSWER:_____

C–245

Jose found the same fertilizer on sale at 4 bags for $31.81. He needed fertilizer for 25,322 square feet. How much did Jose pay for his fertilizer?

a. $6 \times \$31.81$

c. $\$31.81 + (\$31.81 \div 4)$

b. $\$31.81 + (\$31.81 \div 2)$

d. $\$31.81 + 2 \times (\$31.81 \div 4)$

ANSWER:_____

C–246

Taxi cab rates are $1.30 for the first 3/10 of a mile and 20¢ for each additional 1/10 of a mile. The distance from the train station to the nearest hotel is 1 3/4 miles. What is the cab fare for the journey?

a. $17 \times 20¢$

c. $\$1.30 + (15 \times 20¢)$

b. $\$1.30 + (17 \times 20¢)$

d. $\$1.30 + (14 \times 20¢)$

ANSWER:_____

COMPARING LENGTHS

Pairs of lines are drawn on a grid.
Complete each statement by placing one of the symbols >, <, or = in the box.

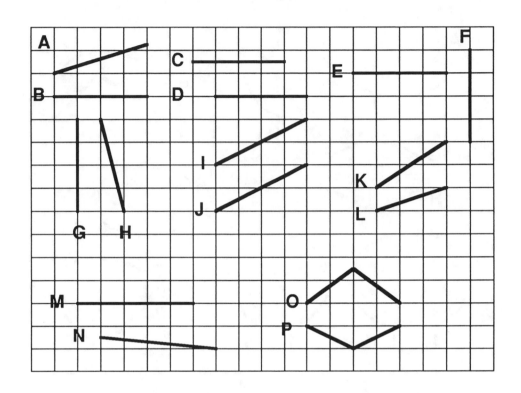

Example length of A [>] length of B   **D–4** length of I [　] length of J

D–1 length of C [　] length of D   **D–5** length of K [　] length of L

D–2 length of E [　] length of F   **D–6** length of M [　] length of N

D–3 length of G [　] length of H   **D–7** length of O [　] length of P

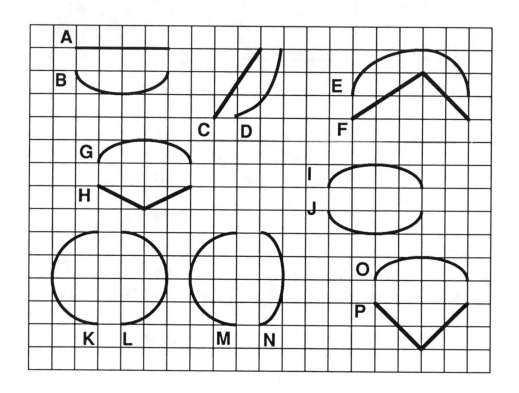

COMPARING LENGTHS

Paths and lines are drawn on a grid.
Complete each statement by placing one of the symbols >, <, or = in the box.

Example length of A **<** length of B   **D–11** length of I ☐ length of J

D–8 length of C ☐ length of D   **D–12** length of K ☐ length of L

D–9 length of E ☐ length of F   **D–13** length of M ☐ length of N

D–10 length of G ☐ length of H   **D–14** length of O ☐ length of P

COMPARING LENGTHS

Name the longest and the shortest line segment pictured in each figure.

Example

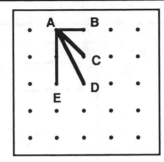

Longest: $\overline{AD}$

Shortest: $\overline{AB}$

D–15

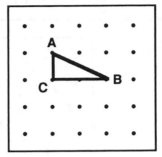

Longest: _____

Shortest: _____

D–16

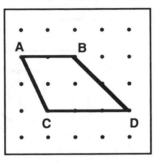

Longest: _____

Shortest: _____

D–17

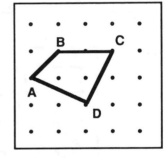

Longest: _____

Shortest: _____

D–18

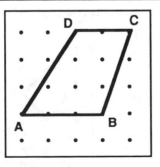

Longest: _____

Shortest: _____

D–19

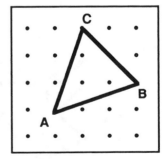

Longest: _____

Shortest: _____

COMPARING PATHS

Compare the length of path AB to the length of path XY.
Indicate the relationship by placing one of the symbols <, >, or = in the box.

Example

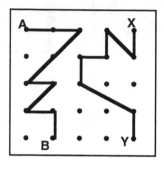

AB > XY

D–20

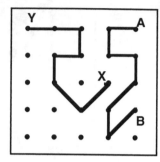

AB ☐ XY

D–21

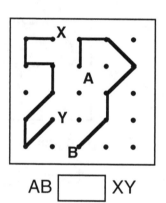

AB ☐ XY

D–22

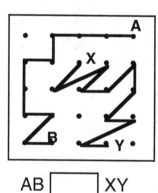

AB ☐ XY

D–23

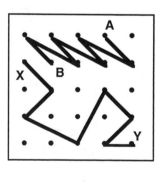

AB ☐ XY

D–24

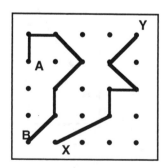

AB ☐ XY

COMPARING PERIMETERS

Circle the letter of the figure which has the largest perimeter.

Example

A   (B)   C

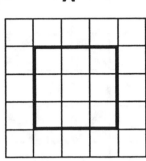 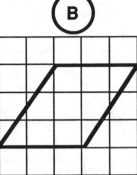 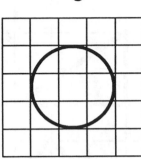

D–25

A   B   C

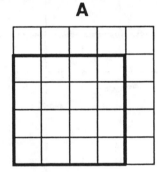 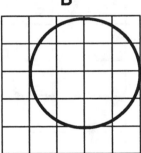 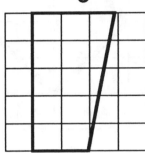

D–26

A   B   C

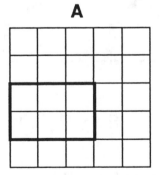 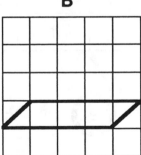 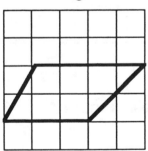

D–27

A   B   C

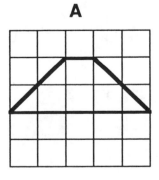 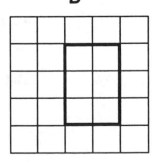 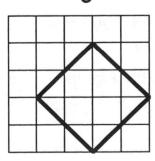

P.O. BOX 448, PACIFIC GROVE, CA 93950

ESTIMATING PERIMETERS

For each figure, estimate the perimeter in grid units.
Circle the best estimate.

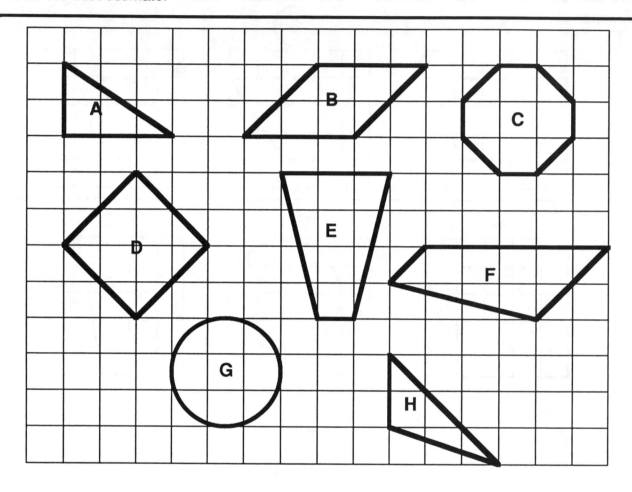

Example	Figure A :	3	7	(9)	**D–31** Figure E :	8	12	14

Example Figure A : 3   7   ⑨   **D–31** Figure E : 8   12   14

D–28 Figure B : 6   10   12   **D–32** Figure F : 7   10   13

D–29 Figure C : 7   9   12   **D–33** Figure G : 7   9   12

D–30 Figure D : 8   11   14   **D–34** Figure H : 3   7   9

COMPARING PERIMETERS

Complete each statement by placing one of the symbols >, <, or = in the box .
Assume one unit is the length of an edge of a square in the grid.

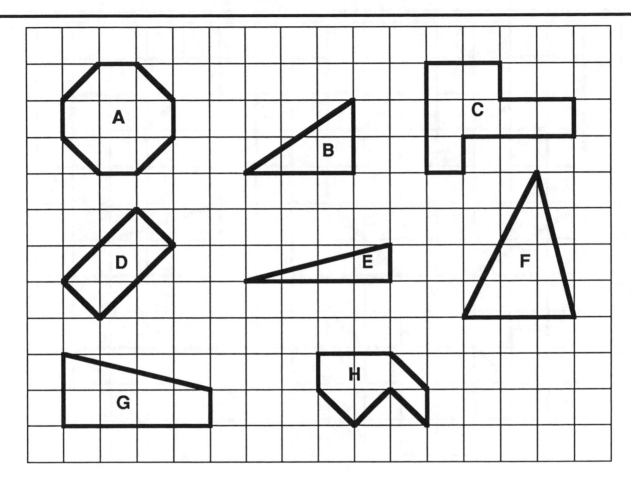

Example perimeter of A $\boxed{>}$ 8 units   **D–38** 10 units $\boxed{}$ perimeter of E

D–35 perimeter of B $\boxed{}$ 8 units   **D–39** 11 units $\boxed{}$ perimeter of F

D–36 perimeter of C $\boxed{}$ 14 units   **D–40** 12 units $\boxed{}$ perimeter of G

D–37 perimeter of D $\boxed{}$ 6 units   **D–41** 8 units $\boxed{}$ perimeter of H

COMPARING PERIMETERS

Complete each statement by placing one of the symbols >, <, or = in the box .
Assume one unit is the length of an edge of a square in the grid.

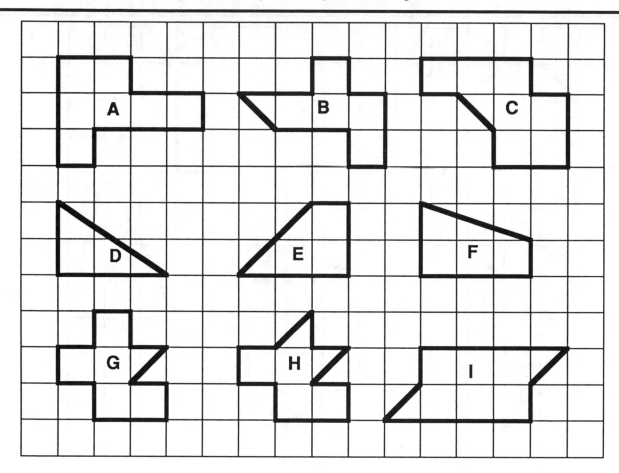

Example   perimeter of A **>** perimeter of B   **D–45** perimeter of E ☐ perimeter of F

D–42 perimeter of B ☐ perimeter of C   **D–46** perimeter of G ☐ perimeter of H

D–43 perimeter of A ☐ perimeter of C   **D–47** perimeter of H ☐ perimeter of I

D–44 perimeter of D ☐ perimeter of E   **D–48** perimeter of G ☐ perimeter of I

COMPUTING PERIMETERS

The lengths of some edges are marked on each figure.
Write the missing lengths in the circles and compute the perimeter of each figure.

Example

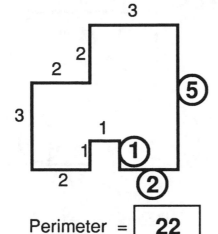

Perimeter = $\boxed{22}$

D–49

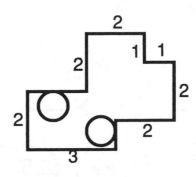

Perimeter = ☐

D–50

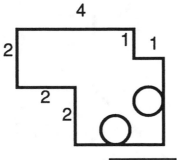

Perimeter = ☐

D–51

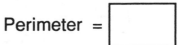
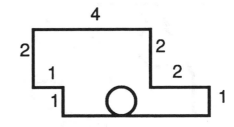

Perimeter = ☐

D–52

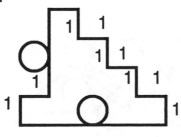

Perimeter = ☐

D–53

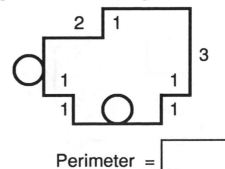

Perimeter = ☐

---

183   P.O. BOX 448, PACIFIC GROVE, CA 93950

COMPUTING PERIMETERS

The lengths of some edges are marked on each figure.
Write the missing lengths in the circles, and compute the perimeter of each figure.

Example

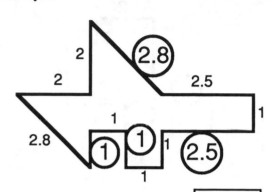

Perimeter = 20.6

D–54

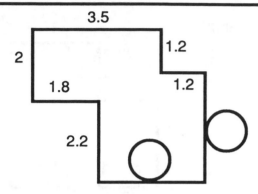

Perimeter = ☐

D–55

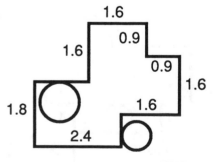

Perimeter = ☐

D–56

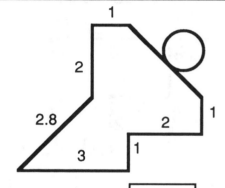

Perimeter = ☐

D–57

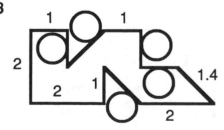

Perimeter = ☐

D–58

Perimeter = ☐

COMPUTING PERIMETERS

Each of the figures below have line symmetry.
Some lengths are marked on the figure.
Find the perimeter of each figure.

Example

Perimeter = 12.96

D–59

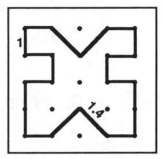

Perimeter =

D–60

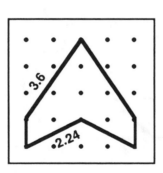

Perimeter =

D–61

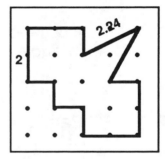

Perimeter =

D–62

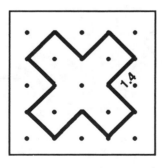

Perimeter =

D–63

Perimeter =

185   P.O. BOX 448, PACIFIC GROVE, CA 93950

FINDING PERIMETERS OF POLYGONS

In each exercise a polygon is identified.
The lengths of some of the sides of the polygon are given.
Determine the perimeter of the polygon, if possible.
If you cannot determine the perimeter, place a "?" in the answer column.

	Polygon	Lengths	Perimeter
Example	Rhombus	4	16
D–64	Rectangle	3, 7	
D–65	Isosceles Triangle	3, 6	
D–66	Parallelogram	3, 7	
D–67	Trapezoid	3, 4, 7	
D–68	Square	4	
D–69	Right Triangle	3, 4	

COMPARING PERIMETERS

The figures in each exercise are similar.
Find the missing lengths, and compute the perimeter of each figure.

Example

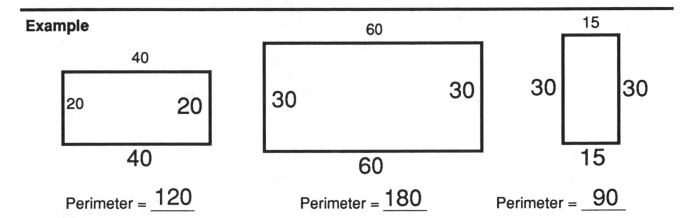

Perimeter = __120__   Perimeter = __180__   Perimeter = __90__

D–70

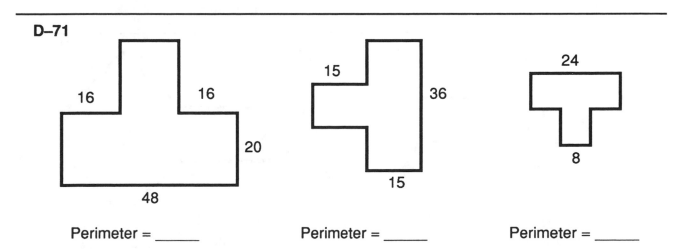

Perimeter = _____   Perimeter = _____   Perimeter = _____

D–71

Perimeter = _____   Perimeter = _____   Perimeter = _____

                   P.O. BOX 448, PACIFIC GROVE, CA 93950

COMPARING PERIMETERS

All figures below are similar and have line symmetry.
Find the perimeter of each figure.

Example

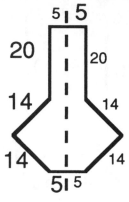

5 ⎸ 5

20   20

14   14

14   14

5 ⎸ 5

Perimeter = __116__

D–72

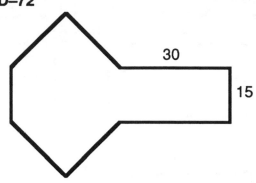

30

15

Perimeter = _____

D–73

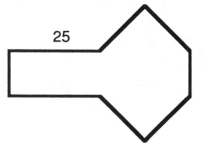

25

Perimeter = _____

D–74

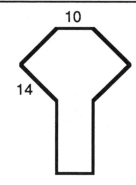

10

14

Perimeter = _____

D–75

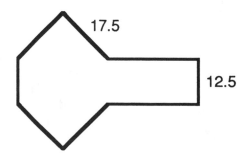

17.5

12.5

Perimeter = _____

D–76

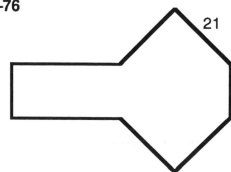

21

Perimeter = _____

USING SIMILARITY TO COMPUTE PERIMETERS

In each exercise the triangles pictured are similar.
The lengths of some sides are given.
Find the lengths of the indicated segments and the perimeter of triangle ABC.

Example

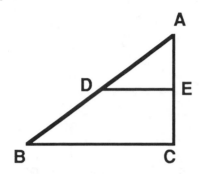

AE = 3   EC = 3   DE = 4

AD = 5   BC = _8_   BD = _5_

Perimeter △ ABC = _24_

D–77

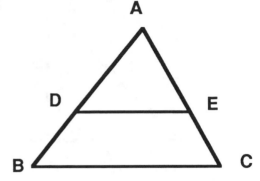

AE = 5   DB = 3   DE = 6

AD = 4   EC = ____   BC = ____

Perimeter △ ABC = ____

D–78

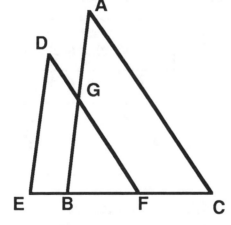

BG = 5   BF = 4   FC = 4

FG = 6   DG = 3   AC = ____

DE = ____   AG = ____

Perimeter △ ABC = ____

D–79

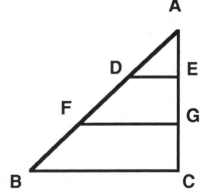

AE = 1   AC = 3   DE = 1

EG = 1   AF = 2.8   AD = ____

BF = ____   AB = ____   BC = ____

Perimeter △ ABC = ____

USING SIMILARITY TO COMPUTE PERIMETERS

The lengths of some sides are given for each polygon.
Find the lengths of the indicated segments and the perimeter of the indicated polygon.

Example

All triangles
are similar.

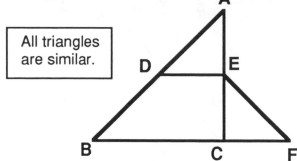

AE = 1   EC = 1   DE = 1

AD = 1.4   BC = __2__   BD = __1.4__

EF = __1.4__   CF = __1__

Perimeter ABFE = __8.2__

D–80

All triangles
are similar.

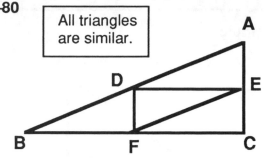

AE = 2.5   EC = 2.5   BD = 6.5

AD = 6.5   BC = 12   BF = _____

DF = _____   DE = _____   EF = _____

Perimeter △ EFC = _____

D–81   ABCD is a rectangle.
           All right triangles are similar.

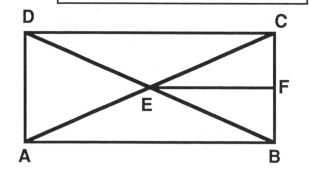

AB = 12   EC = 6.5   CF = 2.5

CB = 5   AE = _____   EF = _____

DA = _____   DB = _____

Perimeter △ BEF = _____

D–82   ABCD is a rhombus.
           All triangles are similar.

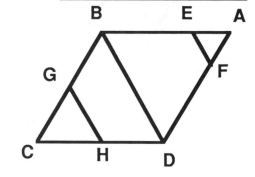

AB = 8   AF = 2   CG = 4

BD = 8   GH = _____   BE = _____

DF = _____   EF = _____   DH = _____

Perimeter EFDHGB = _____

P.O. BOX 448, PACIFIC GROVE, CA 93950

PERIMETERS OF CONGRUENT AND SIMILAR FIGURES

The perimeter, rounded to the nearest tenth, of figure A = 9.2, figure B = 6.8, and figure C = 6.4.
Determine the perimeter of each figure below to the nearest tenth.

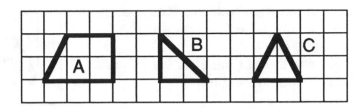

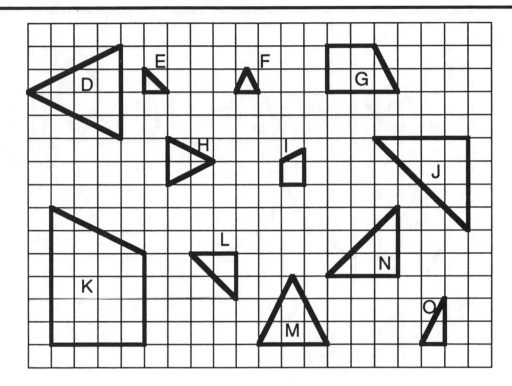

Example
 perimeter of D = <u>12.8</u>

D–83
 perimeter of E = _____

D–84
 perimeter of F = _____

D–85
 perimeter of G = _____

D–86
 perimeter of H = _____

D–87
 perimeter of I = _____

D–88
 perimeter of J = _____

D–89
 perimeter of K = _____

D–90
 perimeter of L = _____

D–91
 perimeter of M = _____

D–92
 perimeter of N = _____

D–93
 perimeter of O = _____

PERIMETERS OF CONGRUENT AND SIMILAR FIGURES

The perimeter, rounded to the nearest tenth, of figure A = 9.2, figure B = 6.8, and figure C = 6.4.
Determine the perimeter of each figure below to the nearest tenth.

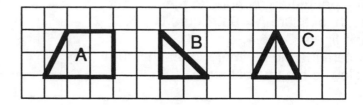

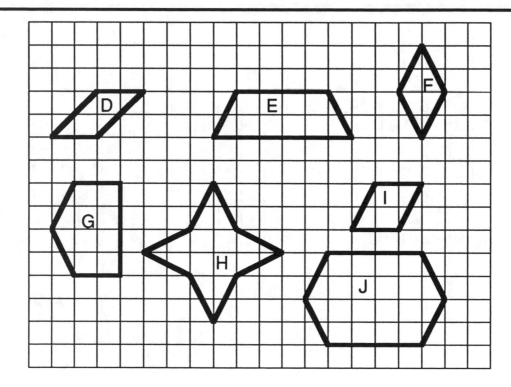

Example
perimeter of D = __9.6__

D–94
perimeter of E = _____

D–95
perimeter of F = _____

D–96
perimeter of G = _____

D–97
perimeter of H = _____

D–98
perimeter of I = _____

D–99
perimeter of J = _____

P.O. BOX 448, PACIFIC GROVE, CA 93950

DRAWING POLYGONS

On the isometric geoboards below, draw each described polygon.

Example   A parallelogram with perimeter 10

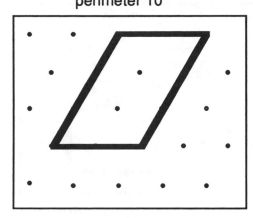

D–100   A parallelogram different from the Example with perimeter 10

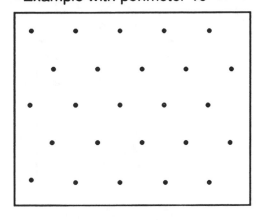

D–101   A triangle with perimeter 12

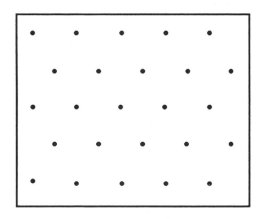

D–102   A trapezoid with perimeter 11

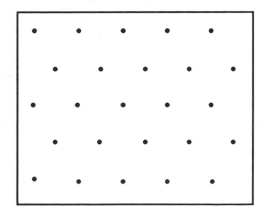

D–103   A hexagon with perimeter 10

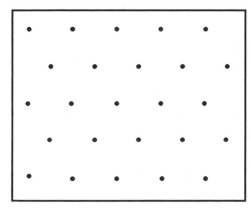

D–104   A pentagon with perimeter 9

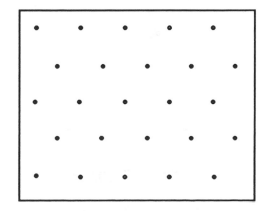

DRAWING POLYGONS

Draw a polygon similar to the given polygon.
Make your drawing as large as possible on the given grid.
Determine the perimeter of your drawing.

Example

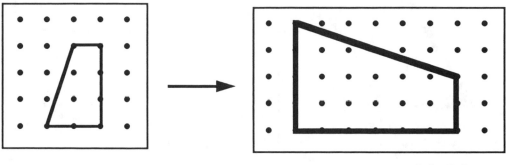

Perimeter = 9.16   Perimeter = $\underline{18.32}$

D–105

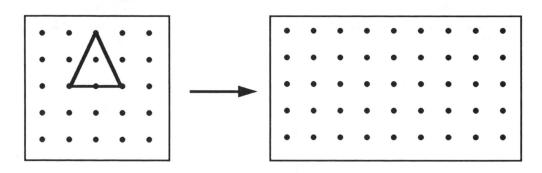

Perimeter = 6.47   Perimeter = _____

D–106

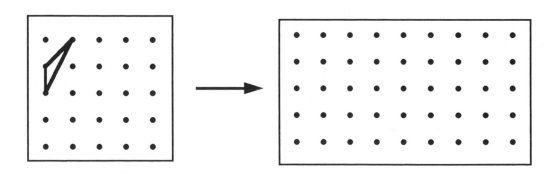

Perimeter = 4.65   Perimeter = _____

COMPARING PERIMETER AND CIRCUMFERENCE

The diameter of each circle is 4 centimeters.
Find the perimeter of each inscribed and circumscribed polygon.
Use each set of perimeters to approximate the circumference of the circle.

Example

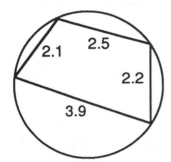

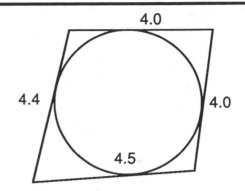

Approximate
Circumference

__13.8__

Perimeter = __10.7__   Perimeter = __16.9__

D–107

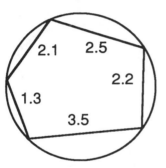

Approximate
Circumference

———

Perimeter = _____   Perimeter = _____

D–108

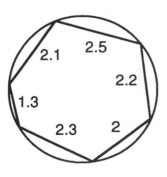

Approximate
Circumference

———

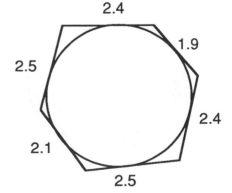

Perimeter = _____   Perimeter = _____

                 P.O. BOX 448, PACIFIC GROVE, CA 93950

COMPARING PERIMETER AND CIRCUMFERENCE

The diameter of each circle is 4 centimeters.
Find the perimeter of each regular inscribed and circumscribed polygon.
Use each set of perimeters to approximate the circumference of the circle.

Example

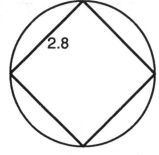

2.8

Approximate
Circumference

13.6

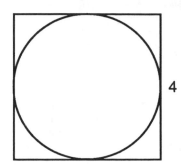

4

Perimeter = **11.2**

Perimeter = **16**

D–109

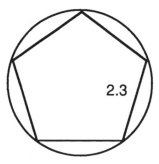

2.3

Approximate
Circumference

_____

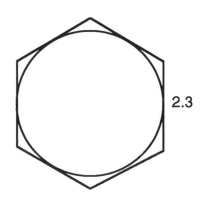

3

Perimeter = _____

Perimeter = _____

D–110

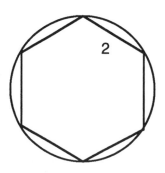

2

Approximate
Circumference

_____

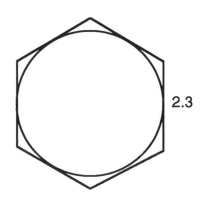

2.3

Perimeter = _____

Perimeter = _____

                   P.O. BOX 448, PACIFIC GROVE, CA 93950

COMPARING AREAS

Compare each polygon with polygon A.
Separate the polygons into two sets, the first with figures having areas less than that of
A and the second with areas greater than figure A.

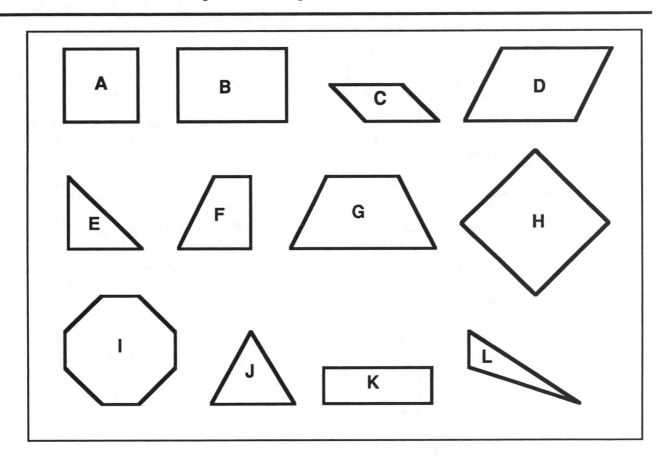

D–111　Polygons with area less than the area of polygon A

D–112　Polygons with area greater than the area of polygon A

COMPARING AREAS

Figure A has an area of 4 square centimeters.

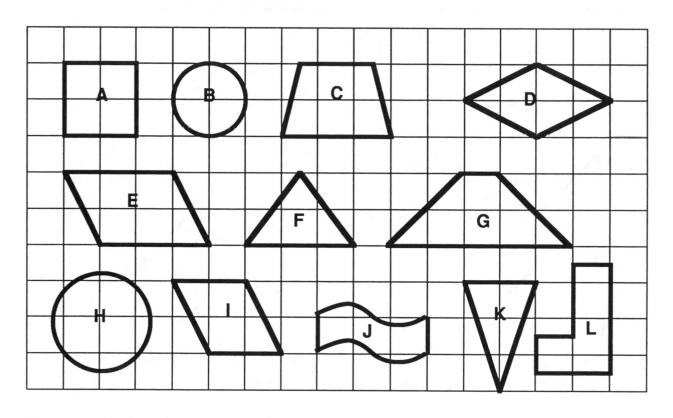

D–113 List the letters of all figures with areas less than 4 square centimeters.

D–114 List the letters of all figures with areas greater than 4 square centimeters.

D–115 List the letters of all figures with areas equal to 4 square centimeters.

COMPARING AREAS

Polygon ABCDE is divided into 8 regions.
Compare the areas of the polygons formed by combining the regions listed. Place one of the symbols <, =, or > in the box.
If it is impossible to determine a solution, place a "?" in the box.

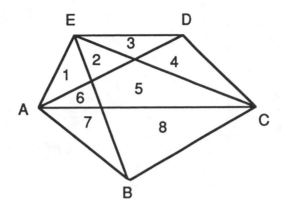

Example	Area of regions 1, 2, 3	>	Area of regions 1, 2, 6
D–116	Area of regions 2, 5		Area of regions 4, 5
D–117	Area of regions 2, 3, 5		Area of regions 2, 3, 4
D–118	Area of regions 3, 4		Area of regions 2, 5
D–119	Area of regions 1, 2, 3		Area of regions 3, 4
D–120	Area of regions 1, 6, 7		Area of regions 1, 2, 3

COMPUTING AREA BY COUNTING

Separate each figure into unit squares and half squares.
Write the area of each figure in the box.

Example

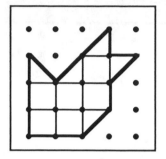

Area of figure = $8 \frac{1}{2}$

D–121

Area of figure = ☐

D–122

Area of figure = ☐

D–123

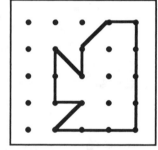

Area of figure = ☐

D–124

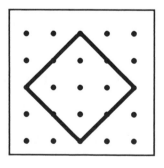

Area of figure = ☐

D–125

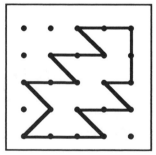

Area of figure = ☐

                                       P.O. BOX 448, PACIFIC GROVE, CA 93950

COMPUTING AREA BY SUBTRACTION

Add one or more regions to each figure to form a rectangle with horizontal and vertical sides. Write the area of each figure in the appropriate box.

Example

AREA

Completed figure	9
Added regions	6
Original figure	3

D–126

AREA

Completed figure	
Added regions	
Original figure	

D–127

AREA

Completed figure	
Added regions	
Original figure	

D–128

AREA

Completed figure	
Added regions	
Original figure	

D–129

AREA

Completed figure	
Added regions	
Original figure	

D–130

AREA

Completed figure	
Added regions	
Original figure	

P.O. BOX 448, PACIFIC GROVE, CA 93950

DRAWING FIGURES

One side of a polygon is drawn on a geoboard design.
Complete the figure described in each exercise.

Example   Parallelogram ABCD with
area of 6 square units

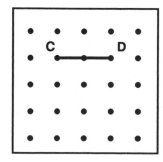

D–131   Rectangle ABCD with
area of 6 square units

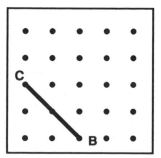

D–132   Triangle ABC with
area of 8 square units

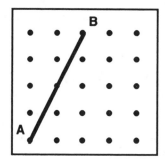

D–133   Square ABCD with
area of 8 square units

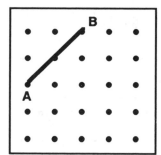

D–134   Trapezoid ABCD with
area of 7 1/2 square units

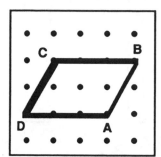

D–135   Isosceles triangle ABC with
area of 6 square units

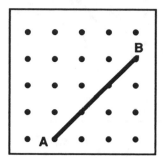

                           P.O. BOX 448, PACIFIC GROVE, CA 93950

DRAWING FIGURES

One side of a polygon is drawn on a geoboard design.
Complete the figure described in each exercise.

Example Triangle ABC with the smallest possible area

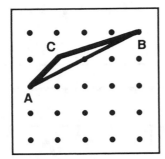

D–136 Rectangle ABCD with the largest possible area

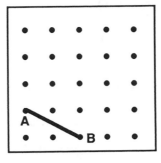

D–137 Quadrilateral ABCD with the smallest possible area

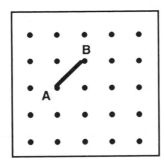

D–138 Triangle ABC with the largest possible area

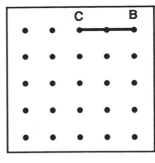

D–139 Triangle ABC with the largest possible area

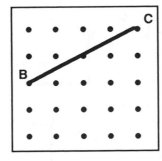

D–140 Quadrilateral ABCD with the smallest possible area

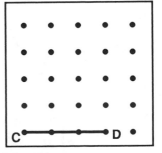

P.O. BOX 448, PACIFIC GROVE, CA 93950

AREA IN TRIANGULAR UNITS

On the isometric grid to the right, figure A has an area of one triangular unit, and figure B has an area of 1/2 triangular unit.

Separate each figure in the exercises into triangular and 1/2 triangular units.

Write the area of the original figure in terms of triangualr units.

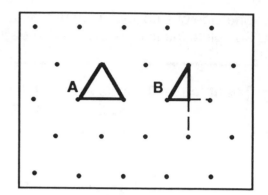

Example

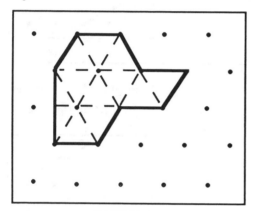

Area = ☐ 11 ☐

D–141

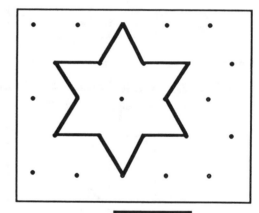

Area = ☐

D–142

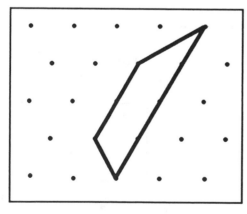

Area = ☐

D–143

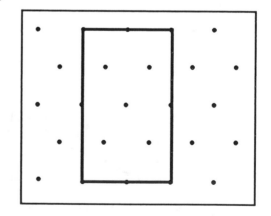

Area = ☐

　　204　　P.O. BOX 448, PACIFIC GROVE, CA 93950

DRAWING FIGURES

One side of a polygon is drawn on an isomorphic grid.
The area of each polygon is given in triangular units.
Draw a polygon that satisfies the description.

Example

Triangle ABC with an area of 9

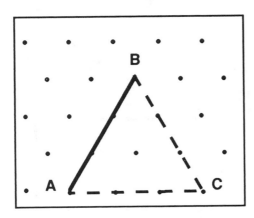

D–144

Parallelogram ABCD with an area of 12

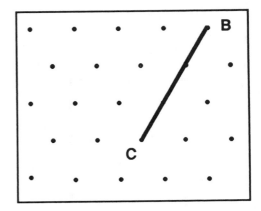

D–145

Rectangle ABCD with an area of 8

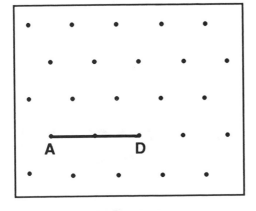

D–146

Right triangle ABC with an area of 8

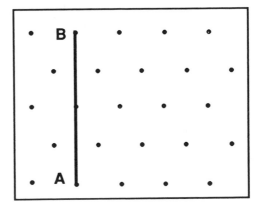

205   P.O. BOX 448, PACIFIC GROVE, CA 93950

PERIMETER AND AREA

Find the perimeter and area of each rectangle.

Example

9

3 | Perimeter = __24__

Area = __27__

D–147

10

2

Perimeter = _____

Area = _____

D–148

6

6 | Perimeter = _____

Area = _____

D–149

8

4 | Perimeter = _____

Area = _____

D–150

5

7

Perimeter = _____

Area = _____

D–151

$7\frac{1}{2}$

$4\frac{1}{2}$ | Perimeter = _____

Area = _____

D–152

$8\frac{1}{2}$

$3\frac{1}{2}$ | Perimeter = _____

Area = _____

---

206   P.O. BOX 448, PACIFIC GROVE, CA 93950

PERIMETER AND AREA

The length of each side of a rectangle is shown.
Find the perimeter and area of each rectangle.

Example

15

2

Perimeter = _34_

Area = _30_

D–153

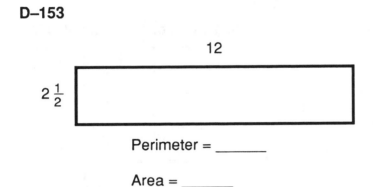

12

$2\frac{1}{2}$

Perimeter = _____

Area = _____

D–154

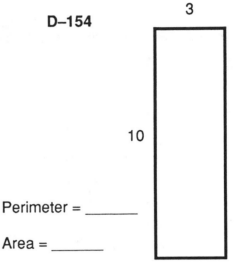

3

10

Perimeter = _____

Area = _____

D–155

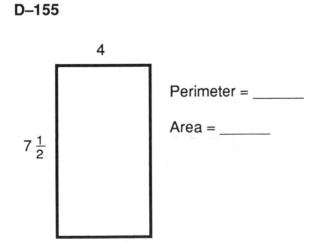

4

$7\frac{1}{2}$

Perimeter = _____

Area = _____

D–156

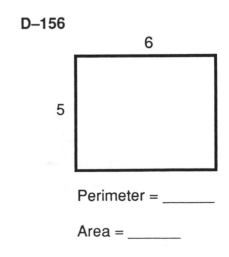

6

5

Perimeter = _____

Area = _____

207   P.O. BOX 448, PACIFIC GROVE, CA 93950

PERIMETER AND AREA

Each figure below is a part of a rectangle which has an area of 36 square units. Use the given information to shade in unit squares to complete each rectangle. Find the perimeter of each rectangle.

Example   A rectangle with one side equal to 2 units

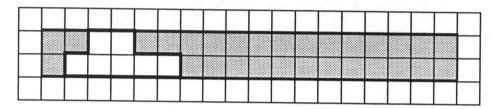

Perimeter = __40__

D–157

A rectangle with one side equal to 3 units

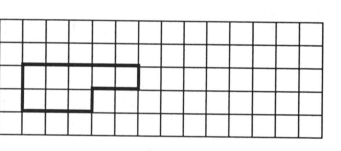

Perimeter = _____

D–158

A rectangle with one side equal to 6 units

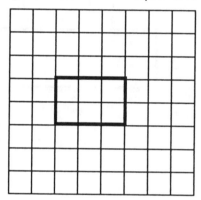

Perimeter = _____

D–159

A rectangle with one side equal to 8 units

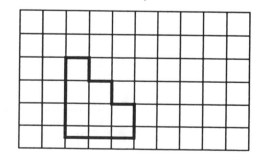

Perimeter = _____

D–160

A rectangle with one side equal to 9 units

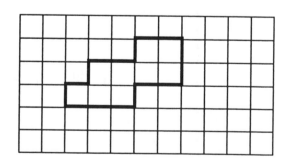

Perimeter = _____

PERIMETER AND AREA

Each figure below is part of a rectangle which has a perimeter of 20 units.
Use the given information to shade in unit squares to complete each rectangle.
Find the area of each rectangle.

Example   A rectangle with one side equal to 8 units

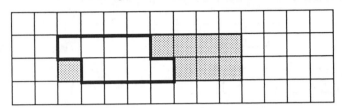

Area = __16__

D–161

A rectangle with one side equal to 6 units

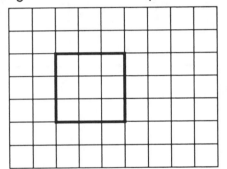

Area = _____

D–162

A rectangle with one side equal to 3 units

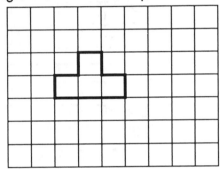

Area = _____

D–163

A rectangle with one side equal to 5 units

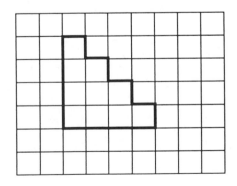

Area = _____

D–164

A rectangle with one side equal to 4 1/2 units

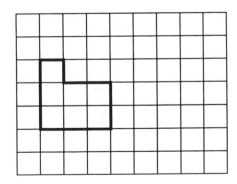

Area = _____

                   P.O. BOX 448, PACIFIC GROVE, CA 93950

PERIMETER AND AREA

The perimeter of each parallelogram is 26 units.
Estimate the area of each parallelogram in square units.

Example

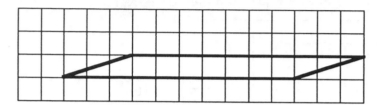

Area = <u>10</u>

D–165

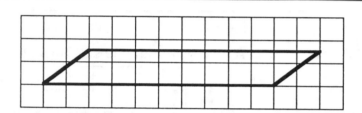

Area = _____

D–166

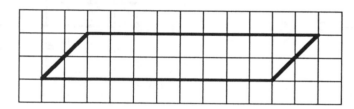

Area = _____

D–167

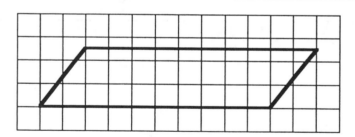

Area = _____

D–168

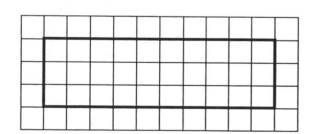

Area = _____

COMPUTING AREA

The lengths of some sides are given for each figure.
Divide each figure into rectangular regions.
Write the area of each region inside the rectangle.
Then compute the area of the given figure by adding the areas of the regions.

Example

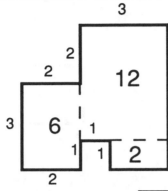

Area of figure = 20

D–169

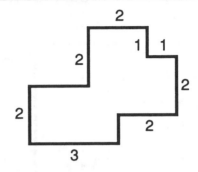

Area of figure =

D–170

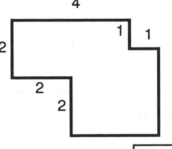

Area of figure =

D–171

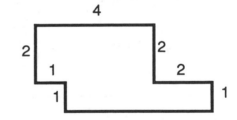

Area of figure =

D–172

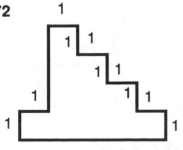

Area of figure =

D–173

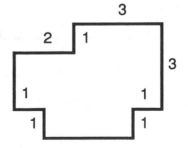

Area of figure =

COMPUTING AREA

The lengths of some sides are given for each figure.
Make each figure into a rectangle by adding regions to the figure.
Write the area within each added region.
Then fill in the boxes with the appropriate areas.

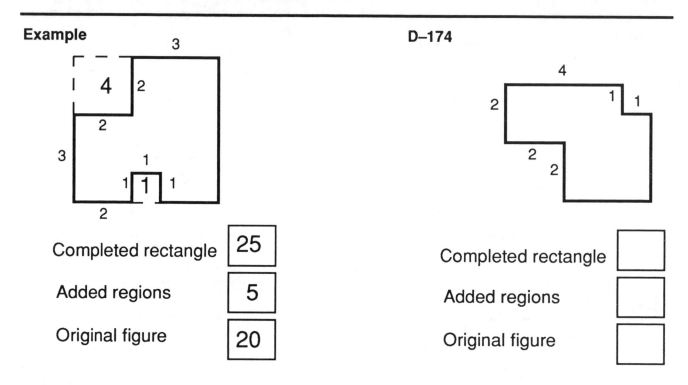

Example

Completed rectangle [25]

Added regions [5]

Original figure [20]

D–174

Completed rectangle [ ]

Added regions [ ]

Original figure [ ]

D–175

Completed rectangle [ ]

Added regions [ ]

Original figure [ ]

D–176

Completed rectangle [ ]

Added regions [ ]

Original figure [ ]

MATHEMATICAL REASONING–2

MEASUREMENT

COMPUTING AREA

The length of some sides are given for each figure.
Divide each figure into triangular or rectangular regions.
Write the area within each region.
Then compute the area of the original figure by adding areas.

Example

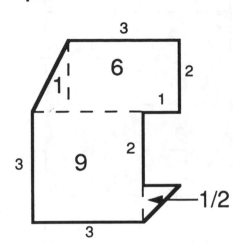

Area of figure = 16 1/2

D–177

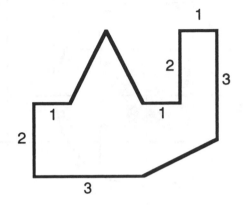

Area of figure =

D–178

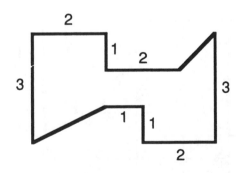

Area of figure =

D–179

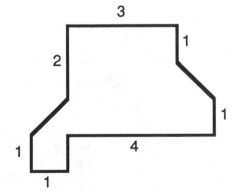

Area of figure =

P.O. BOX 448, PACIFIC GROVE, CA 93950

FINDING AREA

Find the number of shaded squares in each exercise.
Circle the number in the box that is the best estimate of the area of the circle.

Example   Shaded squares = __4__   **D–180**   Shaded squares = _____

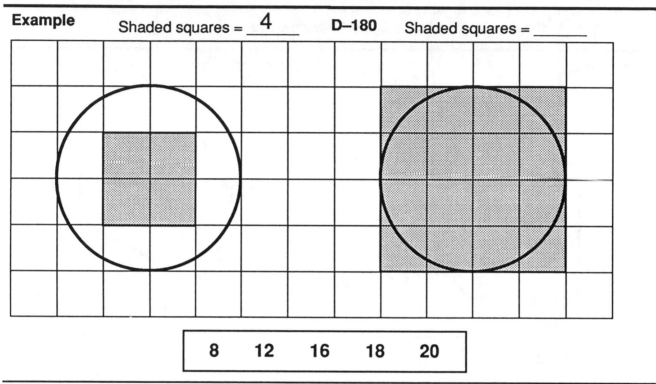

| 8 | 12 | 16 | 18 | 20 |

D–181   Shaded squares = _____   **D–182**   Shaded squares = _____

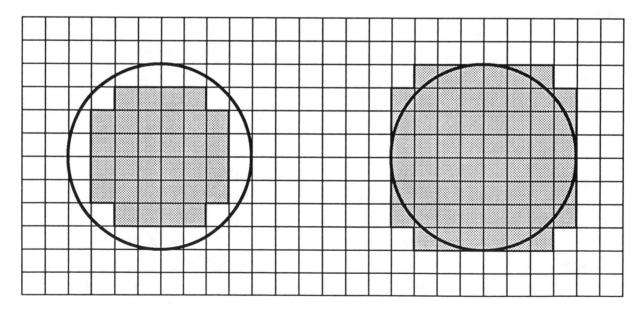

| 32 | 40 | 42 | 50 | 54 | 60 |

214   P.O. BOX 448, PACIFIC GROVE, CA 93950

FINDING AREA

Find the number of shaded squares in each exercise.
Circle the number in the box that is the best estimate of the area of the circle.

Example   Shaded squares = __12__   **D–183**   Shaded squares = _____

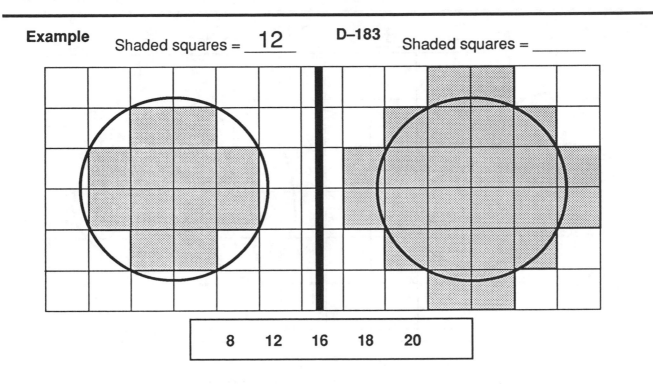

| 8 | 12 | 16 | 18 | 20 |

D–184   Shaded squares = _____   **D–185**   Shaded squares = _____

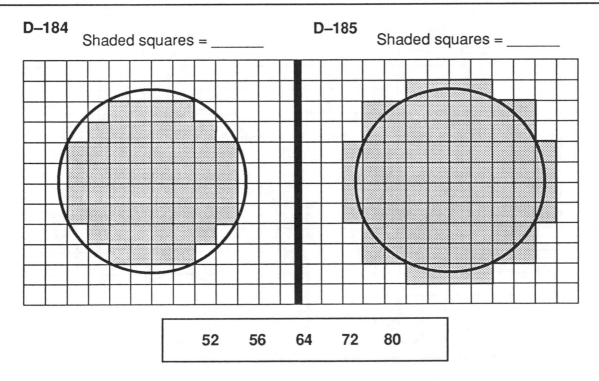

| 52 | 56 | 64 | 72 | 80 |

ESTIMATING AREA

Find the number of shaded squares in each exercise.
Circle the number in the box that is the best estimate of the area of the shape.

Example   Shaded squares = ___8___   **D–186**   Shaded squares = _____

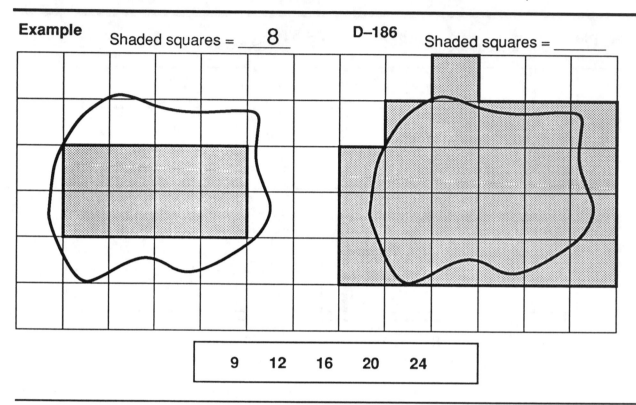

| 9 | 12 | 16 | 20 | 24 |

D–187   Squares contained entirely inside of the shape = _____   **D–188**   Squares containing any part of the shape = _____

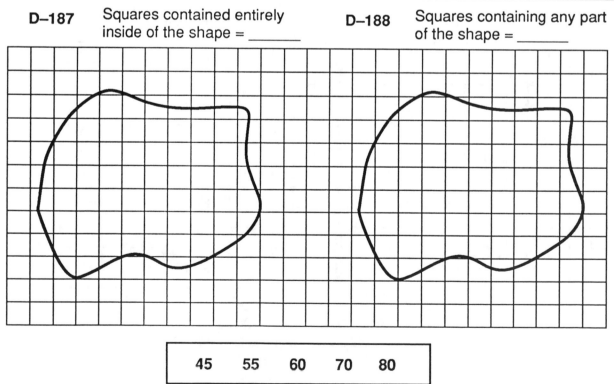

| 45 | 55 | 60 | 70 | 80 |

216   P.O. BOX 448, PACIFIC GROVE, CA 93950

COMPARING CIRCLES

Each table lists information about the radius, diameter, circumference,
or area for the two circles.
In each exercise complete the table.

Example

	r	d	C	A
A	0.5	1	3.14	0.79
B	1	2	6.28	3.14

D–189

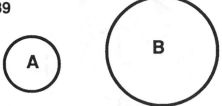

	r	d	C	A
A		1.5		
B	1.5			

D–190

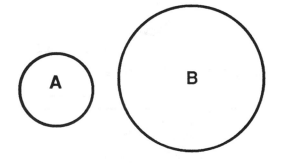

	r	d	C	A
A	1			
B			12.56	

D–191

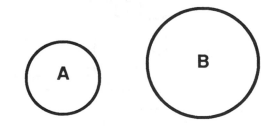

	r	d	C	A
A				3.14
B		3		

COMPUTING AREAS

In each exercise, the diameter of the larger circle is 4 units, and the smaller circle is 2 units in diameter. Find the area of the shaded regions.

Example

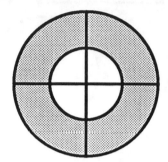

Area of shaded region = **9.42**

D–192

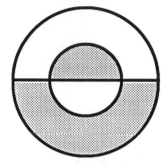

Area of shaded region =

D–193

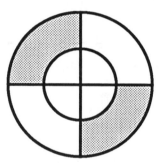

Area of shaded region =

D–194

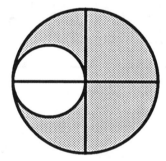

Area of shaded region =

D–195

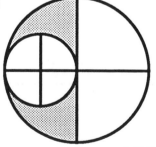

Area of shaded region =

D–196

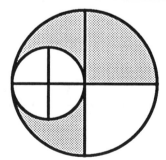

Area of shaded region =

P.O. BOX 448, PACIFIC GROVE, CA 93950

RECTANGULAR SOLIDS

Rectangular solids are pictured on an isometric grid.
Indicate the number of unit cubes in each solid.

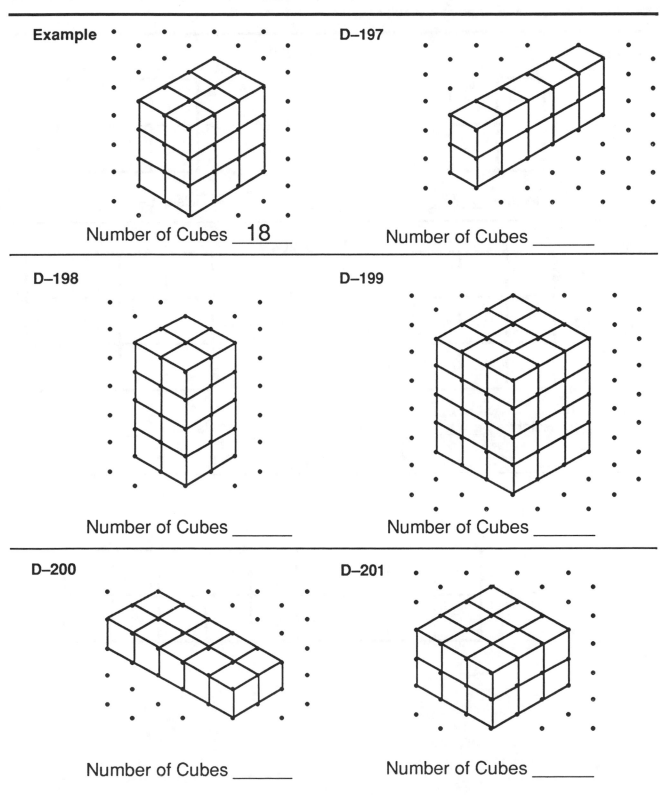

Example

Number of Cubes ___18___

D–197

Number of Cubes _____

D–198

Number of Cubes _____

D–199

Number of Cubes _____

D–200

Number of Cubes _____

D–201

Number of Cubes _____

219   P.O. BOX 448, PACIFIC GROVE, CA 93950

RECTANGULAR SOLIDS

In each exercise below, 36 cubes are used to build a rectangular solid.
Each exercise pictures the base on which the solid is built.
Determine the height of each rectangular solid.

Example

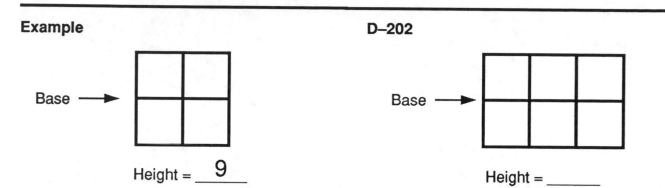

Base ➞

Height = ___9___

D–202

Base ➞

Height = _____

D–203

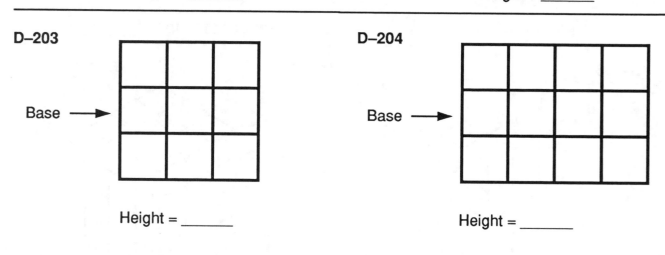

Base ➞

Height = _____

D–204

Base ➞

Height = _____

D–205

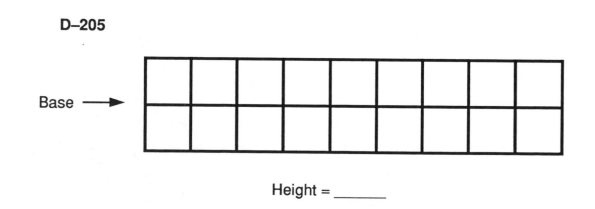

Base ➞

Height = _____

                   P.O. BOX 448, PACIFIC GROVE, CA 93950

COUNTING CUBES IN SOLIDS

The following solids are built from cubes.
Indicate the number of cubes in each solid.
Assume that all nonvisible parts of the figures are solid.

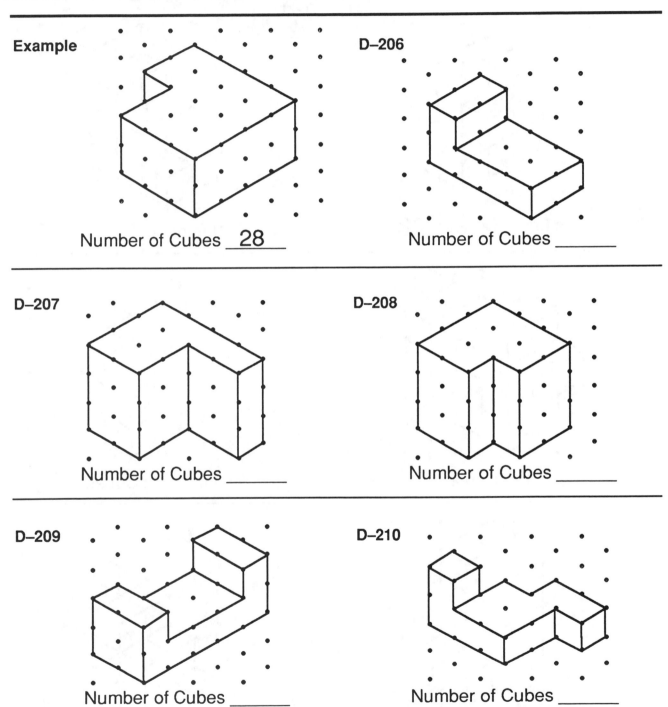

Example

Number of Cubes __28__

D–206

Number of Cubes _____

D–207

Number of Cubes _____

D–208

Number of Cubes _____

D–209

Number of Cubes _____

D–210

Number of Cubes _____

                   P.O. BOX 448, PACIFIC GROVE, CA 93950

VOLUME OF SOLIDS

Determine the number of cubes needed to build each figure.
Assume all nonvisible parts of the figures are solid.

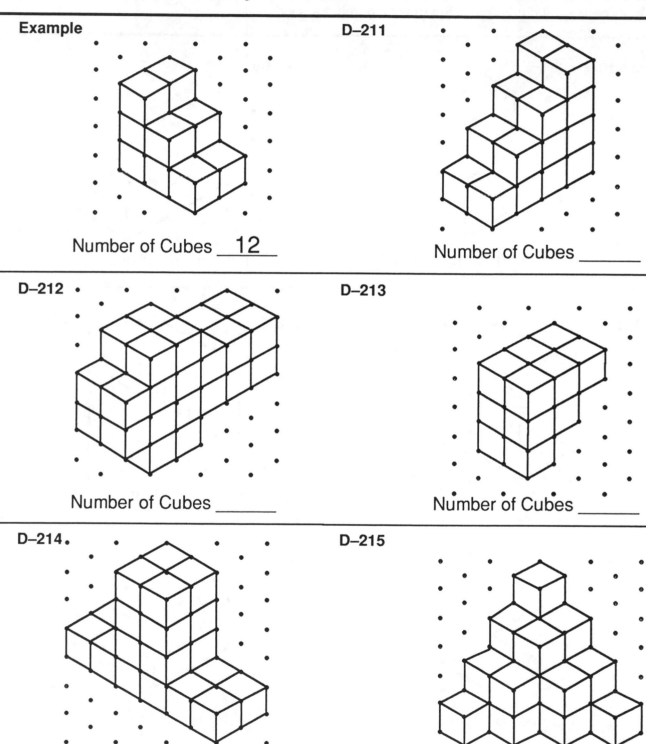

Example

Number of Cubes __12__

D–211

Number of Cubes _____

D–212

Number of Cubes _____

D–213

Number of Cubes _____

D–214

Number of Cubes _____

D–215

Number of Cubes _____

222   P.O. BOX 448, PACIFIC GROVE, CA 93950

MAKING SOLIDS BY FOLDING

When cut out and folded, each pattern forms one of the solids pictured.
Draw lines connecting each pattern to its corresponding solid.
Then determine the volume of the solid in unit cubes.

Example

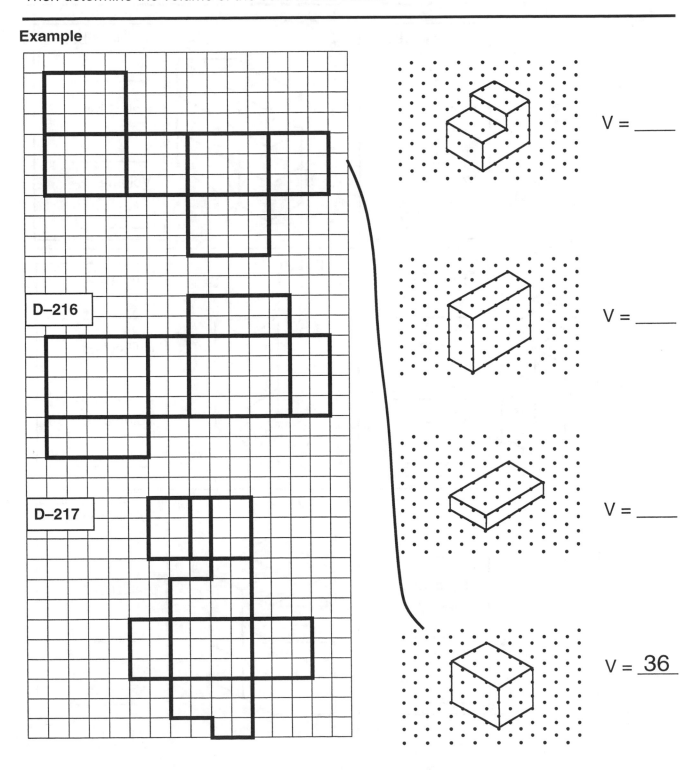

D–216

D–217

V = ____

V = ____

V = ____

V = _36_

               P.O. BOX 448, PACIFIC GROVE, CA 93950

COUNTING CUBES IN SOLIDS

The solids below are constructed with cubes and half cubes.
In each exercise determine the number of cubes, the number of half cubes, and the volume.

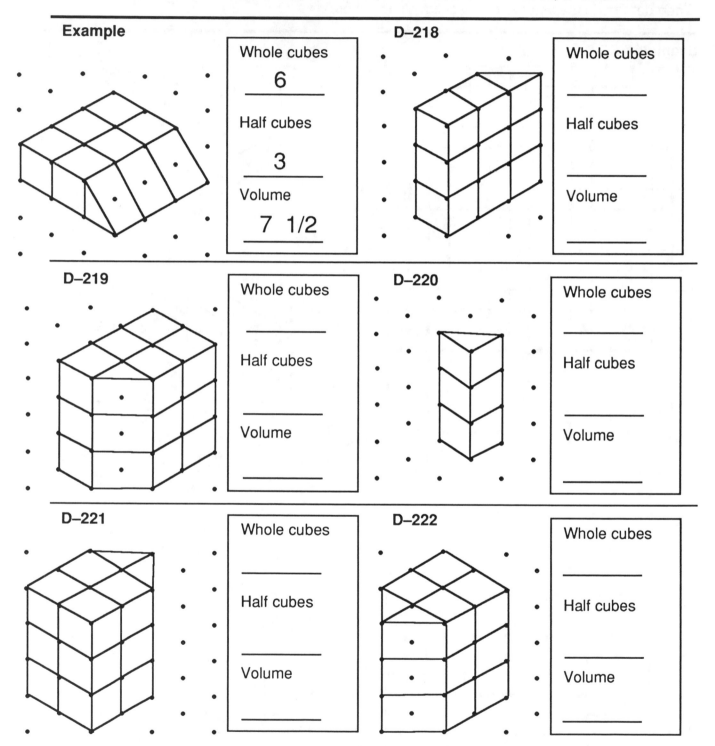

Example

Whole cubes

_____6_____

Half cubes

_____3_____

Volume

____7 1/2____

D–218

Whole cubes

_____

Half cubes

_____

Volume

_____

D–219

Whole cubes

_____

Half cubes

_____

Volume

_____

D–220

Whole cubes

_____

Half cubes

_____

Volume

_____

D–221

Whole cubes

_____

Half cubes

_____

Volume

_____

D–222

Whole cubes

_____

Half cubes

_____

Volume

_____

MAKING SOLIDS BY FOLDING

When cut out and folded, each pattern forms one of the solids pictured.
Draw lines connecting each pattern to its corresponding solid.
Then determine the volume of the solid in unit cubes.

Example

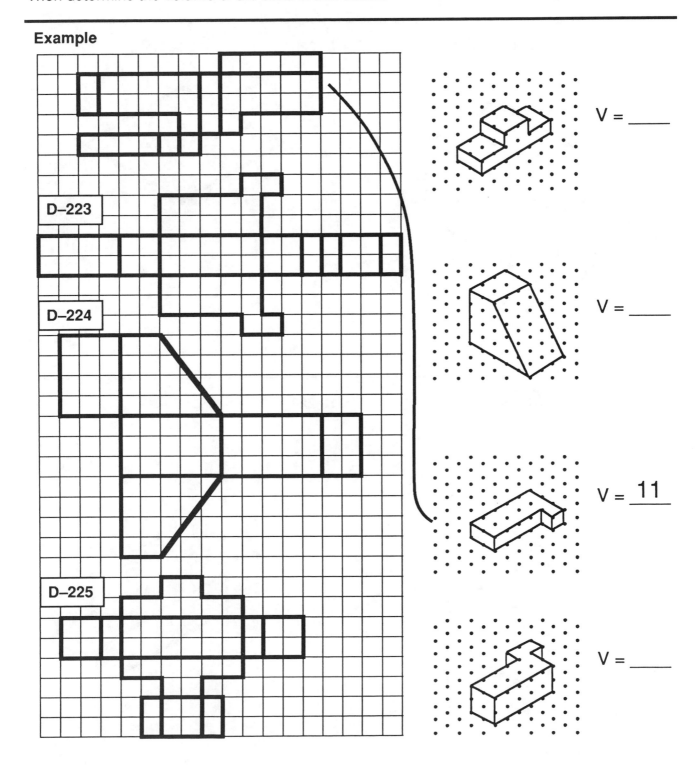

D–223

D–224

D–225

V = ____

V = ____

V = _11_

V = ____

DRAWING SOLIDS

One surface of a solid is drawn on an isometric grid.
The volume of each solid is given in unit cubes.
Complete the drawing of the solid.

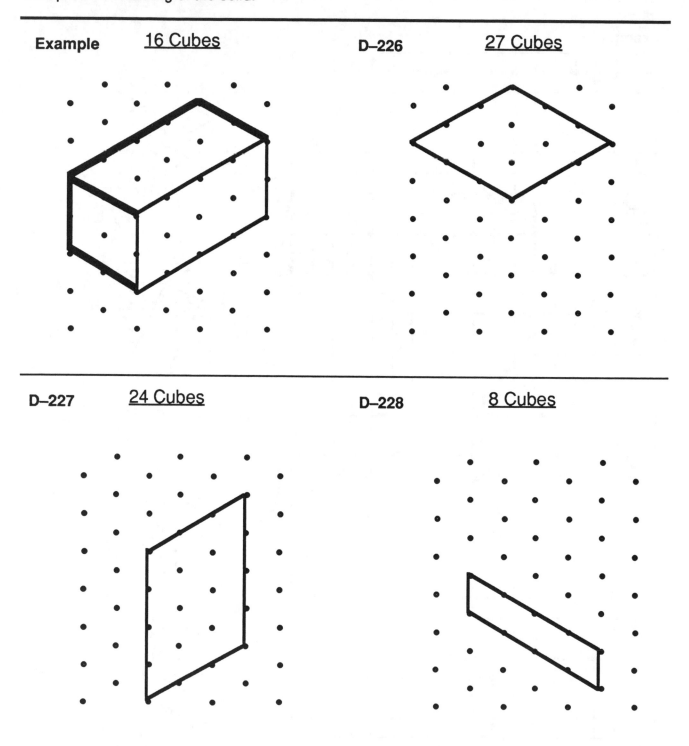

Example   <u>16 Cubes</u>

D–226   <u>27 Cubes</u>

D–227   <u>24 Cubes</u>

D–228   <u>8 Cubes</u>

         P.O. BOX 448, PACIFIC GROVE, CA 93950

COMPUTING VOLUME

The length of the diagonal line that indicates the depth of each solid is 4 units.
Compute the volume of each solid.

Example   **D–229**   **D–230**

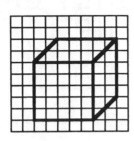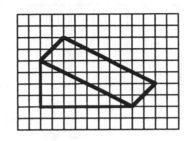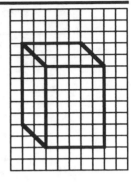

V = _100_   V = _____   V = _____

D–231   **D–232**

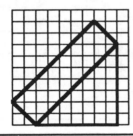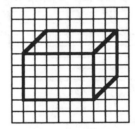

V = _____   V = _____

D–233   **D–234**

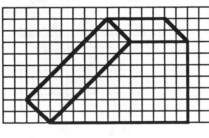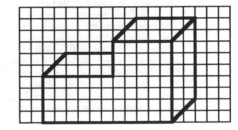

V = _____   V = _____

D–235   **D–236**

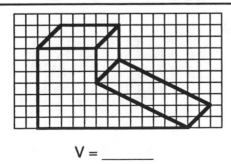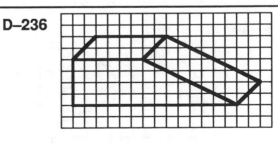

V = _____   V = _____

DECOMPOSING SOLIDS

The volumes of three solids are given.
Use the composition of these solids to compute the volumes of the other solids.

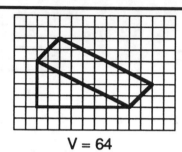

V = 64

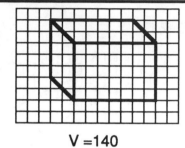

V =140

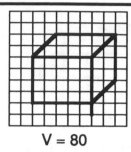

V = 80

Example

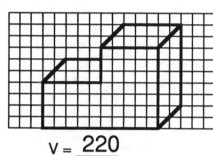

V = 220

D–237

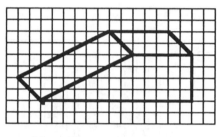

V = _____

D–238

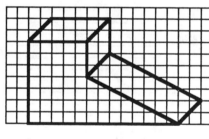

V = _____

D–239

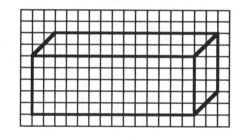

V = _____

D–240

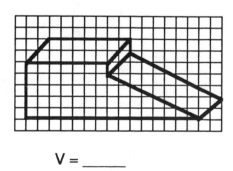

V = _____

D–241

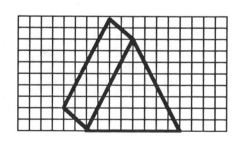

V = _____

               P.O. BOX 448, PACIFIC GROVE, CA 93950

FINDING THE DIMENSIONS OF A SOLID

The volume of each rectangular solid is given.
Select the letter that indicates the most likely dimensions of the solid.
Write the dimensions of each solid in the blanks.

a. 5, 5, 10	b. 3, 4, 6	c. 5, 6, 3	d. 3, 3, 10	e. 2, 8, 6
f. 3, 4, 8	g. 4, 6, 10	h. 3, 3, 8	i. 10, 12, 2	j. 5, 2, 25

Example

g

V = 240

4   10

6

D–242

V = 96

____   ____

____

D–243

V = 90

____

____

D–244

V = 250

____

____

D–245

V = 90

____   ____

____

D–246

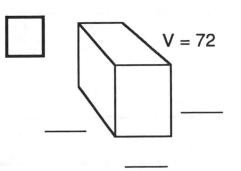

V = 72

____

____

ESTIMATING VOLUME

Some of the dimensions are given for each rectangular solid.
Circle the number in the box that is the best esimate of its volume.

Example

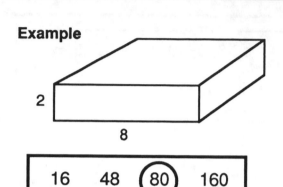

2
8

| 16 | 48 | (80) | 160 |

D–247

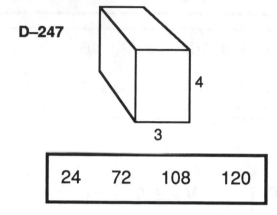

4
3

| 24 | 72 | 108 | 120 |

D–248

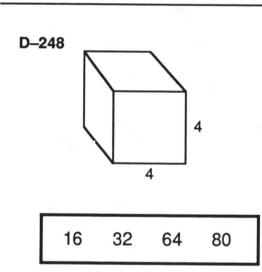

4
4

| 16 | 32 | 64 | 80 |

D–249

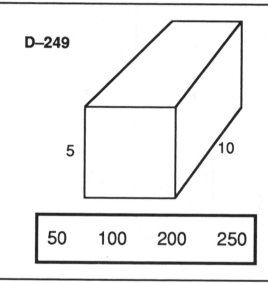

5
10

| 50 | 100 | 200 | 250 |

D–250

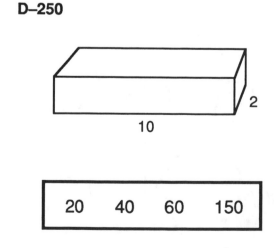

2
10

| 20 | 40 | 60 | 150 |

D–251

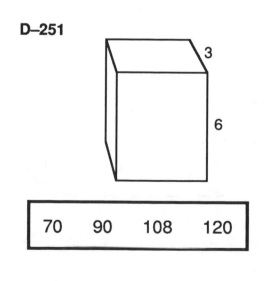

3
6

| 70 | 90 | 108 | 120 |

                   P.O. BOX 448, PACIFIC GROVE, CA 93950

COMPARING NUMBERS

Circle the largest number in each set.
Draw a box around the smallest number in each set.

Example

$$\frac{3}{4} \quad \boxed{\frac{2}{8}} \quad \frac{2}{5}$$

$$\textcircled{$\frac{8}{9}$} \quad \frac{3}{10} \quad \frac{1}{2}$$

E–1

$$\frac{3}{12} \quad \frac{1}{6} \quad \frac{7}{10}$$

$$\frac{4}{8} \quad \frac{3}{5} \quad \frac{4}{6}$$

E–2

$$\frac{3}{8} \quad \frac{1}{2} \quad \frac{7}{16}$$

$$\frac{11}{16} \quad \frac{3}{4} \quad \frac{2}{8}$$

E–3

$$\frac{4}{10} \quad \frac{3}{4} \quad \frac{4}{9}$$

$$\frac{2}{3} \quad \frac{3}{5} \quad \frac{3}{8}$$

E–4

$$\frac{3}{8} \quad \frac{7}{20} \quad \frac{2}{5}$$

$$\frac{3}{10} \quad \frac{1}{2} \quad \frac{1}{4}$$

E–5

$$\frac{3}{5} \quad \frac{5}{6} \quad \frac{5}{8}$$

$$\frac{2}{3} \quad \frac{3}{4} \quad \frac{4}{9}$$

E–6 Which is the largest number in all the sets? _____

E–7 Which is the smallest number in all the sets? _____

COMPARING NUMBERS

Circle the largest number in each set.
Draw a box around the smallest number in each set.

Example

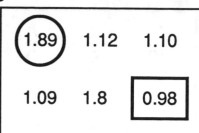

1.89   1.12   1.10

1.09   1.8   0.98

E–8

0.08   0.01   0.59

0.61   0.09   0.16

E–9

0.375   0.057   0.735

0.537   0.705   0.037

E–10

0.2   0.102   0.02

0.21   0.1   0.021

E–11

$\frac{3}{8}$ 1.8 $\frac{8}{9}$

0.62 $\frac{8}{5}$ 0.8

E–12

$2\frac{1}{4}$ 1.09 $\frac{4}{3}$

1.98 $\frac{7}{3}$ 2.05

E–13 Which is the largest number in all the sets? _____

E–14 Which is the smallest number in all the sets? _____

ORDERING NUMBERS

The symbols below are used to compare numbers.
Write the correct symbol in each box.

is greater than	is less than	is equal to
>	<	=

Example

$$1 \boxed{<} \frac{3}{8} + \frac{3}{4}$$

E–15

$$\frac{1}{2} \times \frac{3}{4} \ \Box \ \frac{3}{4}$$

E–16

$$\frac{6}{7} \div \frac{6}{7} \ \Box \ 1$$

E–17

$$\frac{1}{2} \ \Box \ \frac{1}{2} \div 5$$

E–18

$$\frac{1}{4} - \frac{1}{12} \ \Box \ \frac{1}{8}$$

E–19

$$3 \times \frac{1}{2} \ \Box \ 3 \div \frac{1}{2}$$

E–20

$$\frac{7}{8} \div \frac{3}{5} \ \Box \ \frac{5}{3} \times \frac{7}{8}$$

E–21

$$\frac{3}{5} \div \frac{1}{2} \ \Box \ \frac{5}{3} \times \frac{2}{1}$$

FINDING COMMON MULTIPLES

Circle all the numbers that are common multiples of the two numbers above each box.
Then list 3 other numbers that are common multiples of the two numbers.

Example

6 and 9

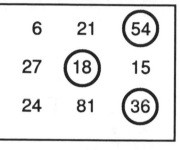

6   21   (54)

27   (18)   15

24   81   (36)

_72, 90, 108_

E–22

3 and 4

15	52	24
18	36	28
12	48	16

_____

E–23

8 and 12

64	24	36
4	32	96
48	60	56

_____

E–24

10 and 15

60	20	90
5	120	70
45	30	150

_____

What is the smallest number that is a common multiple of each of the
following pairs of numbers?

E–25
        6 and 9 _____

E–26
        3 and 4 _____

E–27
        8 and 12 _____

E–28
        10 and 15 _____

USING COMMON FACTORS

Circle the numbers in the box that are factors of each number.
Use these factors to reduce each fraction to lowest terms.

Example	72	(4)	5	(6)	7	(8)	(36)	48
E–29	80	4	6	7	8	12	16	24
E–30	256	4	8	12	14	16	32	48
E–31	144	4	7	9	32	48	72	81
E–32	81	3	6	9	12	15	27	31
E–33	360	7	8	9	14	36	72	108

E–34

$$\frac{72}{80} = \underline{\qquad}$$

E–35

$$\frac{256}{360} = \underline{\qquad}$$

E–36

$$\frac{81}{144} = \underline{\qquad}$$

E–37

$$\frac{80}{256} = \underline{\qquad}$$

E–38

$$\frac{144}{360} = \underline{\qquad}$$

E–39

$$\frac{81}{360} = \underline{\qquad}$$

USING ORDER RELATIONS

A number is missing from each sentence.
Circle all the numbers that will make a true statement.

Example

$$3\frac{3}{8} + \bigcirc < 4\frac{1}{2}$$

$$\boxed{\left(\frac{7}{8}\right) \quad 1\frac{1}{8} \quad 2\frac{1}{8} \quad \left(\frac{3}{4}\right)}$$

E–40

$$\bigcirc - 2\frac{2}{3} > 1\frac{2}{9}$$

$$\boxed{3\frac{1}{3} \quad 1\frac{4}{9} \quad 4 \quad 3\frac{8}{9}}$$

E–41

$$2\frac{3}{4} \div \bigcirc < 3\frac{1}{4}$$

$$\boxed{1\frac{1}{2} \quad \frac{3}{4} \quad \frac{1}{2} \quad \frac{11}{13}}$$

E–42

$$\frac{2}{3} \times \bigcirc < \frac{7}{8} \times \frac{2}{3}$$

$$\boxed{\frac{9}{10} \quad \frac{7}{8} \quad \frac{3}{4} \quad \frac{4}{5}}$$

E–43

$$2\frac{2}{3} \times 1\frac{1}{2} > 1\frac{3}{8} \times \bigcirc$$

$$\boxed{2\frac{1}{2} \quad 3\frac{1}{8} \quad 2\frac{2}{3} \quad 1\frac{3}{8}}$$

E–44

$$5\frac{1}{2} + 3\frac{1}{4} < 10 - \bigcirc$$

$$\boxed{1\frac{1}{8} \quad \frac{7}{8} \quad 1\frac{1}{4} \quad 2\frac{1}{8}}$$

E–45

$$11\frac{2}{3} - 7\frac{1}{2} < 13\frac{2}{3} - \bigcirc$$

$$\boxed{10\frac{1}{4} \quad 9\frac{1}{2} \quad 8\frac{3}{8} \quad 11\frac{1}{3}}$$

E–46

$$7\frac{5}{8} \times 3\frac{1}{4} > 7\frac{5}{8} \div \bigcirc$$

$$\boxed{\frac{4}{13} \quad \frac{5}{13} \quad 3\frac{1}{8} \quad \frac{1}{12}}$$

　　　　236　　　　P.O. BOX 448, PACIFIC GROVE, CA 93950

USING ORDER RELATIONS

Two numbers are missing from each sentence.
Circle all the ordered pairs that will make a true statement.
The first number in each pair must go in the circle and the second number in the box.

Example $2.98 - \bigcirc > 1.4 + \boxed{}$

(2.05, 0.97)   (1.89, 0.08)   (0.25, 1.32)   (1.89, 1.48)

E–47 $3.04 \times \bigcirc < 4.75 \times \boxed{}$

(4.8, 2.98)   (4.25, 3.15)   (4.75, 3.04)   (6.08, 9.50)

E–48 $19.25 - \bigcirc > \boxed{} - 7.75$

(7.75, 19.25)   (7.25, 19.50)   (8.25, 19.15)   (1.25, 20)

E–49 $135 \div \boxed{} < 135 \div \bigcirc$

(5, 6)   (6, 5)   (7, 7)   (5, 7)

USING ARITHMETIC OPERATIONS

In each box place one of the four operations (+, −, ×, ÷) to make a true statement.

Example   3 $\boxed{+}$ (4 + 2) < 9 $\boxed{\times}$ 2

E–50   (5 $\boxed{}$ 7) $\boxed{}$ 9 > 7 $\boxed{}$ (9 $\boxed{}$ 5)

E–51   3 $\boxed{}$ (4 $\boxed{}$ 5) = (3 $\boxed{}$ 4) $\boxed{}$ (3 $\boxed{}$ 5)

E–52   1.85 $\boxed{}$ 3.75 < 1.85 $\boxed{}$ 3.75

E–53 $\dfrac{7}{8} \div 1\dfrac{1}{2} < \dfrac{2}{3}$ $\boxed{}$ $\dfrac{7}{8}$

E–54 $3\dfrac{3}{4}$ $\boxed{}$ $4\dfrac{1}{4} = 4\dfrac{1}{4}$ $\boxed{}$ $3\dfrac{3}{4}$

USING OPERATIONS AND RELATIONS

In each box place one of the operations (+, −, ×, +) or
one of the relations (<, =, >) to make a true sentence.

Example   3 $\boxed{+}$ 2 $\boxed{<}$ 7 + 4

E–55   9 × 7 $\square$ 7 $\square$ 9

E–56 $\dfrac{3}{8}$ + $\dfrac{5}{8}$ $\square$ $\dfrac{7}{8}$ $\square$ $\dfrac{8}{7}$

E–57   4.54 − 3.85 $\square$ 4.54 $\square$ 3.85

E–58   3 $\square$ 4 $\square$ 5 $\square$ 6

E–59   12.75 $\square$ 9.50 $\square$ 6.75 $\square$ 4.95

E–60   1 $\square$ 0 $\square$ 0 $\square$ 1

CONTINUING THE SEQUENCE

Place numbers in the blank spaces to continue the sequence.

Example   1, 2, 4, 7, 11, __16__ , __22__ , __29__

E–61   5, 6, 8, 11, 15, _____, _____, _____

E–62   1, 2, 5, 10, 17, _____, _____, _____

E–63   1, 3, 6, 10, 15, _____, _____, _____

E–64   1, 4, 9, 16, 25, _____, _____, _____

E–65   9, 11, 12, 14, 15, _____, _____, _____

E–66   4, 7, 13, 22, 34, _____, _____, _____

E–67   1, 5, 12, 22, 35, 51, _____, _____, _____

E–68   3, 5, 8, 13, 20, 31, _____, _____, _____

SEQUENCES OF NUMBERS

The three dots mean that the sequence continues.
Circle all the numbers that belong to the sequence.

Example

2, 5, 8, 11, 14, . . .

a. (38)   b. 36

c. 24   d. (23)

E–69

9, 13, 17, 21, . . .

a. 32   b. 33

c. 40   d. 41

E–70

4, 9, 14, 19, 24, . . .

a. 27   b. 54

c. 39   d. 43

E–71

8, 10, 14, 20, 28, 38, . . .

a. 49   b. 98

c. 51   d. 48

E–72

8, 12, 16, 20, 24, . . .

a. 48   b. 62

c. 254   d. 96

E–73

8, 10, 13, 18, 25, 36, . . .

a. 85   b. 64

c. 75   d. 108

SEQUENCES OF NUMBERS

Each exercise below begins a sequence.
Circle the row that continues the sequence.

Example   a. 21, 22, 24, 25

     1, 2, 4, 5, 7, 8, 10, . . .   b. 17, 18, 19, 20

                                               (c.) 22, 23, 25, 26

E–74   a. 28, 29, 30, 32

     1, 2, 3, 5, 6, 7, 9, 10, 11, . . .   b. 31, 32, 33, 35

                                             c. 21, 22, 23, 25

E–75   a. 19, 20, 21, 23

     1, 2, 4, 5, 6, 8, 9, 10, 12, 13, . . .   b. 24, 25, 26, 28

                                           c. 25, 26, 27, 29

E–76   a. 33, 34, 36, 37

     3, 5, 6, 8, 9, 11, 12, 14, 15, 17, . . .   b. 33, 35, 36, 38

                                           c. 47, 48, 50, 51

E–77   a. 63, 65, 66, 68

     3, 5, 6, 8, 10, 11, 13, 15, . . .   b. 65, 67, 69, 70

                                           c. 45, 46, 48, 50

         P.O. BOX 448, PACIFIC GROVE, CA 93950

PAIRING NUMBERS

The arrows show how numbers are paired.
Fill in the circles with the missing numbers.

Example

1	2	3	4	5	6 ...	26 ...	33 ...	41
↓	↓	↓	↓	↓	↓	↓	↓	↓
2	4	6	8	10	12	(52)	(66)	(82)

E–78

1	2	3	4	5	6 ...	26 ...	33 ...	41
↓	↓	↓	↓	↓	↓	↓	↓	↓
3	5	7	9	11	13	◯	◯	◯

E–79

3	4 ... 7		8 ... 11 ... 14 ...			19 ...	23 ...	36
↓	↓	↓	↓	↓	↓	↓	↓	↓
9	12	21	24	33	42	◯	◯	◯

E–80

3	4 ... 7		8 ... 11 ... 14 ...			19 ...	23 ...	36
↓	↓	↓	↓	↓	↓	↓	↓	↓
11	14	23	26	35	44	◯	◯	◯

E–81

3	4	5	6 ... 8		9 ...	14 ...	31 ...	39
↓	↓	↓	↓	↓	↓	↓	↓	↓
5	7	9	11	15	17	◯	◯	◯

P.O. BOX 448, PACIFIC GROVE, CA 93950

PAIRING NUMBERS

The arrows show how numbers are paired.
Fill in the circles with the missing numbers.

Example

1	2	3	4	5	6 . . .	10 . . .	15 . . .	23
↓	↓	↓	↓	↓	↓	↓	↓	↓
1	4	9	16	25	36	(100)	(225)	(529)

E–82

1	2	3	4	5	6 . . .	11 . . .	16 . . .	22
↓	↓	↓	↓	↓	↓	↓	↓	↓
2	5	10	17	26	37	( )	( )	( )

E–83

1	2	3	4	5	6 . . .	12 . . .	17 . . .	25
↓	↓	↓	↓	↓	↓	↓	↓	↓
2	8	18	32	50	72	( )	( )	( )

E–84

3	4	5	6	7	8 . . .	12 . . .	17 . . .	25
↓	↓	↓	↓	↓	↓	↓	↓	↓
8	15	24	35	48	63	( )	( )	( )

E–85

3	4	5	6	7	8 . . .	12 . . .	17 . . .	25
↓	↓	↓	↓	↓	↓	↓	↓	↓
19	33	51	73	99	129	( )	( )	( )

        244   P.O. BOX 448, PACIFIC GROVE, CA 93950

PAIRING NUMBERS

The arrows show how numbers are paired.
Fill in the circles with the missing numbers.

Example

1	2	3	4	5	6 . . .	9 . . .	14 . . .	20
↓	↓	↓	↓	↓	↓	↓	↓	↓
1	0	1	0	1	0	(1)	(0)	(0)

E–86

1	2	3	4	5	6 . . .	10 . . .	15 . . .	24
↓	↓	↓	↓	↓	↓	↓	↓	↓
2	1	4	3	6	5	◯	◯	◯

E–87

1	2	3	4	5	6 . . .	15 . . .	18 . . .	26
↓	↓	↓	↓	↓	↓	↓	↓	↓
2	4	4	8	6	12	◯	◯	◯

E–88

1	2	3	4	5	6 . . .	14 . . .	19 . . .	25
↓	↓	↓	↓	↓	↓	↓	↓	↓
2	1	4	2	6	3	◯	◯	◯

E–89

1	2	3	4	5	6 . . .	11 . . .	16 . . .	33
↓	↓	↓	↓	↓	↓	↓	↓	↓
1	1	2	2	3	3	(1)	(0)	(0)

MATCHING A TABLE TO A RULE

Each table contains a set of values for A and B.
Match each table with the rule which tells the relationship between A and B.

Example

Table

A	B
1	4
2	7
3	10
4	13
5	16

Rule

a. $B = (5 \times A) - 1$

b. $A = 1 + (3 \times B)$

c. $B = (3 \times A) + 1$ ⟲

d. $4 \times A = B$

E–90

Table

A	B
1	1
2	3
3	5
4	7
5	9

Rule

a. $A = (2 \times B) - 1$

b. $B = A + 1$

c. $A = B$

d. $B = (2 \times A) - 1$

E–91

Table

A	B
1	3
2	6
3	9
4	12
5	15

Rule

a. $B = 3 \times A$

b. $B = A + 2$

c. $A = 3 \times B$

d. $B - A = 2$

E–92

Table

A	B
1	14
2	13
3	12
4	11
5	10

Rule

a. $B = 14 - A$

b. $A + B = 15$

c. $B = A + 13$

d. $B = 2 \times A$

E–93

Table

A	B
4	16
7	13
11	9
17	3
20	0

Rule

a. $A = B + 20$

b. $B = A \times 4$

c. $B = 20 - A$

d. $B = 3 \times A$

E–94

Table

A	B
0	0
2	3
4	6
10	15
12	18

Rule

a. $3 \times B = 2 \times A$

b. $B = (2 \times A) + 1$

c. $B = 3 \times A$

d. $2 \times B = 3 \times A$

COMPLETING A TABLE FROM A RULE

Each rule tells the relationship between numbers represented by A and B.
Use the rule to complete the table.

Example

Rule

$B = 2 \times A$

Table

A	B
0	0
2	4
3	6
5	10
8	16

E–95

Rule

$B = A - 3$

Table

A	B
7	___
9	___
10	___
___	14
___	30

E–96

Rule

$\dfrac{A}{B} = \dfrac{1}{2}$

Table

A	B
6	___
8	___
1	___
___	6
___	8

E–97

Rule

$B = (2 \times A) - 1$

Table

A	B
1	___
3	___
4	___
7	___
___	9

E–98

Rule

$A < B + 2$

Table

A	B
0	___
1	___
3	___
4	___
___	12

E–99

Rule

$B = A^2$

Table

A	B
0	___
___	1
3	___
___	49
10	___

SEQUENCES OF ORDERED PAIRS

Fill in the missing numbers in the following sequences of ordered pairs.

Example   (1, 4)   (2, 7)   (3, 10)   (4, <u>13</u>)   (5, 16)   (6, <u>19</u>)

E–100   (3, 5)   (4, ___)   (5, 7)   (6, 8)   (7, 9)   (8, ___)

E–101   (1, 3)   (2, 6)   (3, ___)   (4, 12)   (5, ___)   (6, 18)

E–102   (2, 1)   (3, 1.5)   (4, 2)   (5, ___)   (6, 3)   (7, ___)

E–103   (3, ___)   (4, ___)   (5, 17)   (6, 20)   (7, 23)   (8, 26)

E–104   (1, 1)   (2, 4)   (3, ___)   (4, ___)   (5, 25)   (6, 36)

E–105   (3, 1)   (___, 2)   (9, 3)   (___, 4)   (15, 5)   (18, ___)

E–106   (1, 4)   (2, ___)   (3, ___)   (4, 16)   (___, 20)   (6, 24)

SEQUENCES OF ORDERED PAIRS

Fill in the missing numbers in the following sequences of ordered pairs.
The three dots indicate that the sequence continues.

Example (4, 1)   (5, 1.25)   (6, 1.5)   (7, 1.75)   (8, _2_) • • • (15, _3.75_)

E–107   (2, 7)   (3, 8)   (4, ___)   (5, 10)   (6, 11) • • • (12, ___)

E–108   (1, ___)   (2, 10)   (3, ___)   (4, 20)   (5, 25) • • • (19, ___)

E–109   (3, 7)   (4, 9)   (5, 11)   (6, 13)   (7, ___) • • • (10, ___)

E–110   (1, 4)   (2, ___)   (3, 10)   (4, 13)   (5, 16) • • • (11, ___)

E–111   (4, 2) (9, 3) (16, 4)   (___, 5)   (36, 6) • • • (___, 12)

E–112   (2, 3)   (4, 6)   (6, 9)   (8, 12)   (___, 15) • • • (___, 36)

E–113   (5, 1) (___, 1.2) (7, 1.4) (8, ___) (___, 1.8) • • • (___, 2.4)

MATCHING ORDERED PAIRS TO A RULE

In each ordered pair, the first number is the "A" value and
the second number is the "B" value.
Circle the ordered pairs that satisfy the rule.

Example	Rule	Ordered Pairs

$A + B < 10$

(3, 5)   (7, 4)   (5, 5)   (5, 3)

(10, 0)   (4, 10)   (1, 6)   (4, 7)

E–114   Rule   Ordered Pairs

$B = A^2$

(6, 12)   (1, 1)   (25, 5)   (3, 9)

(9, 3)   (0, 0)   (12, 144)   (4, 4)

E–115   Rule   Ordered Pairs

$B = (2 \times A) + 1$

(3, 1)   (5, 11)   (3, 7)   (9, 17)

(1, 3)   (1, 0)   (11, 5)   (0, 1)

E–116   Rule   Ordered Pairs

$\dfrac{A}{B} = \dfrac{1}{3}$

(3, 1)   (2, 6)   (1, 3)   (1, 6)

(6, 2)   (12, 36)   (3, 9)   (5, 7)

E–117   Rule   Ordered Pairs

$A = 2 \times B$

(1, 2)   (3, 6)   (6, 3)   (7, 5)

(5, 10)   (10, 12)   (2, 1)   (10, 5)

     P.O. BOX 448, PACIFIC GROVE, CA 93950

MATCHING A RULE TO ORDERED PAIRS

In each ordered pair, the first number is the "A" value and
the second number is the "B" value.
Identify the rule that each of the six ordered pairs satisfies.

Example   Ordered Pairs

(2, 7)   (5, 16)   (3, 10)

(0, 1)   (10, 31)   (1, 4)

Rule

a. $A = (3 \times B) + 1$
b. $B > A + 3$
c. $(3 \times A) + 1 = B$
d. $B = A + 5$

E–118   Ordered Pairs

(1, 5)   (3, 11)   (4, 16)

(5, 19)   (0, 2)   (10, 33)

Rule

a. $B = (3 \times A) + 2$
b. $B > (3 \times A) + 1$
c. $A > (3 \times B) + 1$
d. $A + B > 5$

E–119   Ordered Pairs

(7, 35)   (4, 20)   (0, 0)

(1, 5)   (3, 15)   (10, 50)

Rule

a. $5 \times B = A$
b. $A + B > 5$
c. $B = A + 28$
d. $B = 5 \times A$

E–120   Ordered Pairs

(0, 1)   (1, 2)   (4, 17)

(2, 5)   (5, 26)   (10, 101)

Rule

a. $B = A + 1$
b. $B = (A \times A) + 1$
c. $A = (B \times B) + 1$
d. $6 \times A > B$

E–121   Ordered Pairs

(2, 3)   (3, 4)   (0, 1)

(5, 6)   (7, 8)   (10, 18)

Rule

a. $B = A + 1$
b. $2 \times A > B$
c. $B < A + 9$
d. $B - A = 1$

SATISFYING NUMBER PROPERTIES

Circle all the pairs of numbers that satisfy the given properties.

Example The product of the numbers is less than 24 and their sum is 10.

5 and 5	(8 and 2)
4 and 6	(0 and 10)
(1 and 9)	5 and 4

E–122 Both numbers are multiples of 3 and their difference is greater than 6.

9 and 12	12 and 3
15 and 25	18 and 6
36 and 30	0 and 15

E–123 One number is 2 more than the other and their product is an odd number.

7 and 5	4 and 6
2 and 3	5 and 9
13 and 11	0 and 2

E–124 Both numbers are prime numbers and their product is less than 20.

7 and 5	4 and 2
3 and 5	5 and 9
13 and 11	2 and 7

E–125 The sum of the two numbers is less than 9 and one number is twice the other.

3 and 6	4 and 2
4 and 8	2 and 6
3 and 5	2 and 1

SATISFYING NUMBER PROPERTIES

Find 3 pairs of whole numbers that satisfy the given properties.

Example One number is greater than the square of the other number.

<u>10 and 3</u>

<u>24 and 4</u>

<u>30 and 5</u>

E–126 Three times the sum of the two numbers is less than the product of the numbers.

_____

_____

_____

E–127 One number plus 3 is greater than 2 times the other number.

_____

_____

_____

E–128 The square of one number equals twice the other number.

_____

_____

_____

E–129 The sum of the squares of the two numbers is less than 13.

_____

_____

_____

INFERENCES

The two sentences below give information about two numbers, **m** and **n**.

m and **n** are both whole numbers.
(**m** + **n**) is an even number.

Decide whether the following statements are always true, always false, or cannot be determined (CBD).

Example	**m** and **n** are even numbers.	**CBD** _____
E–130	(**m** + **n**) is divisible by 2.	_____
E–131	(**m** + **n**) is divisible by 4.	_____
E–132	Suppose **n** is an even number. Then **m** is an odd number.	_____
E–133	**m** and **n** are different numbers.	_____
E–134	If **m** = 2 × **n** then **m** is an even number.	_____
E–135	Suppose **m** = 2 × **n**. Then **n** is an odd number.	_____
E–136	(**m** + **n**) is not a prime number.	_____
E–137	If **n** is greater than 2, then (**m** + **n**) is not a prime number.	_____
E–138	Suppose **n** is an odd number. Then **m** is an odd number.	_____

INFERENCES

The two sentences below give information about two numbers, **m** and **n**.

m and **n** are both whole numbers.
m is equal to (**n** + 1).

Decide whether the following statements are always true, always false, or cannot be determined (CBD).

Example	(**m** + **n**) is an even number.	False
E–139	(**m** × **n**) is an even number.	_____
E–140	**m** is an odd number.	_____
E–141	(**m** + **m**) is an odd number.	_____
E–142	(**n** + 1) is not divisible by 2.	_____
E–143	**m** could be equal to **n**.	_____
E–144	When **n** is an even number, (**m** + **n**) is an even number.	_____
E–145	(**n** + **n**) is an odd number.	_____
E–146	(**m** + **m**) is an even number.	_____
E–147	When **n** is an odd number, (**m** + **n**) is an odd number.	_____

MATCHING GRAPHS WITH LABELS

Select the bar graph that fits the given description.

Example Daily high temperatures in degrees Fahrenheit for June 1–7   <u>C</u>

F–1   Average number of hours of homework done for a math class for one week   <u>   </u>

F–2   Number of absences for a school of 1100 for one week   <u>   </u>

F–3   Number of tickets sold in one week for a 500 ticket raffle   <u>   </u>

F–4   Number of hours worked per day for one week in a summer job   <u>   </u>

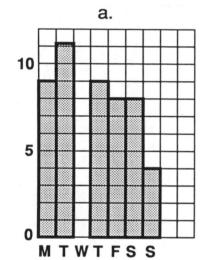

a.

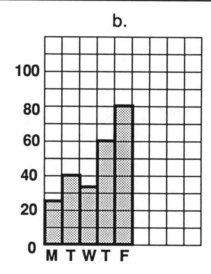

b.

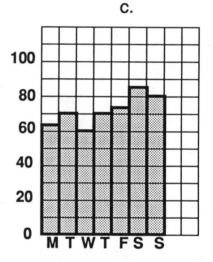

c.

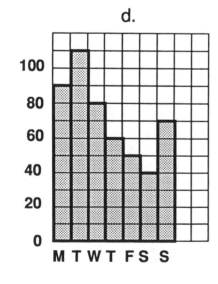

d.

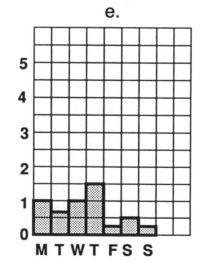

e.

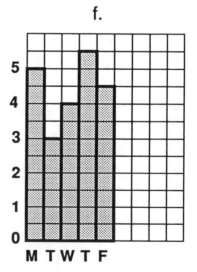

f.

                   P.O. BOX 448, PACIFIC GROVE, CA 93950

INTERPRETING A BAR GRAPH

Use the graph to answer the questions below.

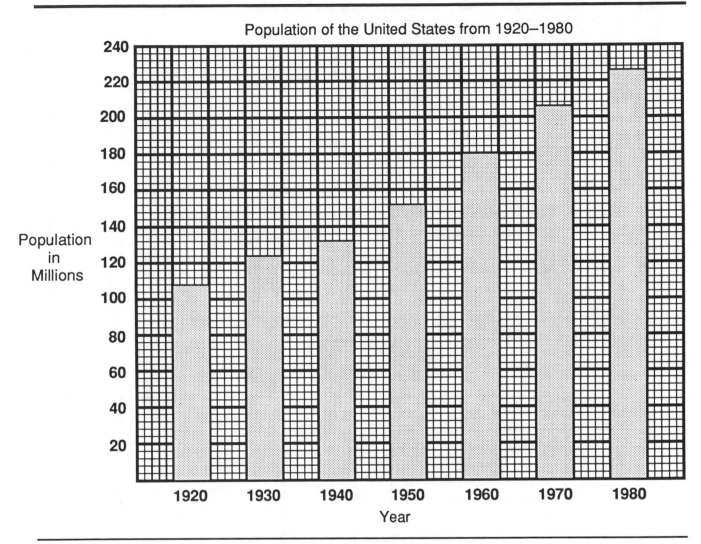

Population of the United States from 1920–1980

Population in Millions

Year

Example In what year was the population about 150 million? _____1950_____

F–5 What was the increase in population during the 1940s? _____

F–6 During which decade was the population increase the greatest? _____

F–7 During which decade was the population increase the smallest? _____

F–8 What do you think the population was in 1990? _____

F–9 What do you think the population was in 1910? _____

SUMS OF WHOLE NUMBERS

Write the area of the rectangle in the circle.
Count the number of squares with Xs in each row of the rectangle.
Use the information to complete the table in F–13.

Example

$\boxed{12}$ (in circle)

1	X
2	X X
3	X X X

F–10

(empty circle)

X
X X
X X X
X X X X
X X X X X

F–11

(empty circle)

X
X X
X X X
X X X X

F–13

1 + 2 =	
1 + 2 + 3 =	6
1 + 2 + 3 + 4 =	
1 + 2 + . . . + 5 =	
1 + 2 + . . . + 6 =	
1 + 2 + . . . + 7 =	

F–12

(empty circle)

X
X X

258   P.O. BOX 448, PACIFIC GROVE, CA 93950

COUNTING CHORDS

Draw chords connecting point A with each of the other points on the circle.
In the table, write the number of chords drawn.
Draw additional chords that connect point B with the other points on the circle.
In the table, write the number of additional chords drawn.
Continue until each pair of points is connected and the table is completed.

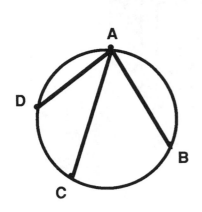

Example How many chords are drawn from point A?

3

F–14 How many additional chords can be drawn from point B?

F–15 How many additional chords can be drawn from point C?

F–16

POINT	A	B	C
NUMBER OF CHORDS	3		

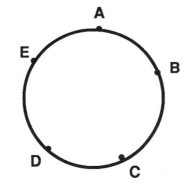

F–17

POINT	A	B	C	D
NUMBER OF CHORDS				

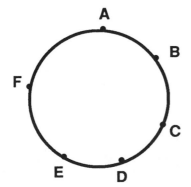

F–18

POINT	A	B	C	D	E
NUMBER OF CHORDS					

                   P.O. BOX 448, PACIFIC GROVE, CA 93950

SURFACE AREA

A $3 \times 3 \times 3$ cube is constructed with 27 unit cubes.
An X is placed on the outside surface of each of the unit cubes.

Example

How many Xs are on the front of the cube?

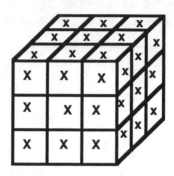

_____9_____

F–19 How many Xs are on the top of the cube?

_____

F–20 How many Xs are on the bottom of the cube?

_____

F–21 How many Xs are on the back of the cube?

_____

F–22 Complete the table.

SURFACE	# OF X'S
FRONT	9
BOTTOM	
BACK	
LEFT SIDE	
RIGHT SIDE	
TOP	
TOTAL	

SURFACE AREA

The 3 × 3 × 3 cube from the previous activity has been enlarged to form a 4 × 4 × 4 cube.

Example
How many unit cubes were needed to
make the 3 × 3 × 3 cube?   27

F–23
What is the total number of unit cubes
in the 4 × 4 × 4 cube?   _____

F–24
How many cubes were added to the 3 ×
3 × 3 cube to make the 4 × 4 × 4 cube? _____

Suppose Xs are placed on the OUTSIDE surfaces of each of the NEW unit cubes.

F–25   How many Xs are on the front   **F–26**   How many Xs are on the bottom
of the 4 × 4 × 4 cube?   of the 4 × 4 × 4 cube?

_____   _____

F–27   Complete the Table.

SURFACE	# OF X'S
FRONT	16
BOTTOM	
BACK	
LEFT SIDE	
RIGHT SIDE	
TOP	
TOTAL	

SURFACE AREA

Xs were placed on the outside surface of each of the unit cubes in the figure below.
Then the $3 \times 3 \times 3$ cube is disassembled.
The unit cubes are sorted according to the number of Xs on each.

Example

What is the GREATEST number of Xs
appearing on a unit cube?

<u>   3   </u>

Describe the location of the unit cubes that have three Xs.

<u>   each of the 8 corners of the cube   </u>

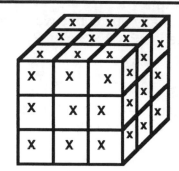

F–28 How many unit cubes have three Xs? _____

F–29 How many unit cubes have only two Xs? _____

F–30 How many unit cubes have only one X? _____

F–31 Are there any unit cubes that do not have any Xs? _____

F–32 How many unit cubes have no Xs? _____

F–33 Complete the Table.

NUMBER OF X'S	NUMBER OF CUBES
3	
2	
1	
0	

USING TABLES TO COMPUTE PARKING FEES

The hourly parking fees for the Metroplex Parking System are shown in the table.
Compute the parking fee for each ticket.

PARKING RATES   METROPLEX PARKING SYSTEM

ARRIVE BEFORE 8:00 a.m. **SAVE $1.00**	First 1/2 hour	$1.00
	Next 1/2 hour to 2 hours	additional 50¢ per 1/2 hour
	Next 2 hours to 4 hours	additional 25¢ per 1/2 hour
	each additional hour over 4 hours	25¢ per hour
	Maximum Charge per 24 Hours	$8.00

PARK FREE ON HOLIDAYS

Example The first 1/2 hour costs $1.00, the next three 1/2 hours cost 3 X .50 = 1.50, and the final 1/2 hour costs .25.

dep:	02/16/92 12:46 a.m.
arr:	02/16/92 10:16 a.m.

time __2 1/2 hrs__ fee __$2.75__

F–34

dep:	06/06/89 11:05 a.m.
arr:	06/06/89 8:35 a.m.

time _____ fee _____

F–35

dep:	10/11/90 11:45 a.m.
arr:	10/11/90 7:45 a.m.

time _____ fee _____

F–36

dep:	04/29/88 4:56 p.m.
arr:	04/29/88 9:56 a.m.

time _____ fee _____

F–37

dep:	07/04/89 1:42 p.m.
arr:	07/04/89 11:12 a.m.

time _____ fee _____

F–38

dep:	09/16/91 6:39 a.m.
arr:	09/15/91 7:39 p.m.

time _____ fee _____

                   P.O. BOX 448, PACIFIC GROVE, CA 93950

USING TABLES TO COMPUTE PARKING FEES

The hourly parking fees for the Metroplex Parking System are shown in the table. Compute the parking fee for each ticket.

PARKING RATES   METROPLEX PARKING SYSTEM

ARRIVE BEFORE 8:00 a.m.	First 1/2 hour	$1.00	PARK FREE ON HOLIDAYS
	1/2 hour to 2 hours	additional 50¢ per 1/2 hour	
	2 hours to 4 hours	additional 25¢ per 1/2 hour	
SAVE $1.00	each additional hour over 4 hours	25¢ per hour	
	Maximum Charge per 24 Hours	$8.00	

Example

dep:	07/30/91	1:37 a.m.
arr:	07/29/91	4:15 p.m.

time <u>9 hrs 22 min</u>   fee <u>$5.00</u>

F–39

dep:	09/10/89	9:52 a.m.
arr:	09/10/89	7:39 a.m.

time _____   fee _____

F–40

dep:	10/18/88	4:03 p.m.
arr:	10/17/88	2:39 p.m.

time _____   fee _____

F–41

dep:	02/01/89	6:51 a.m.
arr:	01/31/89	4:52 p.m.

time _____   fee _____

F–42

dep:	01/01/90	2:51 p.m.
arr:	12/31/89	9:08 p.m.

time _____   fee _____

F–43

dep:	03/01/88	5:56 p.m.
arr:	02/28/88	3:27 p.m.

time _____   fee _____

                   P.O. BOX 448, PACIFIC GROVE, CA 93950

USING TABLES TO COMPUTE COST

The price charts below show the cost of purchasing tape cassettes.
Use the two charts to complete each sales slip and compute the total cost of each purchase.

Tape Prices

TAPE	1 TAPE	2 TAPES
A	$3.99	$7.79
B	$4.59	$8.98
C	$5.95	$10.67
D	$6.83	$13.39
E	$7.49	$14.49
F	$8.25	$15.95

Quantity Discount

TOTAL PURCHASE	SAVE
$10.00–19.99	$2.00
$20.00–29.99	$3.00
$30.00–34.99	$4.50
$35.00–39.99	$5.00
over $40.00	$6.00

**Buy 8 or more tapes,
save an additional $2.00.**

Example

2 A tapes	7.79
3 D tapes	20.22
1 E tape	7.49
Subtotal	35.50
Discount	5.00
Total	30.50

F–44

2 F tapes	_____
1 D tape	_____
3 C tapes	_____
Subtotal	_____
Discount	_____
Total	_____

F–45

3 A tapes	_____
3 C tapes	_____
2 E tapes	_____
Subtotal	_____
Discount	_____
Total	_____

USING TABLES TO COMPUTE COST

Use the price charts on the previous page to complete each sales slip for tape cassettes. Compute the total cost of each purchase.

F–46

3 A tapes _____

3 B tapes _____

1 F tape _____

  Subtotal _____

  Discount _____

  Total _____

F–47

3 A tapes _____

4 B tapes _____

1 F tape _____

  Subtotal _____

  Discount _____

  Total _____

F–48

4 A tapes _____

3 B tapes _____

1 F tape _____

  Subtotal _____

  Discount _____

  Total _____

F–49

3 D tapes _____

1 C tape _____

1 A tape _____

2 B tapes _____

  Subtotal _____

  Discount _____

  Total _____

F–50

3 C tapes _____

2 F tapes _____

3 A tapes _____

2 B tapes _____

  Subtotal _____

  Discount _____

  Total _____

F–51

3 F tapes _____

2 D tapes _____

1 C tape _____

1 A tape _____

  Subtotal _____

  Discount _____

  Total _____

P.O. BOX 448, PACIFIC GROVE, CA 93950

USING TABLES TO COMPUTE AIRCRAFT FUEL

Commerical airlines calculate the amount of aviation fuel needed for aircraft in pounds.
Each 1000 pounds of fuel will allow an aircraft to fly a given amount of time.
In addition each take off or landing requires an extra 1450 pounds of fuel.
Use the charts below to calculate the amount of fuel needed for each flight.
Round each flight time up to the next half hour and the answer to the nearest one hundred pounds.

	Atlanta	Boston	Chicago	Dallas	Detroit	New York	San Diego
Atlanta	X	2:46	1:10	1:39	1:24	2:23	4:28
Boston	2:46	X	1:58	3:12	1:19	0:55	5:58
Chicago	1:10	1:58	X	2:09	0:40	1:46	4:00
Dallas	1:39	3:12	2:09	X	2:13	2:53	2:49
Detroit	1:24	1:19	0:40	2:13	X	1:24	4:37
New York	2:23	0:55	1:46	2:53	1:24	X	5:40
San Diego	4:28	5:58	4:00	2:49	4:37	5:40	X

Minutes per 1000 lbs.

M–80	45
727	35
737	40
757	40
DC–9	30
DC–10	35

Example A flight from New York to San Diego through Dallas—
New York to Dallas, M–80; Dallas to San Diego, 737

14,300

F–52 A flight from Boston to Chicago through Detroit—
Boston to Detroit, DC–9; Detroit to Chicago, 727

_____

F–53 A flight from Dallas to Detroit through Atlanta—
Dallas to Atlanta, DC–10; Atlanta to Detroit, M–80

_____

F–54 A flight from San Diego to Chicago through Dallas—
San Diego to Dallas, 737; Dallas to Chicago, 757

_____

F–55 A flight from from Boston to San Diego through Chicago—
Boston to Chicago, DC–10; Chicago to San Diego, M–80

_____

F–56 A flight from San Diego to New York through Dallas and Chicago—
San Diego to Dallas, 737; Dallas to Chicago, 757;
Chicago to New York, DC–9

_____

SUMS OF ORDERED PAIRS

The points on the grid represent all ordered pairs that could result when two dice are rolled.

Example

Which ordered pairs are on the diagonal line in the figure?

$$(1, 2) \text{ and } (2, 1)$$

What is the sum of the two numbers in each of these ordered pairs?

$$3$$

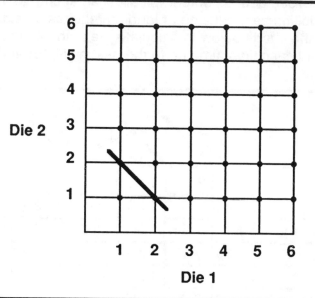

Die 2

Die 1

F–57   Draw the diagonal line that connects the ordered pairs that have a sum of 6.

F–58   List the ordered pairs that have a sum of 6.

_____

F–59   How many ordered pairs have a sum of 6?   _____

F–60   Use other diagonal lines to complete the table.

SUM	2	3	4	5	6	7	8	9	10	11	12
NUMBER OF PAIRS	1	2									

F–61   How many different ordered pairs are possible?   _____

F–62   Which sum has the greatest number of ordered pairs?   _____

                   P.O. BOX 448, PACIFIC GROVE, CA 93950

SUMS OF ORDERED PAIRS

The points on the grid represent all ordered pairs that could result when an octahedron (numbered 1–8) and a die (numbered 1–6) are rolled.

Example

Which ordered pairs are on the diagonal line in the figure?

$$(1, 2) \text{ and } (2, 1)$$

What is the sum of the two numbers in each of these ordered pairs?

3

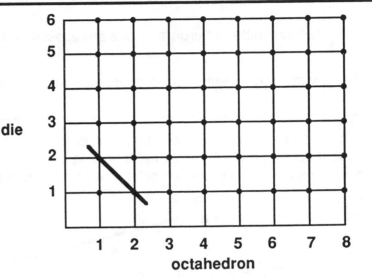

die

octahedron

F–63 Draw the diagonal line that connects the ordered pairs that have a sum of 11.

F–64 List the ordered pairs that have a sum of 11.

F–65 How many ordered pairs have a sum of 11? _____

F–66 Use other diagonal lines to complete the table.

SUM	2	3	4	5	6	7	8	9	10	11	12	13	14
NUMBER OF PAIRS	1	2											

F–67 How many different ordered pairs are possible? _____

F–68 Which sum has the greatest number of ordered pairs? _____

SUMS OF ORDERED PAIRS

One person has two dice and another person has a die and an octahedron.
Use the completed tables in the last two activities to answer the questions below.

F–69 How many different ordered pairs are possible with the two dice? _____

F–70 How many different ordered pairs are possible with the die and octahedron? _____

The left column gives the sums that result from rolling two dice or a die and an octahedron.
The right column gives the chances of rolling a particular sum.
Match the statements in the left column with those in the right column.

Example 2 dice: sum of 2   a. 6 out of 36

F–71 die and octahedron: sum of 2   b. 1 out of 36

F–72 2 dice: sum of 7   c. 1 out of 12

F–73 die and octahedron: sum of 7   d. 1 out of 48

F–74 die and octahedron: sum of 5   e. 6 out of 48

F–75 2 dice: sum of 5   f. 1 out of 4

F–76 die and octahedron: sum of 5 or 11   g. 1 out of 9

F–77 2 dice: sum of 8 or 9   h. 8 out of 48

SUMS OF ORDERED PAIRS

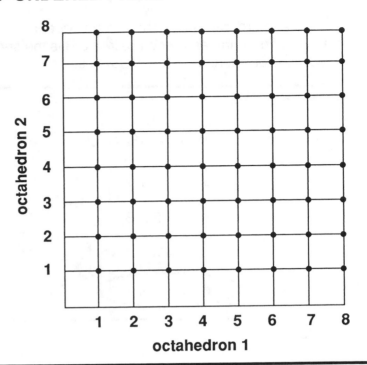

Two octahedra are rolled and the data is recorded on the grid.

Example

Which ordered pairs have a sum of 14?

_(6, 8), (7, 7), (8, 6)_

F–78 Which ordered pairs have a sum of 12? _____

F–79 What is the largest possible sum? _____

F–80 How many ordered pairs have a sum of 15? _____

F–81 How many ordered pairs have a sum of 10? _____

F–82 Complete the table.

SUM	2	3	4	5	6	7	8	9	10	11	12	13	14	15	16
NUMBER OF PAIRS															

        271   P.O. BOX 448, PACIFIC GROVE, CA 93950

GRAPHING SEQUENCES OF ORDERED PAIRS

Graph each ordered pair in the given sequence.
If A is the first number in each pair and B is the second number,
select the correct rule for the sequence.

Example

(0, 0), (1, 2), (2, 4), (3, 6), (4, 8)

      RULE: a. $A = B + 2$

                b. $A = 2 \times B$

                c. $B = A + 2$

                d. $B = 2 \times A$

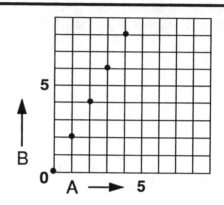

F–83

(0, 1), (1, 4), (2, 7), (3, 10), (4, 13)

      RULE: a. $A = (3 \times B) + 1$

                b. $A = 3 \times B$

                c. $B = (3 \times A) + 1$

                d. $B = A + 3$

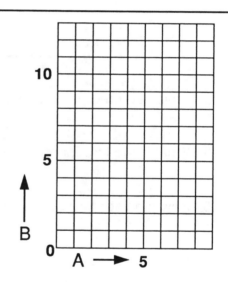

F–84

(0, 3), (1, 5), (2, 7), (3, 9), (4, 11)

      RULE: a. $B = (2 \times A) + 3$

                b. $B = (3 \times A) + 2$

                c. $A = (2 \times B) + 3$

                d. $B = A + 4$

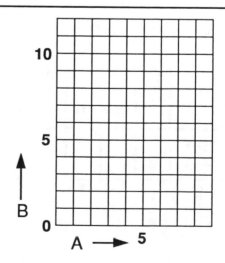

GRAPHING SEQUENCES OF ORDERED PAIRS

Graph each ordered pair in the given sequence.
If A is the first number in each pair and B is the second number,
select the correct rule for the sequence.

F–85

(0, 0), (1, 3), (2, 6), (3, 9), (4, 12)

RULE: a. $B = A + 2$

b. $A = B - 3$

c. $B = 3 \times A$

d. $A = 3 \times B$

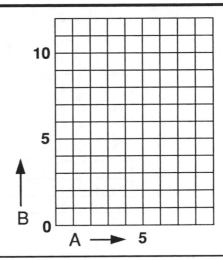

F–86

(0, 7), (1, 6), (2, 5), (3, 4), (4, 3)

RULE: a. $B = A + 7$

b. $B = 6 \times A$

c. $A = 7 - B$

d. $B = 7 - A$

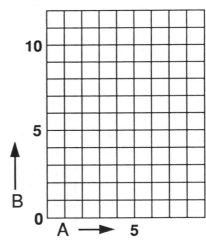

F–87

(0, 9), (1, 7), (2, 5), (3, 3), (4, 1)

RULE: a. $A = 9 - (2 \times B)$

b. $A + B = 9$

c. $B = 9 - (2 \times A)$

d. $B = (2 \times A) + 5$

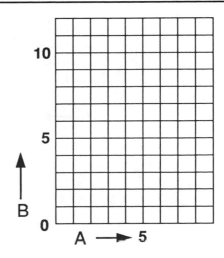

GRAPHING ORDERED PAIRS

A and B represent numbers in a given relationship.
Complete the table, and graph the resulting ordered pairs of numbers.

Example

$B = (2 \times A) + 1$

A	B
0	**1**
1	**3**
2	**5**
3	**7**
4	**9**

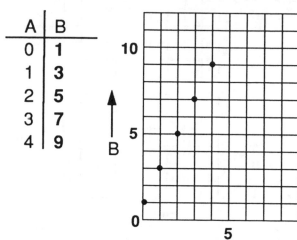

F–88

$B = (2 \times A) + 2$

A	B
0	
1	
2	
3	
4	

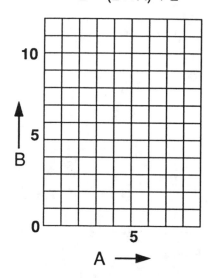

F–89

$A + B = 10$

A	B
0	
1	
2	
3	
4	

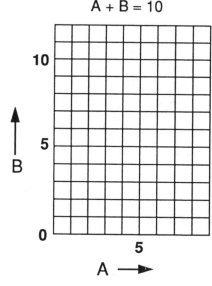

F–90

$B = 2 \times A$

A	B
0	
1	
2	
3	
4	

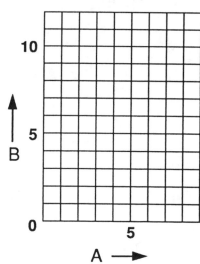

---

274   P.O. BOX 448, PACIFIC GROVE, CA 93950

READING ORDERED PAIRS

Use the graph to complete the table.
Then select the correct rule.

Example

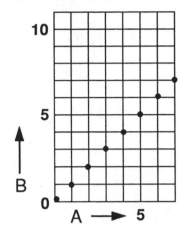

A	B
0	**0**
1	**1**
2	**2**
3	**3**
4	**4**
5	**5**
6	**6**
7	7

RULE:

a. $B = A + 1$

b. $A + B = 2$

(c.) $B = A$

d. $A = B + 1$

F–91

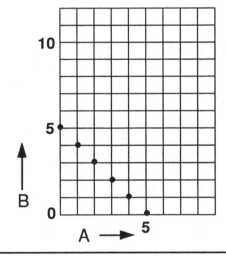

A	B
0	
1	
2	
3	
4	
5	

RULE:

a. $B = A + 3$

b. $B = A - 5$

c. $B - A = 3$

d. $B = 5 - A$

F–92

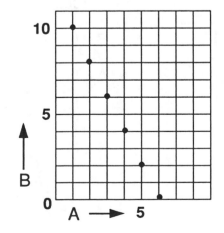

A	B
1	
2	
3	
4	
5	
6	

RULE:

a. $B + A = 11$

b. $A = 12 - (2 \times B)$

c. $B = 12 - (2 \times A)$

d. $7 = A + B$

 P.O. BOX 448, PACIFIC GROVE, CA 93950

READING ORDERED PAIRS

Use the graph to complete the table.
Then select the correct rule.

F–93

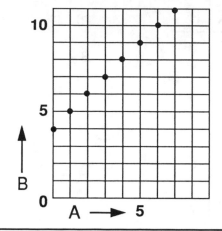

A	B
0	
1	
2	
3	
4	
5	
6	
7	

RULE:

a. A = B

b. B – A = 5

c. B – A = 4

d. A = B + 4

F–94

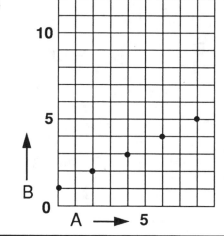

A	B
0	
2	
4	
6	
8	

RULE:

a. B = A

b. $2 \times B = A + 2$

c. A = (1/2 × B) + 1

d. $B + 2 = 2 \times A$

F–95

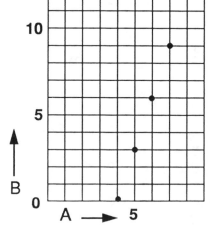

A	B
4	
5	
6	
7	
8	

RULE:

a. B = (2 × A) – 8

b. A = (3 × B) – 12

c. B = (3 × A) + 12

d. B = (3 × A) – 12

                   P.O. BOX 448, PACIFIC GROVE, CA 93950

MATCHING RULES WITH GRAPHS

Match each rule with the correct graph.

Example	$3 \times A = 2 \times B$	GRAPH	$\underline{\quad C \quad}$
F–96	$A + B = 10$	GRAPH	$\underline{\qquad\qquad}$
F–97	$2 \times B = A + 3$	GRAPH	$\underline{\qquad\qquad}$
F–98	$B = 12 - (3 \times A)$	GRAPH	$\underline{\qquad\qquad}$

a.
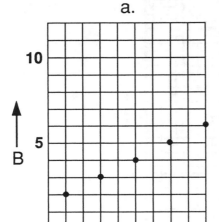

b.
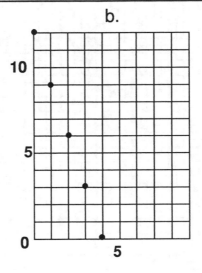

c.
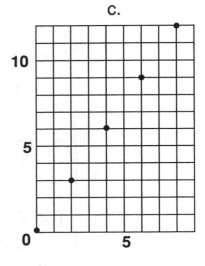

d.
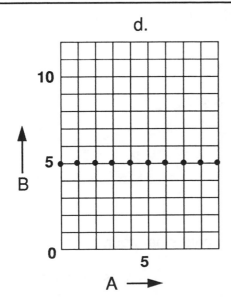

e.
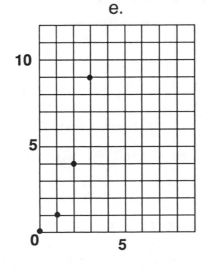

f.
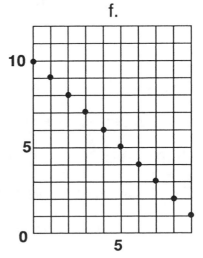

USING A GRAPH FOR CONVERSION

The graph below relates distances in miles to distances in kilometers.
Use the graph to answer the questions below.

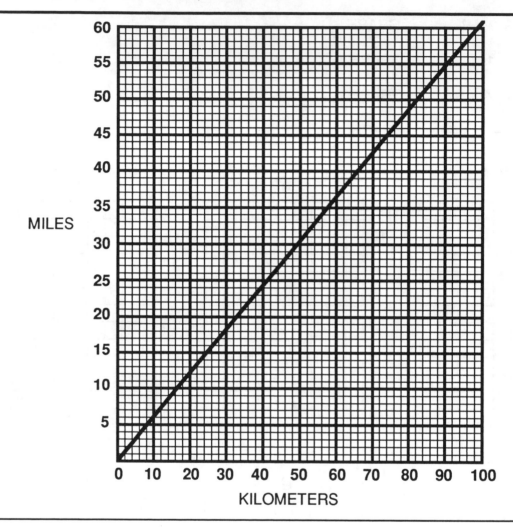

Example A distance of 50 kilometers is about _____31_____ miles.

F–99 A distance of 50 miles is about _____ kilometers.

F–100 Which is longer, a kilometer or a mile? _____

F–101 One kilometer is about _____ miles.

F–102 A speed of 55 miles per hour is about _____ kilometers per hour.

F–103 A car that travels 60 km on a gallon of gas will travel _____ miles per gallon.

USING A GRAPH FOR CONVERSION

On the grid below, plot the two well-known Centigrade/Fahrenheit equivalents:
0° C = 32° F and 100° C equals 212° F.
Connect these two points with a straight line.
Use the resulting graph to estimate the temperature equivalents.

F–104 50° F = _____ ° C.   **F–105** 20° C = _____ ° F.

F–106 100° F = _____ ° C.   **F–107** 50° C = _____ ° F.

F–108 98.6° F = _____ ° C.   **F–109** 70° C = _____ ° F.

F–110 At what value does the temperature have the same Centigrade and
Fahrenheit temperature?

_____

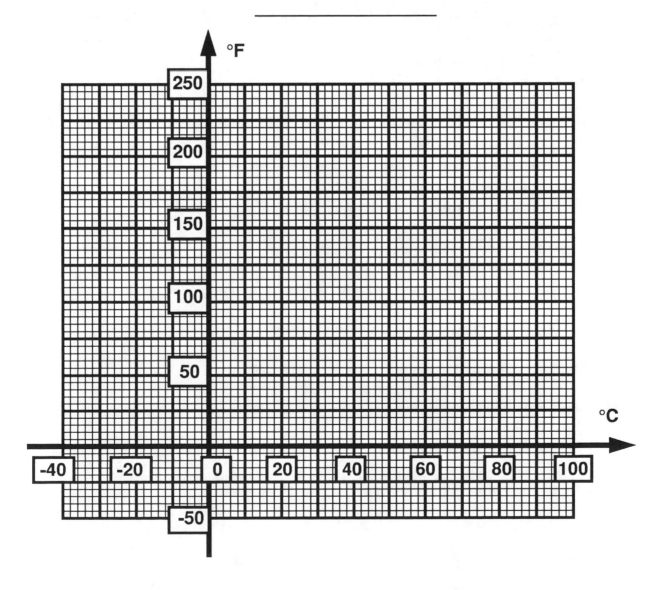

USING TWO GRAPHS FOR CONVERSION

Use the two conversion graphs to answer the questions below.

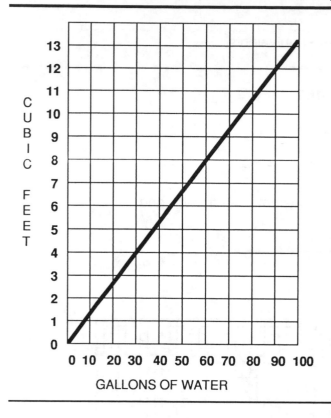

GALLONS OF WATER

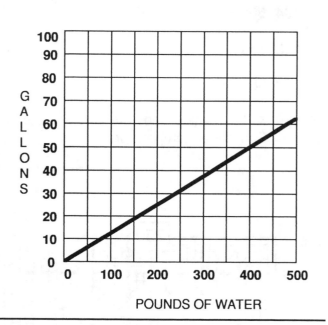

POUNDS OF WATER

Example A 5 cubic foot water tank holds about _____38_____ gallons.

F–111 When full, a 5 cubic foot water tank holds about _____ pounds of water.

F–112 By weighing, it is determined that a water truck is carrying 475 pounds of water.

It is carrying about _____ gallons of water.

F–113 350 pounds of water is about _____ cubic feet.

F–114 130 gallons of water is about _____ cubic feet.

F–115 1000 pounds of water is about _____ gallons.

F–116 1000 pounds of water is about _____ cubic feet.

INTERPRETING A GRAPH

The graph below relates time measured in hours to the total distance traveled.
Use the graph to answer the questions.

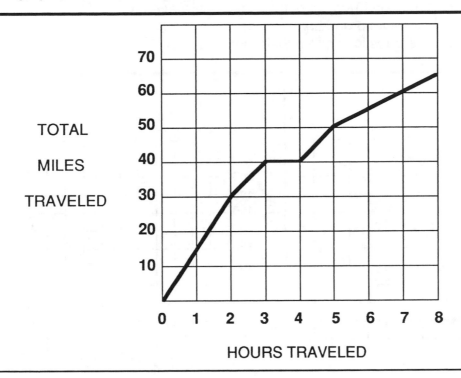

TOTAL

MILES

TRAVELED

HOURS TRAVELED

Example How many miles were traveled in the first 4 hours?   40 miles

F–117 What do you think happened between the 3rd and 4th hour? _____

F–118 How many miles were traveled in 8 hours? _____

F–119 Was the traveler going faster in the first 3 hours or the last 3 hours? _____

F–120 What was the average rate of speed during the first 3 hours? _____

F–121 What was the average rate of speed during the last 3 hours? _____

F–122 What are two likely modes of travel? _____

INTERPRETING GRAPHS

The Kim and Jones families are traveling 220 miles from Westville to Center Port by car.
On the trip they must travel 40 miles by ferry.
The Kim family leaves at 2 p.m. on Friday and the Jones family at 4 p.m.
The graph below shows their travel progress.
Use the graphs to answer the questions about their trips.

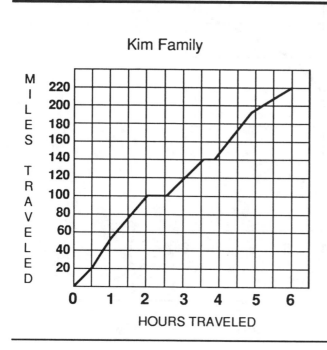

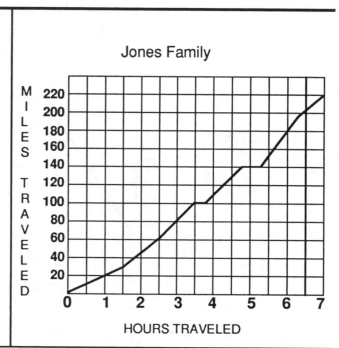

Example

At what time did each family arrive in Center Port? Kim 8 p.m., Jones 11 p.m.

F–123 Explain the two horizontal lines in each graph. _____

F–124 How far do you think the ferry is from Westville? _____

F–125 How long did the ferry trip take? _____

F–126 Which family drove faster to the ferry? _____

F–127 Which family drove faster from the ferry to Center Port? _____

F–128 What was the speed of the ferry? _____

MATCHING GRAPHS WITH LABELS

Select the graph that best illustrates the stated relationship.

Example Conversion of inches to centimeters   GRAPH   d

F–129 Radius of a circle and the area of the circle   GRAPH _____

F–130 Hours traveled and miles traveled on a bus trip   GRAPH _____

F–131 Conversion of meters to centimeters   GRAPH _____

F–132 Weeks of growth and height of a plant (in cm)   GRAPH _____

a.

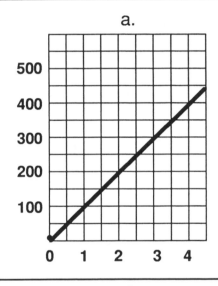

b.

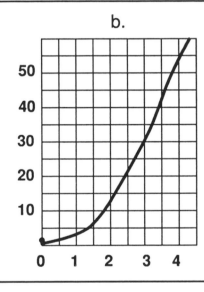

c.

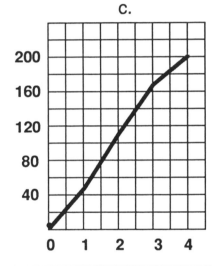

d.

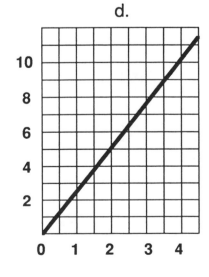

e.

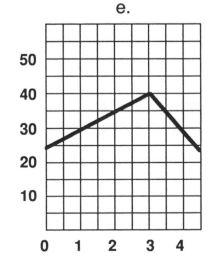

f.

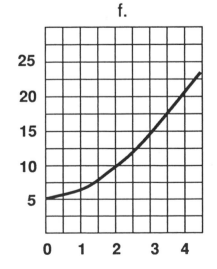